Doctor Bruce Goldberg has captivated the mind ᵥ
ancient Egypt. A must-read.

- George Noory, Coast to Coast AM

# EGYPT: AN
# EXTRATERRESTRIAL
# AND TIME TRAVELER EXPERIMENT

by

**Dr. Bruce Goldberg**

Dr. Bruce Goldberg
4300 Natoma Ave.
Woodland Hills, CA 91364
(818) 713-8190

Published by

**Bruce Goldberg, Inc.**
**4300 Natoma Ave.**
**Woodland Hills, CA 91364**
**Telephone: (800) KARMA-4-U or**
**FAX: (818) 704-9189**
**Email: drbg@sbcglobal.net**
**Web Site:**
**www.drbrucegoldberg.com**

**Printed in the United States of America**


**ISBN 1-57968-017-8**

# ABOUT THE AUTHOR

Dr. Bruce Goldberg holds a B.A. degree in Biology and Chemistry, is a Doctor of Dental surgery, and has an M.S. degree in counseling psychology. He retired from dentistry in 1989, and has concentrated on his hypnotherapy practice in Los Angeles. In 1975 Dr. Goldberg was trained by the American Society of Clinical Hypnosis in the techniques and clinical applications of hypnosis.

Dr. Goldberg has been interviewed on the *Donahue, Oprah, Leeza, Joan Rivers, Regis, Tom Snyder, Jerry Springer, Jenny Jones,* and *Montel Williams* shows; by *CNN, CBS News, NBC* and many others.

Through lectures, television and radio appearances, and newspaper articles, including interviews in *TIME, The Los Angeles Times*, and *The Washington Post*, he has conducted more than 35,000 past-life regressions and future-life progressions since 1974, helping thousands of patients empower themselves through these techniques. His CDs, cassette tapes and DVDs teach people self-hypnosis, and guide them into past and future lives. He gives lectures and seminars on hypnosis, regression and progression therapy, time travel, and conscious dying; he is also a consultant to corporations, attorneys, and the local and network media. His first edition of *The Search for Grace*, was made into a television movie by CBS. His third book, the award-winning *Soul Healing*, is a classic on alternative medicine and psychic empowerment. *Past Lives, Future Lives* is Dr. Goldberg's international bestseller and is the first book written on future lives (progression hypnotherapy).

Dr. Goldberg distributes CDs, cassette tapes and DVDs to teach people self-hypnosis and to guide them into past and future lives and time travel. For information on self-hypnosis tapes, speaking engagements, or private sessions, Dr. Goldberg can be contacted directly by writing to:

**Bruce Goldberg, D.D.S., M.S.**
**4300 Natoma Avenue, Woodland Hills, CA 91364**
**Telephone: (800) KARMA-4-U or (800) 527-6248**
**Fax: (818) 704-9189**
**email: drbg@sbcglobal.net**
**Web Site: www.drbrucegoldberg.com**

Please include a self-addressed, stamped envelope with your letter.

# EGYPT:  AN EXTRATERRESTRIAL AND TIME TRAVELER EXPERIMENT

## OTHER BOOKS BY DR. BRUCE GOLDBERG

*Past Lives, Future Lives*
*Soul Healing*
*The Search for Grace:  A Documented Case of Murder and Reincarnation*
*Spirit Guide Contact Through Hypnosis*
*Peaceful Transition:  The Art of Conscious Dying and the Liberation of the Soul*
*New Age Hypnosis*
*Past Lives, Future Lives Revealed*
*Unleash Your Psychic Powers*
*Look Younger and Live Longer:  Add 25 to 50 Quality Years to Your Life, Naturally*
*Protected by the Light:  The Complete Book of Psychic Self-Defense*
*Time Travelers from Our Future:  A Fifth Dimension Odyssey*
*Astral Voyages:  Mastering the Art of Interdimensional Travel*
*Self-Hypnosis:  Easy Ways to Hypnotize Your Problems Away*
*Custom Design Your Own Destiny*
*Karmic Capitalism:  A Spiritual Approach to Financial Independence*
*Dream Your Problems Away:  Heal Yourself While You Sleep*
*Lose Weight Permanently and Naturally*

*NOTE TO THE READER*
　　　This book is the result of the professional experiences accumulated by the author since 1974, working individually with over 14,000 patients.  The material included herein is intended to complement, not replace, the advice of your own physician, psychotherapist or other health care professional, whom you should always consult about your circumstances prior to starting or stopping any medication or any other course of treatment, exercise regimen or diet.

　　　At times the masculine pronoun has been used as a convention.  It is intended to imply both male and female genders where this is applicable. All names and identifying references, except those of celebrities, have been altered to protect the privacy of my patients.  All other facts are accurate and have not been altered.

# EGYPT: AN EXTRATERRESTRIAL AND TIME TRAVELER EXPERIMENT

## DEDICATION

This book is dedicated to my readers, who have been most kind and generous in expressing their interest in my various books, workshops and self-hypnosis tapes. None of what you will read in this work would have appeared in print without their support.

The main impetus for this manuscript originated from the reports of my patients with their communication and contact with time travelers from our future. I therefore further dedicate this small contribution to a field of rewriting the history of civilization so that the truth of our heritage will be known. Lastly, I dedicate this book to the universe with all of its wonders and manifestations.

## Acknowledgments

I would like to eternally thank my patients who were kind enough to share their experiences with the time travelers. As unusual as it may sound, I also express my gratitude to the time travelers for providing both insight to and a specific mechanism for assisting our spiritual growth. In addition, I thank the universe for providing the opportunity to each of us to learn how to become a better soul.

# EGYPT: AN EXTRATERRESTRIAL AND TIME TRAVELER EXPERIMENT

## CONTENTS

# INTRODUCTION

We have all been exposed to the conventional history of Egypt. Historians and Egyptologists clearly state that Egypt was first unified at approximately 3000 B.C., the pyramids at Giza and the Sphinx were constructed at about 2500 B.C. and so on.

Although there were no transitional civilizations to account for Egypt's phenomenal technological and artistic achievements, the establishment's position remains dogmatically unchanged. Despite recent water erosion establishing evidence that the Sphinx must be at least 5000 years older than proposed, new history books are still clinging to old chronological paradigms.

Throughout this book we will learn the true origin of Egypt. Its history doesn't go back a mere 5,000 or 6,000 years, but at least 18,000 years!

Be prepared for some rather shocking revelations. We shall see throughout this book how Egypt developed under the influence of four main sources. These were:

- Lemuria (Mu)
- Atlantis
- Extraterrestrials
- Time Travelers

We shall explore in great detail how Egypt's sudden rise was assisted by very advanced civilizations who came and went at various periods throughout Egyptian prehistory and history. Long before the first Egyptian scribe recorded events of their day, these highly advanced societies possessed technology equal to ours today. There was also considerable interaction with extraterrestrials and time travelers from our future.

We will also see how the Mystery schools developed and the mechanism of secret pacts made between the Egyptian priests, extraterrestrials and these time travelers. Men In Black (MIB) were active during these ancient times to repress esoteric knowledge from the masses, not unlike what occurs today. These MIB also performed clean-up operations to remove any evidence of advanced helpers to humanoid's development.

Such topics as anti-gravity devices, Egyptian masonry, and other less frequently reported accomplishments, will also be thoroughly discussed. In writing this book I have researched psychology, mythology, religion, theosophy, Egyptology, quantum physics and the various esoteric traditions of the ages to arrive at my conclusions. We must not forget the many hundreds of past life regressions I conducted on my patients who lived in ancient Lemuria, Atlantis and Egypt. Along with these are the UFO and time traveler abductees, who were kind enough to share their experience with my hypnotic regressions.

The fascinating concept of time travel is a constant theme throughout this book. For those of you that would like to experience this discipline yourself, chapter 7 presents several self-hypnosis exercises to guide you into the past or future.

I quite realize that the material included in this book will be considered controversial and unbelievable to many. The scientific support for my conclusions are detailed and independently corroborated.

It is important for us to know and understand Egypt's true origins, since all civilization modeled itself after it. The Greeks stole their mathematics, the Romans their military might and organization, and the rest of the world its very essence from its medicine to the concept of monarchies.

By studying Egyptian history we are truly looking into our own "Mirror of Karma," since we have all had past lives there. Read on and discover both your past and your destiny.

# CHAPTER 1  CONVENTIONAL HISTORY VS. FORBIDDEN ARCHAEOLOGY

Before I begin to dissect the conventional data, concerning the origins of the Egyptian civilization, a survey of the history of mankind is in order. The origins of our species, *Homo sapiens sapiens*, can be briefly summarized as follows:

Our planet came into being approximately 4.6 billion years ago when our solar system was formed. About 3.5 billion years ago a certain physical stimulus (scientists do not agree what that was) somehow caused certain chemical reactions to occur so that primordial organic molecules interacted with sustained vigor to create life. Life existed only as single-celled organisms until about 630 million years ago, when simple multicellular life arose.

An explosive proliferation took place some 590 million years ago resulting in the production of invertebrate marine life. The first fish appeared 505 million years ago, followed by amphibians (408 million years ago), reptiles (360 million years ago) and mammals (248 million years ago). Apes appeared 38 million years ago for the first time.

As we now move forward to approximately twelve million years ago in Africa, the lush forests of the Miocene era gradually disappeared as rainfall declined. Grasslands now replaced these forests seven million years later (Pliocene era), and our ancestor *Ramapithecus* descended from the trees to roam the savannahs.

Paleontologists trace our species back to a small, bipedal hominid who lived in the Ethiopian region of East Africa's Great Rift Valley abut three and a half million years ago. This 1974 find was named "Lucy," and had a brain capacity of 400 cc (about one third that of ours).

This specimen was neither human nor ape, and some consider it the "missing link." Her human-like features included an upright gait and the anatomy of her posterior teeth and pelvis. Her technical name is Australopithecus afarenis, and she is considered our earliest direct ancestor.

Lucy was a meat eater that stood approximately four feet tall. The other Australopithecus existing at that time was a vegetarian and, due to its large height, was named *Australopithecus robustus*. This latter ape gave rise to the apes we see today.

| Era | Period | Start in Millions of Years Ago |
|---|---|---|
| Cenozoic | Holocene | .01 |
| | Pleistocene | 2 |
| | Pliocene | 5 |
| | Miocene | 25 |
| | Oligocene | 38 |
| | Eocene | 55 |
| | Paleocene | 65 |
| Mesozoic | Cretaceous | 144 |
| | Jurassic | 213 |
| | Triassic | 248 |
| Paleozoic | Permian | 286 |
| | Carboniferous | 360 |
| | Devonian | 408 |
| | Silurian | 438 |
| | Ordovician | 505 |
| | Cambrian | 590 |

**Figure 1   Geological Eras and Periods**

As the Pleistocene era began two million years ago, the ice age began with its preceding rains that lasted for 65,000 years.  Following this there were warm periods that created deserts and four ice ages.  Our predecessor, Australopithecus (the earliest known hominid) quickly evolved into man, first *Homo habilis*, then *Homo erectus* around 1.5 million years ago.  The size of the brain doubled from that of Australopithecus.  Modern man (*Homo sapiens sapiens*) evolved from H*omo erectus* about 300,000 to 400,00 years ago by way of several intermediaries.

This rapid evolution breaks every rule of biology, and was surpassed by another increase in brain size of one third between half a million years ago and modern times.  The majority of this growth took place in the cerebrum, the part of our brain that deals with higher mental processes.

Robert Ardrey offers an interesting explanation for this explosion in his book *African Genesis*.  He alludes to the fact that a giant meteorite, or small asteroid, exploded over the Indian Ocean about 700,000 yeas ago, scattering very small fragments called *tektites* over an area of twenty million square miles.

In addition, the Earth's North and South poles reversed (as it had several times during the history of our planet for completely unknown reasons).  This left the Earth devoid of a magnetic field and vulnerable to cosmic ray bombardment, which produced genetic mutations.  Ardrey uses this explanation to account for our "brain explosion," resulting in man evolving faster in half a million years than he had in the preceding three million years.[1]

*Homo sapiens Neanderthalensis* (Neanderthal Man) first came on the scene about 300,000 years ago. This primitive man had a larger brain than us (1400 cc as compared to our 1360 cc), and dominated the planet until about 40,000 years ago. Neanderthal Man was a failed experiment, and was killed off by Cro-Magnon, the latter supposedly gave rise to our species (*Homo sapiens sapiens*). We shall see that this was not the case.

There has always been a debate among scholars concerning whether Neanderthal man was our direct ancestor. Recent DNA studies on the skeleton of Neanderthal Man revealed 27 differences between our respective species. Our present species typically differ in no more than eight of the DNA base pairs. This basically eliminates Neanderthal Man from our family tree and suggests that they were a separate species (failed experiment) that lived in Europe and Western Asia 100,000 to 300,000 years ago.

As we shall see this corresponds with the ancient civilization of Lemuria (Mu). To be fair, some scientists still feel we have a common ancestry with Neanderthal Man, but went on our own separate genetic paths about 500,000 years ago. Did some extraterrestrial or time traveler alter our genetic coding? We shall see.

Some scientists state that our species appeared as early as 117,000 years ago, as a result of the Border Cave Finds in South Africa.[2] Synchronistically, about 18,000 years ago, during the Ice Age, farming was discovered when seeds dropped into cracks in the mud near the edge of lakes and streams grew into crops that could be harvested with stone sickles.

At about this time in Lascaux, France, cave paintings demonstrated that hunters devised how to construct rope to lure animals into traps. Approximately 12,000 B.C. the last Ice Age ended and two thousand years after man domesticated wolves into dogs. Sheep and goats were domesticated 1,000 years later.

The Jordan valley was the site of the first walled town called Jericho in 8,600 B.C. Wheat was harvested at first, and 1,000 years later a genetic "accident" between wheat and goat grass resulted in a heavier and plumper variety known as emmer. This later evolved into bread wheat, whose tightly packed and heavy grains coincidentally will not scatter in the wind. This marked the end of hunter-gather cultures for the most part, and gave rise to farming.

---

[1] Robert Ardrey, *African Genesis*. (New York: Atheneum, 1961).

[2] Roger Lewin, *Human Evolution*. (Oxford, England: Blackwell Scientific Publications, 1984).

The farming man now included cattle in his livestock, learned how to irrigate his fields and began weaving goat and sheep wool into cloth. For totally unknown reasons, this farming revolution spread throughout the world; in Africa and China, millet was cultivated; in America, beans and maize, in New Guinea, sugar cane, in Indochina, rice.

By 6,000 B.C. pottery and bread were baked in ovens, copper was beaten into blades and axes and arrow heads were constructed. The addition of arsenic to copper created tin, an alloy that could take an edge. Bronze was later discovered by combining copper with tin and swords were produced. This resulted in the building of walled towns to protect farmers from these warrior swordsmen.

At this time oxen were utilized to hoe the soil and the development of the harness allowed the plough to break up the fine, dry soil of the Middle East.

5,600 years ago in Sumer, Mesopotamia clay tokens were used as a form of money. Writing was created to make this system more efficient and to vastly increase man's own knowledge. At first a pictographic form of writing was used, with wedge-shaped cuneiform figures replacing them. The North Semite script of Aramaic languages eventually became the mode of written communication some time later.

Approximately 4,000 years ago the greatest invention of man, the wheel, surfaced. An axle attached to these wheels resulted in carts that enabled heavy loads to be transported.

The two most important technological developments in antiquity, the wheel and writing, was produced by Mediterranean man. By combining the discovery of bronze with the domestication of the horse, a new warrior class was created. This led to conquest of other people and the establishment of empires.

The first empire was established in the northern part of Babylon in Mesopotamia (present day Iraq) in a place called Akkad. Since the pictographs of the Sumerians was not an efficient enough form of communication, a form of writing was created in Mesopotamia that was based upon human language, rather than on pictures of objects. By having a symbol stand for a syllable, the basics of modern language was born.

Egypt is derived from the Greek word *Aigyptos*, which is a transcription of *Hikuptah*. Ha-Ka-Ptah was the Egyptian god's Path temple in Memphis. The Land of the *Neters*' (gods), or *Ta_Nutri* is another name for Egypt.

This ancient civilization was composed of the "Land of the North," and consists of the territories within the Nile delta from Memphis to the Mediterranean. Its symbol is the papyrus and its king wears the red crown. We refer to this part of Egypt as Lower Egypt.

The "Land of the South" includes the region from Memphis to the southern border of Egypt and is known as Upper Egypt. Its sovereign wears the white crown and his attribute is the reed *scirpus*. This reed and the papyrus, united in a monogram represent the "Two-Lands", North and South. The Pharaoh, "Lord of the Two-Lands" wears the double crown, the *pshent*, which consists of the white crown supported by the red crown.

The Nile River is Egypt's only river and flows from south to north. That is why the southern component is called Upper Egypt, while the northern section is labeled Lower Egypt. Its length is 4,000 miles and north of Memphis it fans out into seven arms that spread out into the Mediterranean. Today only two arms of importance remain: the Phatmetic, which reaches the sea at Damietta, and the Bolbitine at Rosetta, between those two stretches the delta is irrigated by numerous canals.

The Nile begins to rise at the summer solstice and reaches its greatest height between September 30th and October 10th, after which it gradually subsides. Along the Nile are located nomes, or regions of this land. There are 20 nomes in Lower (Northern) Egypt, and 22 in Upper (Southern) Egypt, which gives a total of 42 nomes. Forty two is also the number of the assessors (or functions) of Osiris, and the number of books written by the god Thoth (Hermes), according to some Egyptologists.

## EGYPT'S PREDYNASTIC PERIOD

Conventional Egyptologists know very little about a transition period from about 6500 B.C. to 5500 B.C., during which an organized permanent settlement centered around agriculture was established in Egypt. The Egyptian lifestyle changed from hunting to a diet consisting of domesticated cattle, pigs, goat, sheep, barley and wheat.

Metal replaced stone and pottery, weaving and the tanning of animal hides became evident. Egypt was no longer a land of primitive nomadic tribes. Their burial patterns changed, as now the dead were placed further and further away. Before permanent settlements were established, the departed were buried wherever it was convenient.

Beliefs in life after death now dominated Egyptian life. The dead were buried in a fetal position surrounded with provisions for the journey into the next life. They were positioned to face west in Lower Egypt and east in Upper Egypt.

Prior to 4500 B.C., the rest of the known world was quite primitive. In Egypt pottery was painted in figurines and tableware were manufactured. The Arratian period, or Naqada I, at around 4200 B.C. was characterized by a form of urban planning and great advances in architecture.

Naqada II occurred at about 3700 B.C., during which Lower Egypt manifested a growing influence on the people of Upper Egypt. This would result in a blending of the people both genetically and culturally in Naqada II (3700 B.C. to 3250 B.C.). In the latter period we see geometric motifs and highly realistic depictions of animals and people in their art.

The first representation of gods, usually shown riding in ships, can be seen in Naqada III (3250 B.C. to 3050 B.C.). A high level of civilization is evident now and the Cult of Osiris would result from their theology. A growing tension between Upper and Lower Egypt brought about their unification sometime between 3150 and 3000 B.C. under the legendary Menes.

Scholars disagree over who conquered whom. One reason for this discord is that although it appears Upper Egypt defeated Lower Egypt, the social system that resulted resembled the north (Lower Egypt) far more. Many archeologists feel that the south (Upper Egypt) conquered the north and simply adopted much of the northern culture into their new system.

The Narmer Palette depicted a king named Nar-Mer in its hieroglyphics as the pharaoh of this unified Egypt. He is shown wearing the white crown of the south and holding a mace as he prepares to crush the head of a northern Egyptian. The historian Eratosthenes stated that this king Narmer, or Aha, is the legendary king Meni or Menes.

Mummification was discovered in 2600 B.C., and the great pyramids of Gizah and the Sphinx were constructed at about 2450 B.C. These ancient Egyptians had somehow developed sophisticated mathematics and science (including astronomy and medicine) with absolutely no predecessors. This is what the accepted historical and archaeological paradigms relate to us as the origins of Egypt.

# CHRONOLOGY OF EGYPTIAN CIVILIZATION

| | |
|---|---|
| Prehistoric Era: | |
| Lower Paleolithic Age | 250,000 – 90,000 B.C. |
| Middle Paleolithic Age | 90,000 – 30,000 B.C. |
| Late Paleolithic Age | 30,000 – BP – 7000 B.C. |
| Neolithic Age | 7000  - 4800 B.C. |
| | |
| Predynastic Period | 4800  - 3050 B.C. |
| Upper Egypt: | |
| Badarian Culture | 4800  - 4200 B.C. |
| Amratian Culture (=Nagada I) | 4200  - 3700 B.C. |
| Gerzean A Culture (=Nagada II) | 3700  - 3250 B.C. |
| Gerzean B Culture (=Nagada III) | 3250  - 3050 B.C. |
| | |
| Lower Egypt: | |
| Fayum A Culture | 4800  - 4250 B.C. |
| Merimde Culture | 4500  - 3500 B.C. |
| | |
| Archaic Period | 3050  - 2705 B.C. |
| Dynasties 1-2 | |
| | |
| Old Kingdom | 2705  - 2213 B.C. |
| Dynasties 3-8 | |
| | |
| First Intermediate Period | 2213  - 1991 B.C. |
| Dynasties 9-11 | |
| | |
| Middle Kingdom | 1991  - 1668 B.C. |
| Dynasties 12-13 | |
| | |
| Second Intermediate Period | 1668  - 1570 B.C. |
| Dynasties 14-17 | |
| | |
| New Kingdom | 1570  - 1070 B.C. |
| Dynasties 18-20 | |
| | |
| Late Period | 1070  - 656 B.C. |
| Dynasties 21-24 | |
| Dynasty 25 (Kushite Domination) | |
| Assyrian Domination | |
| | |
| Saite Period | 685  - 525 B.C. |
| Dynasty 26 | |
| | |
| Persian Period | 525  - 332 B.C. |
| Dynasties 27-31 | |
| | |
| Greek and Roman Period | 332 B.C. – A.D. 395 |

All dates are approximate.

# THREE EPOCHS OF EGYPT'S HISTORY

It appears that our conventional knowledge of Egypt's history depicts three separate epochs, each initiated by a pharaoh who united this and following a period of chaos. The initial epoch was begun by Menes (CA. 3100 B.C., give or take 150 years) which is referred to as the First Dynasty. This period ended in the First Intermediate Period. Each intermediate period was characterized by an exodus of ETs and time travelers, as we shall see. Memphis was the capital of this Old Kingdom.

Thebes replaced Memphis as Egypt's capital when Menthotpe II defeated Herakleopolis during the Eleventh Dynasty. An invasion by Hyksos brought this era to a close and resulted in a Second Intermediate Period. A second Theban era arose as a result of Ahmose defeating the Hyksos. This began the Eighteenth Dynasty.

The problem with identifying Menes as the founder of the First Dynasty rests in contradictory archaeological evidence. Egypt's unification took place over more than one generation, and no single king can claim the role as unifier.

There were three kings from Upper Egypt (Scorpion, Narmer and Hor-Aha). Anyone of these could have been Menes. We find in the Narmer Palette a mace head depicting Narmer as king of both Upper and Lower Egypt. On one side, Narmer, wearing the white crown of Upper Egypt and holding a club in his hand, stands guard over a prisoner. Narmer also appears on the reverse side, this time wearing the red crown of Lower Egypt. The scene includes two panthers with long intertwined necks, suggesting the union of the two regions. Other finds, such as the one showing Scorpion, Narmer's predecessor, (also wearing the crowns of both Upper and Lower Egypt) complicate the picture.[3]

Archaeological finds at the tomb of Queen Neith-Hotep, wife of Narmer and mother of Hor-Aha, suggests a northern (Lower Egypt) source to the First Dynasty. The goddess Neith was a northern deity from Sais. Some scholars deduce from this that Egypt may have united through marriage and not military victories.

The capital city of this First Dynasty was established in the city of Hikuptah, which means "Soul of the House of Ptah." Greek translators pronounced this as Aigyptus and this is the source of the name Egypt as I previously mentioned. The name Memphis came from the Greek form of the Egyptian name Mn-Nfr, so Hikuptah was referred to as Memphis.

From the First Dynasty (my data from past life regressions showed even

---

[3] W. C. Hayes, *Cambridge Ancient History*. (Cambridge, England: Cambridge University Press, 1970).

much earlier) every pharaoh was depicted as a human representative of the god Horus. Memphis now became the seat of Horus' throne and authority. These ancients looked upon their pharaohs as the only legitimate divine right monarchs. Any form of challenge to the Memphis ruler was a challenge to Horus himself and could threaten the very stability of the nation.

## FORBIDDEN ARCHAEOLOGY

There are alternate history theories that are based on some pretty impressive evidence. The flies in the conventional ointment of history, paleontology and archaeology have been ignored by establishment scientists for at least 200 years.

First, the classic descriptions of Neanderthal man were based on the remains of a skeleton that suffered from osteoarthritis. We have no hard evidence to show that the posture of Neanderthal man differed significantly from that of modern man.[4]

What is even more significant is the 1937 discovery in a French cave near Lussac-les-Chateaux by Leon Pericard and Stephane Lwoff dating back from the Upper Paleolithic Period (40,000 years ago). We find in these etchings men and women wearing coats, hats, belts, boots and robes. One woman dressed is dressed in a pants suit with a short-sleeved jacket, a pair of small boots, a decorated hat and a purse. Men are depicted wearing tailored pants and coats, trimmed beards and moustaches.

Despite the establishment's attempts to portray these stone engravings as a fraud, they were authenticated in 1938. Abbé Brevil, among others, showed that humans living during the Magdalemian period of the Upper Paleolithic were well-dressed.

The question arises how did these Stone Age people develop the skill and technology to make these clothes and accessories? This is not the behavior of primitive man. Most of these drawings are withheld from the public and can only be viewed by those individuals with appropriate credentials and obtaining special permission. The pre-history library of Lussac-les-Chateaux and the Muséo de ∝ Homme in Paris exhibits only those stone engravings that are not *too antagonistic* to conventional history.

Prehistoric cave paintings from the Kalahari Desert of Southwest Africa, dated within the Stone Age period, show light-skinned men with blond beards and well-styled hair, wearing boots, tight-fitting pants, multicolored shirts, and coats

---

[4] William L. Straus, Jr., and A. J. A. Cave, "Pathology and the Posture of the Neanderthal Man." *Quarterly Review of Biology*, 32 1957; 348-63.

and gloves. Professor Otto Bader of the Ethnographical Institute of the Academy of Soviet Sciences discovered "Vladimir Man" near Moscow. This prehistoric man was also well-dressed. He wore a large pair of trousers made of fur, an embroidered shirt, and a very practical jacket.

In 1921 a fascinating discovery was made in Rhodesia. A Neanderthal skull was found containing a perfectly round hole of the left side of its skull. If this aperture was caused by a blow to the head, we would expect to observe radial cracks surrounding it. None were observed.

Only a high-speed projectile such as a *bullet* could have made such a hole. The skull directly opposite the hole is shattered, having been blown out from the inside. This same feature is seen in modern victims of head wounds received from shots from a high-powered rifle. No slower projectile could have produced either the neat hole or the shattering effect. Forensic experts in Europe declared that only a bullet could have created this hole in the skull. This skull is on exhibit in the Museum of Natural History in London.

There are some possible explanations for this anomaly. One suggests that Neanderthal man survived until a few hundred years ago and was shot by a European explorer. The other deduction points to a hunter from a very ancient and technologically advanced civilization shooting this primitive man.

Since this skull was found sixty feet below the surface, several thousands of years had to elapse for it to be buried so deep naturally. This could not have occurred in two to three hundred years. This makes the second hypothesis more likely.

Louis Leakey found stone tools well over 200,000 years old at Calico in Southern California. This 1960s discovery contradicts the establishment's paradigm that humans did not enter the subarctic regions of the New World until approximately 12,000 years ago. These convention scientists discount Leakey's finds by stating that they were natural products or simply were not 200,000 years old!

We will see how any evidence that goes against established theories of human origin are ignored, suppressed or conveniently forgotten by the scientific establishment. There is ample evidence to show that tool-using humans lived in the Pliocene (2-5 million years ago), the Miocene (5-25 million years ago) and earlier.[5]

The oldest large-scale metallurgical factory in the world was discovered in 1968 by Dr. Koriun Megurtchian in Medzamer, Armenia. This 4,500 year old

---

[5] M. A. Cremo and R. L. Thompson, *Forbidden Archeology: The Hidden History of the Human Race.* (Los Angeles: Bhaktivendanta Book Pub. Co., 1993)

factory had over 200 furnaces that manufactured spearheads, bracelets, rings, vases, knives and other items.  Mouth-filters and gloves were worn by these workers, who handled copper, lead, zinc, gold, tin, iron, manganese and fourteen types of bronze.  This site is interestingly located within fifteen miles from Mount Ararat – the landing site of Noah's Ark.

On April 10, 1967 American newspapers reported the discovery of an artifact and human skeleton at the Rocky Point Mine in Gulman, Colorado.  This several million year old skeleton was found embedded in a silver vein.  A well-tempered copper arrowhead four inches long was also found at this site.  Neither object belonged there, according to the scientific establishment.  Conveniently, this discovery was forgotten.

On June 9, 1891 a Mrs. S. W. Culp of Morrisonville, Illinois found a gold chain of intricate workmanship embedded in a piece of coal that was dated back to a period of 260 to 320 million years ago.

A gold thread was unearthed eight feet below the surface in a quarry near Rutherford Mills, England on June 22, 1844 by workmen blasting granite out of a pit.  The London Times reported that this gold thread was manufactured artificially and was over 60 million years old!

A businessman named Hiram de Witt brought a piece of auriferous (gold-iron) quartz from California to his home in Illinois.  While showing it to a friend, de Witt dropped this rock on the floor.  A cut-iron six-penny nail was found in the center of this quartz, dating over one million years ago.

Another nail manufactured by man was found in 1845 in a granite block excavated from the Kindgoodie Quarry in Northern England that originated over 60 million years ago.

Cremo and Thompson report a partial shoe sole discovered by mining engineer and geologist John T. Reid in Nevada in 1922.  Professors at Columbia University and the American Museum of Natural History confirmed it was a man-made shoe sole that dated back to the Triassic period of 213-248 million years ago.

William Meister found a shoe print in the Wheeler Shale near Antelope Spring, Utah.  Within the imprint were the remains of an extinct marine arthropod called trilobites.  Since the shale containing these fossils is from the Cambrian period, the shoe print dates back 505 to 590 million years ago.

There is ample evidence that modern humans millions of years ago coexisted with more apelike hominids.  Even more interesting is a report by Professor W. G. Burroughs, head of the department of geology at Berea College in Berea, Kentucky.  He cited human-like tracks on a sand beach in Rockcastle County, Kentucky that dates back over 320 million years ago, when amphibians were the most evolved life on Earth.  This discovery was also reported in Cremo and

Thompson's *Forbidden Archaeology.*

Traditional scientists believe the first apelike mammals appeared some 38 million years ago, while we assume no footprint like that reported by Burroughs could have existed farther back than 4 million years ago.

Ruins of a large settlement of 800 structures carefully laid out in planned blocks and avenues was discovered at Ipiutak on Point Hope in northern Alaska. Several thousand people must have lived in this community, which was not merely a hunting culture.

Evidence exists to show that these people possessed knowledge of mathematics and astronomy on a level similar to that of the ancient Mayans. Archeologists are at a loss to explain how such an advanced civilization could have existed that far north in the Arctic Circle, where modern day Eskimos can barely survive. The only logical explanation is that the people who built this community existed before the last Ice Age, and therefore must have lived 12,000 or more years ago.

The cemetery at Ipiutak depicts the citizens who lived there as being tall and blond. Ancient legends talk about Thule, Numinor and the Hyperborean civilizations of the Arctic. These Norse people were responsible for the disasters of Ragnarok and the destruction of the gods of Valhalla.

We even find evidence of a nuclear war in ancient times. The Hindu *Mahabharata* is an epic poem dating back to 500 B.C. The events depicted originate from 1,500 to 2,500 B.C. and refer to great gods riding in Vimanas or "celestial cars," which were described as "aerial chariots with sides of iron clad with wings."

An eighteen day war is portrayed between the Kauravas and the Pandavas. A second battle took place against the Vrishnis and Andhakas. We find stated in the Mahabharata:

*The valiant Adwattan, remaining steadfast in his Vimana, landed upon the water and from there unleashed the Agneya weapon, incapable of being resisted by the very gods. Taking careful aim against his foes, the preceptor's son let loose the blazing missile of smokeless fire with tremendous force. Dense arrows of flame, like a great shower, issued forth upon creation, encompassing the enemy. Meteors flashed down from the sky. . . Birds croaked madly, and beasts shuddered from the destruction. The very elements seemed disturbed. The sun seemed to waver in the heavens. The earth shook, scorched by the terrible violent heat of this weapon. Elephants burst into flame and ran to and fro in a frenzy, seeking protection from the terror. Over a vast area, other animals crumpled to the ground and died. The waters boiled, and the creatures residing therein also died. . .*

The second is described as follows:

*Gurkha, flying in his swift and powerful Vimana, hurled against the three cities of the Vrishnis and Andhakas a single projectile charged with all the power of the Universe. An incandescent column of smoke and fire, as brilliant as ten thousand suns, rose in all its splendor. It was the unknown weapon, the iron thunderbolt, a gigantic messenger of death which reduced to ashes the entire race of the Vrishnis and Andhakas.*[6]

Events such as a column of rising smoke and fire, the effects of radiation poisoning, the brightness of the blast and the intense shock waves and heat accurately depict a nuclear holocaust. Hindu scholars assign the date 2449 B.C. to this nuclear war, due to detailed astronomical configurations given in the poem.

Nuclear physics was known to the ancients. Ancient Sanskrit books, such as the *Kalpa* or "Day of Brahma" mention a period of 4.32 billion years. The *Bihath Sathka* references the Kashta or three one-hundredth-millionths (0.00000003) of a second. Other than nuclear physics, there is no logical reason why ancient Indians should utilize these extreme numbers.


Other evidence of nuclear explosions in antiquity include:
- A 16-foot level of a layer of fused green glass made of fused quartz sand with green discoloration found in Israel in 1952.
- An engineer named Albion W. Hart found another example of fused green glass in the southern Sahara Desert in Egypt. It had the same appearance to that found in atomic test sites.
- Prehistoric forts in the British Isles and the Lofoten Islands off Norway had their stones fused and walls vitrified by an unknown force.
- Several Scottish castle towers and Irish granite fortresses reveal having been melted to a depth of one foot by some extreme heat force.

We can also wonder why several agricultural centers appeared out of nowhere at approximately the same time in different parts of the world.

It is interesting to note that the Paleolithic cultures we find in Europe originated from the north (Hyperborean?) and west (Atlantis?). The paradigm we commonly observe in ancient myths are an initial era of great knowledge and rulership by god-kings (Lemurians, Atlanteans, extraterrestrials or time travelers), followed by a cataclysm and a period of confusion and a degeneration into primitive cultures. Finally, there appears a sudden proliferation of religion, social organization, architecture and science, which remains fairly unchanged for several hundred to thousands of years.

---

[6] P *Mahabharata.* (Calcutta: Bharata Press, 1978).

Egypt stands out as an example during which there is no gradual transition to a pyramid building civilization. A long preliminary period is necessary to acquire the architectural and mathematics skills needed to transport heavy stones and align them with uncanny accuracy. Conventional archeologists do not delve too deeply into this enigma, they merely accept it.

There is no logical way in which primitive nomads in Egypt around 3,000 B.C. could construct the pyramids we find in Cairo in just 500 years. What is far more likely is the existence of other highly advanced civilizations (Lemuria and Atlantis), which preexisted Egypt by many thousands of years and was destroyed by some form of natural disaster.

The survivors of these advanced civilizations sought refuge in Egypt and other lands and facilitated the technological growth of these regions. A flood, or series of floods, most likely destroyed these advanced civilizations. We know that practically every culture reports a great flood in their history and mythology.

An interesting example of unexplained technology was discovered in Peru. Pre-Inca objects were found that were made out of platinum. A temperature of about 1,750 degrees Celsius is required to melt platinum. How could these primitive people possibly have produced this heat, without the assistance of an advanced civilization? Even the ancient Egyptians did not possess platinum or this technology.

It would be most informative if we had all of the ancient libraries to consult. These great libraries were destroyed and included the following losses:

- The Pisastratus (Pisander) library in Athens was destroyed during the sixth century B.C.
- The papyri of the library of the Temple of Ptah in Memphis, Egypt.
- The library of Pergamus in Asia Minor.
- The Carthage library was burned by the Romans in 146 B.C.
- The Alexandrian library in Egypt was destroyed by Julius Caesar and Omar, the Caliph of Islam in 640 A.D.
- The Emperor Chin in Shih Huang Ti of China burned all historical books in 212 B.C.
- The Inquisitions of the Middle Ages destroyed an inestimable number of priceless manuscripts.

## EGYPTIAN HISTORY

The dynastic history of Egypt has been estimated to have originated not prior to 3400 B.C. and not much later than 3000 B.C. E. A. Wallis Budge states in

*The Book of the Dead*: Papyrus of Ani:

*The evidence derived from the enormous mass of new material which we owe to the all-important discoveries of the mastabah tombs and pyramids by M. Maspero, and to his publications of the early religious texts, proves beyond all doubt that all the essential texts comprised in the Book of the Dead are, in one form or another, far older than the period of Mena (Menes), the first historical king of Egypt. Certain sections, indeed, appear to belong to the predynastic period.*

*The earliest texts bear within themselves proof not only of having been composed, but also of having been revised, or edited, long before the copies known to us were made, and, judging from many passages in the copies inscribed in hieroglyphics upon the pyramids of Unas (the last king of the Fifth Dynasty, about 3333 B.C.), and Teta, Pepi I, Mehti-em-sa-t, the Pepi II (kings of the Sixth Dynasty, about 3300-3166 B.C.), **it would seem even at that remote date, the scribes were perplexed and hardly understood the texts which they had before them.** [Bold italics are mine] . . . . To fix a chronological limit for the arts and civilization of Egypt is absolutely impossible.*[7]

Here we have an expert commentary on the fact that we do not know the precise dates of the origin of Egyptian scriptures. Budge suggests that true sources for the *Book of the Dead* were considerably before the dates accepted by Egyptologists.

## THE SPHINX

Robert Schoch (a Boston geologist) and John West decided to test a hypothesis that the Sphinx in Cairo showed weathering patterns that resembled water erosion, rather than that caused by wind.

West first became attracted to the water erosion theory concerning the Sphinx when he read the work of the French mathematician, R. A. Schwaller de Lubicz. The latter's research from 1937 to 1952 of the Luxor Temple resulted in the publication of a three volume *Temple de ∝ Homme* and *Roi de la théocratie Pharaonique*. The latter work was translated into English as *Sacred Science*, and in it de Lubicz comments on the tremendous floods and rains which devastated Egypt in the eleventh millennium B.C. He states:

*A great civilization must have preceded the vast movements of water that passed over Egypt, which leads us to assume that the Sphinx already existed, sculptured in the rock of the west cliff at Giza – that Sphinx whose leonine body,*

---

[7] E.A.W. Budge, Book of the Dead. (London: Longman & Co., 1895).

*except for the head, shows indisputable signs of water erosion.*[8]

If the water erosion theory was correct, this would place the date of the Sphinx's construction to at least 10,000 B.C. Current paradigms propose that this structure was built at about the same time as the pyramids of Giza, approximately 2500 B.C.

The Sphinx enclosure consists of limestone walls on two sides. Schoch hypothesized that the original rock was carved into its current face at a time when the region was still green. At a later date the body was added, so the builders cutting the softer limestone below and around the head forming a two-sided enclosure that resulted in room to work.

The 200 ton blocks removed during this construction were utilized to build the two temples in front of the Sphinx. West's geophysicist, Dobecki, found an underground chamber a few meters under the Sphinx's front paws. Ancient secrets have been reported by legend to be kept in this chamber.

The Associated Press reported the discovery of an unknown passageway leading down below the body of the Sphinx in 1994. As was expected, any exploration of this chamber was prevented by the Giza plateau authorities under the guise that repairs to the Sphinx were far more important. Does this mentality sound familiar?

The Sphinx must be thousands of years older than the pyramids only 200 yards away, due to the former's weathering pattern. The weathering of the Sphinx temples is far worse then that of the three Old Kingdom pyramids, and is a victim of rain erosion. The three pyramids were eroded by wind.

Wind weathering results in a series of parallel layers, having a profile of humps and hollows. Weathering due to water produces vertical channels in the rock. Water erosion gives rise to a series of bumps, a completely different effect from that of wind erosion. The body of the Sphinx and its enclosure clearly show water erosion and not the smoother effects of wind weathering. The enormous amount of rain required to have caused this damage has not been available since at least 10,000 B.C. The Sphinx must have been built before 10,000 B.C. by a highly advanced civilization.[9]

The Sphinx temples also illustrate an architecture quite unlike that of most Egyptian temples. Most Egyptian temples have a plethora of carvings and cylindrical columns. These temples, however, are simple rectangular pillars surrounded by uncarved blocks of a similar appearance.

Egyptologists know very well that pharaohs were in the habit of adding their

---

[8] R. A. Schwaller de Lubicz, *Sacred Science: The King of Pharaonic Theocracy.* (Rochester, Vermont: Inner Traditions Int., 1988).
[9] John A. West, *Serpent in the Sky.* (New York: Harper & Row, 1979).

own names to monuments that predated them. Simply because Chefren's name was mentioned in the inscription on stelae placed between the paws of the Sphinx, doesn't establish that he built it. The fact that seven statues of Chefren were found buried in the Valley Temple next to the Sphinx Temple also is insufficient evidence of it being built by him. There are no inscriptions in this temple bearing Chefren's name. This would have been the case had he built it.

Another extraordinary piece of evidence places the construction of the Sphinx at about 10,450 B.C. Ancient man used the rising of the sun at both the vernal and autumn equinoxes to designate an astronomical age. The Sphinx faces due east, and in 2500 B.C. the sun on the vernal equinox rises against the background of the constellation Taurus (the bull). In 2000 B.C. the sun rose against the constellation Pisces (fish).

The ancients would have built such a monument to reflect the constellation in the background when the sun rose on the vernal equinox. But the Sphinx is not in the shape of a fish (Pisces – 2000 B.C.) or a bull (Taurus – 2500 B.C.), it is in the shape of a lion (Leo).

We assign the dates of 10,970 to 8,810 B.C. to the Age of Leo. In chapter 4 I will discuss in greater detail how the three pyramids at Giza are aligned to reflect the three stars of Orion's Belt when they reached their lowest point in their precessional cycle. This precessional epoch will not return for 26,000 years (15,000 A.D.), so it appears that the Sphinx was probably built 10,450 B.C., and not during the Fourth, Fifth or Sixth Egyptian Dynasty.[10]

When Schoch presented an abstract of his findings to the Geological Society of America in October 1992 at its annual convention, 275 of his colleagues supported his deduction and wondered why this theory hadn't been presented many years earlier. The only challenge to Schoch's hypothesis came from Mark Lehner, the director of the Giza Mapping Project. This Chicago University Egyptologist could not present any convincing evidence to refute Schoch's conclusions.

It became increasingly obvious that the Sphinx must have been built by an advanced civilization many thousands of years prior to Chefren's reign. West brought another factor into this equation later on by pointing out that the mud-brick tombs surrounding the Step Pyramid of Saqqara revealed none of the weathering features exhibited by the Sphinx. Since this structure is located ten miles away and was built a century before the Great Pyramid, it should have weathered exactly as the Sphinx. It didn't because the Sphinx was constructed thousands of years earlier.

The two Sphinx temples are built from 200 ton blocks to worship Khepera,

---

[10] Graham Hancock, *Fingerprint of the Gods* (London: William Heinemann, 1995).

the creator of the universe and the father of all the other gods. How could these ancients have moved 200 ton blocks? Only a very advanced civilization could be responsible for this feat.

Physically the Sphinx is 240 feet long and 66 feet high. An Arab sheikh in 1380, and later the Mamelukes, were responsible for the present damage to the Sphinx's head, as they used it for target practice. This structure was covered with sand up to its neck until 1817, when it was cleared away revealing a small temple located between the paws.

When this temple was explored, three stelae were discovered. It was reported on one of the stelae that King Thutmose IV (1425 B.C.) had made extensive repairs to the body of the Sphinx. Pharaoh Chefren also was assumed to have repaired it. If Chefren built the Sphinx, it most certainly would not have required repairs so soon.

The Sphinx was well protected by being buried in sand for most of the time since it was built (if you assume it was built by Chefren). For those that argue that the limestone composing the Sphinx began to erode as soon as it was completed, an erosion rate of a foot every hundred years would have resulted in it disappearing in five centuries.

Egyptologists during the nineteenth century assumed the Sphinx was much older than the pyramids. The name of Chefren on the stelae has prejudiced modern Egyptologists into thinking he built it, and that its head is that of Chefren.

## THE GREAT PYRAMID

Egyptologists have always assumed that the three pyramids at Giza were built by three pharaohs of the Fourth Dynasty (2275-2467 B.C.). These three kings were Khufu, Khafre and Menkaure. The Greeks later referred to these rulers respectively as Cheops, Chephren and Mycerinus.

The Greek historian Herodotus of the fifth century B.C. is one source of this chronology. He received this data from his ancient Egyptian tour guide when he visited Egypt. Another form of Egyptian hearsay was exhibited during the first century B.C. when the Greek historian Diodorus Siculus traveled to Egypt. This objective historian received his information from Egyptian priests as to the history of Egypt.

European museums contain two lists of ancient Egyptian pharaohs that are called the Palermo Stone (a Fifth Dynasty document) and the Turin Papyrus (from the Nineteenth Dynasty, or thirteenth century B.C.). A Heliopolitan priest named Manetho compiled a widely respected list of kings and Egyptian history during the third century B.C. What is interesting about these three sources is that they all refer to a *distant* era when the Nile Valley was ruled by gods.

The Royal Papyrus of Turin is the most valuable of these ancient documents because it gave a complete list of Egyptian kings in Upper and Lower Egypt from Menes to the combined Egypt. Included within this list was the duration of each reign. This list also depicted rulers well into pre-history. Although this document was found intact, it was shattered during its relocation to Italy.

Here are two very significant lines from this papyrus:

... *venerables Shemsu-Hor, 13,420 years*
*Reigns up to Shemsu-Hor, 23,200 years*
*King Menes*[11]

The *Shemsu-Hor* translates as "Companions of Horus." This total of 36,620 years before Menes dates from over 3000 B.C., making Egypt a 40,000 year old civilization!

We can look to Diodorus of Sicily and his report that gods and heroes ruled Egypt for 18,000 years, followed by 15,000 of mortal kings. This adds up to 33,000 years of pre-history and history. Some authorities state this total should be 23,000 years, since Diodorus uses this lower figure in Book XXIII.

George the Syncellus sums up the Egyptian civilization by mentioning thirty dynasties preceded by a reign of gods comprising twenty-five Sothic cycles of 1461 years each. This total is 36,525 years.

Manetho speaks of a remote golden age of Egypt he terms the First Time. The writings of the Jewish chronicler Josephus (A.D. 60) and of Christian writers, such as Africanus (A.D. 300), Eusebius (A.D. 340) and George the Syncellus (A.D. 300) record Manetho's descriptions of very ancient Egypt. As is typical of the scientific establishment, Manetho's King list is considered reliable, but his references to the First Time are flatly rejected.[12]

Eusebius reports Manetho's chronology as follows:

*These were the first to hold sway in Egypt. Thereafter, the kingship passed from one to another in unbroken succession. . .through 13,900 years- . . .After the Gods, Demigods reigned for 1255 years; and again another line of kings held sway for 1817 years; then came thirty more kings, reigning for 1790 years; and then again ten kings ruling for 350 years. There followed the rule of the Spirits of the Dead. . .for 5813 years. . .*[13]

The total we obtain from this is 24,925 years. This is a significant figure because as we shall see in later chapters the ancient continents of Lemuria and

[11] James Henry Breasted, *Ancient Records of Egypt: Historical Documents from the Earliest Times to the Persian Conquest.* (London: Histories and Mysteries of Man Ltd., 1988).

[12] James Henry Breasted, op. cit.

[13] George Hart, *Pharaohs and Pyramids.* (London: Guild Publishing, 1991).

Atlantis both suffered major earthquakes and subsequent floods at approximately 24,000 B.C.

What Manetho was reporting was simply that civilizations existed in Egypt many millennia before the First Dynasty (approximately 3100 B.C.). This far distant example of advanced civilizations in Egypt was further confirmed by Diodorus when he stated:

*At first gods and heroes ruled Egypt for a little less than 18,000 years, the last of the gods to rule being Horus, the son of Isis. . .Mortals have been kings of their country, they say, for a little less than 5000 years. . .*[14]

Diodorus dates the origin of Egypt as far back as 23,100 B.C. He is only 1,825 years apart from Manetho's figure.

Another quote from Diodorus drives home the distant past of Egypt:

*The position and arrangements of the stars as well as their motions have always been the subject of careful observation among the Egyptians . . . From ancient times to this day they have preserved the records concerning each of these stars over an incredible number of years . . .*[15]

Our understanding of Egyptian hieroglyphics was made possible with the discovery of the Rosetta Stone in 1799. With its parallel inscriptions in Greek and ancient Egyptian, this key finally unlocked the mysteries of what the ancient Egyptians wanted others to know about their civilization.

In 1222 A.D. much of Cairo was destroyed by a great earthquake. The limestone covering the Great Pyramid was removed to rebuild this devastated city. The historian and physician Abdul Latif in 1220 was one of the last to view the Pyramid while it was still encased in limestone. He stated that the hieroglyphics on its surface would fill thousands of pages. Unfortunately, these writings were lost in building the Grand Mosque and other public buildings from the Pyramid's limestone.

Internally the Great Pyramid represents precision. The walls or ramps on either side of the slot at the center of the Grand Gallery have a series of slots cut into them of two different lengths. The short slots slope and equal the horizontal length of the long holes. We don't know what purpose this intricate accuracy serves.

Some of its blocks weigh 70 tons, yet they are placed with incredible accuracy and precision. We can almost explain how the masons who built the Medieval cathedrals could have acquired their skills over the centuries, but what about the ancient Egyptian masons?

---

[14] Diodorus, *Diodorus Siculus* (trans. C. H. Oldfather), (London, Loeb Classical Library, 1989).
[15] Ibid.

Only the Step Pyramid at Saqqara and the Bent Pyramid at Dahshur preceded the Pyramid at Giza.  These crude pyramids were simply insufficient to supply the necessary experimentation to arrive at the final product as represented by the Great Pyramid.

We normally associate voluminous wall decorations with Egyptian temples.  Granted, there were quite a bit of hieroglyphics on the limestone covering this structure that was removed during the thirteenth century, as I previously explained.  But this bare and bleak pyramid is quite atypical for ancient Egypt.  It would be explained by the fact that the Great Pyramid was a primitive computer and astronomical observatory, rather than a burial chamber.

In the King's Chamber two pharaohs were named in the cartouches.  These were Khufu and Khnem-Khuf.  The latter was at first thought to be a variation of Khufu, but the current thinking is he is another pharaoh entirely.  Since Khnem-Khuf's name appeared in chambers lower than Khufu's name, Khnem-Khuf must have lived prior to Khuf.  This is because a pyramid is constructed from the bottom up.

Many people have contemplated the purpose of the Great Pyramid.  Was it merely a burial chamber for the pharaoh?  Did it have some hidden scientific function?  The London publisher John Taylor proposed the first scientific theory depicting the purpose of this structure in 1864.

Taylor was curious as to why the designers of the Pyramid decided to make it slope at an angle of nearly 52°-51°51!  By sloping at this precise angle, the Pyramid's height in relation to the length of its base exactly parallels the radius of a circle to its circumference.  This principle was later called A (pi) by the Greeks.  The Pyramid represented the hemisphere from the North Pole to the equator.

The Greek grammarian Agatharclides of Cnidus, during the second century B.C., related the fact that the base of the Great Pyramid was exactly one eighth of a minute of a degree in length.  It was therefore an eighth of a minute of a degree of the Earth's circumference, since a minute is one sixtieth of a degree.  By multiplying the length of the Pyramid's base by eight, then 60, then 360, we derive a figure of just under 25,000 miles.  That is important, since it represents the circumference of the Earth.

The technical excellence of the Great Pyramid cannot be understated.  For example, the northern face was aligned, almost perfectly, to true north, the eastern face almost perfectly to true east, the southern to true south, and the western face to true west.  This structure contains an average error of only three minutes of arc.  Engineers today would find that feat nearly impossible to match, and that assumes utilizing modern technology.

Achieving a 0.015 percent error, which is what the three arc minutes translates to, would not be much different than a one percent error to the naked eye. Yet the amount of extra work, time and attention to arrive at this workmanship required enormous skill.

Evidence does exist which shows that Khufu did not build the Great Pyramid. The Inventory Stela, a rectangular limestone discovered by the French archaeologist, Auguste Mariette, shows that both the Sphinx and the Great Pyramid were already constructed long before Khufu became pharaoh. This inscription clearly indicates that the Great Pyramid was dedicated to Isis and refers to her as the "Mistress of the Pyramid." This monument was not dedicated to Khufu at all.

The ancient Egyptians demonstrated their phenomenal knowledge by incorporating the measurements of our planet into a pyramid. This knowledge was thousands of years ahead of its time. Taylor's measurements were confirmed by the Scottish astronomer Charles Piazzi Smyth in 1865.

The Precession of the Equinoxes is a 26,000 year cycle that is required for our solar system to make one complete revolution around our greater parent sun, the Pleiades. The precise figure is 25,827.5 years. Robert Bauval's work demonstrated that the ancient Egyptians possessed this advance knowledge.

For example, a careful study of the Great Pyramid shows:

1.     Each of the two base-diagonals of the Great Pyramid taken together equals 25,827.5, the Precession of the of the Equinoxes, at the rate of an inch per year.

2.     The width of the Grand Gallery of the Great Pyramid times A (3.14159) equals 25,827.5, the Precession of the Equinoxes.

3.     The altitude of the Great Pyramid lying above the floor-plane of the King's Chamber times A (Pi)equals 25,827.5, the Precession of the Equinoxes.

4.     The King's Chamber is situated on the 50th plane of masonry in the Great Pyramid. The outside surface perimeter at this level in original Pyramid inches equals 25,827.5, the length of the Precession of the Equinoxes.

The Great Pyramid is a geophysical computer illustrating the light continuum of the other universes associated with our planet. In addition, it demonstrates the relationship of our own universe within the geophysical foundations of the Earth's biophysical, geophysical, and astrophysical meridians.

One of the most puzzling circumstances for conventional Egyptologists is the fact that there were no predecessors to either the superior pyramids at Giza or the Pyramid texts. The three pyramids at Giza were simply unsurpassed technological achievements. It is perplexing that no pyramids of comparable quality were constructed by these ancients following these three.

The argument that these pyramids were burial chambers for the pharaohs doesn't hold up with the evidence. There is absolutely no evidence that they ever housed the dead body of an Egyptian king. No signs of a royal burial have been found in these structures. Furthermore, Sneferu (Khufu's father) is credited with building the "Bent" and "Red" Pyramids at Dahshur, located about thirty miles south of Giza. Why did this pharaoh need two pyramids to be buried in?

We can look to the only other pyramid builders preceding Khufu, namely Zoser and Sekhemkhet, for a reinforcement of this enigma. Zoser was the second pharaoh of the Third Dynasty, and built the Step Pyramid at Saqqara. His successor was Sekhemkhet, who also built an inferior pyramid at Saqarra.

Smaller and shabbier pyramids were built during the Fifth and Sixth Dynasties. These pyramids house the *Pyramid Texts*. The technical and artistic excellence of these examples of scribal and hieroglyphic art has never been equaled. We can see a connection of sorts between the completely uninscribed (but technically superior)–pyramids at Giza, and the brilliantly inscribed (but technically inferior) pyramids of the Fifth and Sixth Dynasties.

Neither had antecedents and both dominated Egyptian culture for a mere hundred years, never to be reproduced. An advanced civilization from pre-history that came and went is a far more logical explanation than a suddenly inspired Egyptian population, whose ancestors were primitive nomads.

As far as the cataclysms alluded to in ancient times, Chapter CLXXV of the *Book of the Dead* relates the following statement by their god Thoth:

*They have fought fights, they have upheld strifes, they have done evil, they have created hostilities, they have made slaughter, they have caused trouble and oppression. . . [Therefore] I am going to blot out everything which I have made. This earth shall enter into the watery abyss by means of a raging flood, and will become even as it was in primeval time.* [16]

The *Book of Genesis* in the *Old Testament* avers:

*The earth was filled with violence, and God looked upon the earth, and, behold, it was corrupt; for all flesh had corrupted his way upon the earth. And God said unto Noah, "The end of all flesh is come before me; for the earth is filled with violence through them; and behold I will destroy them with the earth."* [17]

The First Time gods, according to Egyptian theology, totalled nine in number. They were named Ra, Shu, Tefnut, Geb, Nut, Osiris, Isis, Nepthys and Set. To these we may add the progeny of these gods, namely Horus and Anubis. Ancient cults were dedicated to the gods Ptah and Thoth.

*Pyramid Texts* show the gods travelling in beautiful, high-powered, streamlined ships built to rather advanced specifications. They are similar to those

---

[16] E. A. Wallis Budge, *From Fetish to God in Ancient Egypt.* (London: Oxford University Press, 1934) p. 155.
[17] Genesis, 6:11-13.

sea vessels illustrated in the Giza pyramids.

There was no need for the ancient Egyptians, a landlocked society, to develop these maritime skills. Only seafaring people master astronomy and sophisticated shipbuilding skills. One explanation is that advanced prehistoric maritime civilizations, such as Lemuria and Atlantis, molded the development of the Egyptian society.

## THE PIRI REIS MAPS AND THE BIBLICAL FOUNDER OF EGYPT

On November 9, 1929 Malil Edhem, director of the Turkish National Museum at the old Imperial Palace at Constantinople, discovered a map painted on a gazelle skin and rolled up on a dusty shelf. This map was prepared by an admiral in the Ottoman Navy named Piri Reis in 1513.

Admiral Reis was an unusual character. His real name was Ahmet Muhidd Ibn Bahriye. He was considered an expert on the lands of the Mediterranean, and was the author of a famous sailing book, the *Kitabi Bahriye*, which accurately charted the Aegean and Mediterranean Seas. Due to some nefarious activities, Reis was beheaded in 1554 or 1555 A.D.

The phenomenal accuracy of this map, which was authenticated as having been drawn in 1513, came to the attention of Professor Charles H. Hapgood. Collaborating with mathematician Richard W. Strachan of Keene State College, Hapgood analyzed the Reis map.

Reis had copied the map from other sources. One source of this map was that of ancient Greece. The map projection was based on an overestimate of four and a half percent in the Earth's circumference. The Greek Eratosthenes was the only ancient world geographer to make that error.

All existing longitude errors were eliminated when the Piri Reis map grid was redrawn to correct the Eratosthenes error. One conclusion Hapgood made from this was that the Greek cartographers used a source for their map that did not contain the Eratosthenes error. An earlier people, who possessed a highly advanced science of map making than the Greeks, had been the ultimate source of the Piri Reis map.

The fact that the Piri Reis map shows an intricately accurate measurement of longitude and latitude demonstrates the work of a highly advanced civilization. The chronometer was not invented until 1765, and without that instrument it was impossible to accurately record longitude readings.

Not only are the Caribbean, Spanish, African and South American coasts on the Piri Reis map in correct positions relative to each other, but even such isolated land areas of the Cape Verde Islands, the Azores, and the Canary Islands are accurately situated by latitude and longitude—the first two without error and the last within less than a degree. This achievement is unparalleled in reference to map makers of the Renaissance, the Middle Ages, the Arab world, or any of the ancient geographers.

The Piri Reis map also shows islands and several locations along the Central and South American coast, which were either briefly explored but not accurately positioned or not discovered at all prior to 1513. These include the Isle of Pines, Andros Island, San Salvador, Jamaica and others.

By far the most significant feature of the Piri Reis map concerns the coastline of Antarctica, especially the area known as Queen Maud Land. Reis' map accurately shows this coast to be a rugged one, with several mountain chains and individual peaks breaking through the current levels of ice. The Piri Reis map does *not* show the ice.

Two bays were indicated on the Reis map where modern seismic maps showed land. A rechecking of measurements resulted in Reis' map being correct. The fact that the Piri Reis map clearly shows subglacial topography and an accurate profile of Queen Maud Land Antarctica beneath the ice is beyond comprehension. We must bear in mind that Antarctica was not discovered until 1818, over 300 years after Reis drew this map!

An advancing ice sheet covered this region of Antarctica completely hiding it from view from at least 4000 B.C. It was not revealed again until seismic surveys were carried out during 1949 by a joint British-Swedish scientific reconnaissance team. Hapgood concluded that someone possessing measuring techniques, which were not employed in Europe until the nineteenth century, mapped Antarctica before the continent was covered with ice. We do not know of any civilization that possessed either the need or the technical skills to survey Antarctica's coast line between 13,000 B.C. and 4,000 B.C.[18]

This advanced civilization predated any of the known ancient cultures, such as the Egyptian, Babylonian, Greek, Roman and Phoenician civilizations. It mastered cartography comparable to what we can do today. They had sophisticated instruments, knew the correct size of the earth; they used spherical trigonometry in their mathematical measurements; and they utilized ultramodern cartographical projections.

To place a date on the original map we have to assume it was drawn shortly after the flood (when the land masses were left in their present forms), but before the ice began to accumulate at the poles. This would mean sometime between

---

[18] Charles Hapgood, *Maps of the Ancient Sea Kings*. (London: Turnstone Books, 1979).

24,000 B.C. and 4,000 B.C. It is also interesting to note that the Piri Reis map was based on a circular projection with the focal point in Egypt. Hapgood came to this latter conclusion when he noted that the Caribbean region was shown at right angles to its normal (Mercator) position. The original source maps from which the Piri Reis map was made must have been drawn using a circular grid based on spherical trigonometry, with the focal point situated in Egypt.

Piri Reis wrote notes on his map informing us that he did not do the original surveying. He admitted copying this map from several other sources. Although Hapgood's theory about Antarctica being free of ice within the last 15,000 years sounds good, most geologists in 1963 (when Hapgood did his research on these Renaissance maps) would have argued that Antarctica remained glaciated during the past several million years.

Experts at the Carnegie Institution in Washington, D.C., Dr. Jack Hough of Illinois University and John G. Weiphaupt from the University of Colorado and a specialist in seismology, gravity and planetary geology, agree that parts of Antarctica were free of ice from 7000 B.C. to 4000 B.C.

Hapgood theorizes that a very advanced civilization from sometime before 4000 B.C. made this map and it found its way to the library in Alexandria, Egypt. Copies were transported to Constantinople and when the Venetians conquered Constantinople during the Fourth Crusade in 1204, these maps were made available to sailors like Piri Reis. Hapgood states:

*Most of these maps were of the Mediterranean and the Black Sea. But maps of other areas survived. These included maps of the Americas and maps of the Arctic and Antarctic Oceans. It becomes clear that the ancient voyagers travelled from pole to pole. Unbelievable as it may appear, the evidence nevertheless indicates that some ancient people explored Antarctica when its coasts were free of ice. It is clear, too, that they had an instrument of navigation for accurately determining longitudes that was far superior to anything possessed by the peoples of ancient, medieval or modern times until the second half of the eighteenth century.*

*This evidence of a lost technology will support and give credence to many of the other hypotheses that have been brought forward of a lost civilization in remote times. Scholars have been able to dismiss most of that evidence as mere myth, but here we have evidence that cannot be dismissed. The evidence requires that all the other evidence that has been brought forward in the past should be re-examined with an open mind.*[19]

Other Medieval and Renaissance maps studied by Hapgood that accurately

---

[19] Charles H. Hapgood, op. cit., preface.

depicted geography which was covered by ice when they were drawn are the Orontius Fineus map of 1531 showing rivers in Antarctica where today mile-thick glaciers flow; the Hadji Ahmed map of 1559 depicts the Ice Age land bridge that existed between Siberia and Alaska; the Andrea Benincasa map of 1508 indicates that northern Europe was covered by the farthest advance of the Ice Age glaciation and the 1380 map of the Zen brothers correctly presents the topography of Greenland below the northern icecap.

## EARTH-CRUST DISPLACEMENT

Hapgood published a book in 1958 titled, *Earth's Shifting Crust: A Key to Some Basic Problems of Earth Science.* In it he proposed what he termed an earth-crust displacement theory.

Hapgood's thesis was that Antarctica was not always covered with ice. A mechanism called *earth-crust displacement* quite simply moved the entire outer crust of the Earth, in a manner similar to the skin of an orange shifting over the inner part of the orange in one piece, assuming the skin was loose.

This displacement transported Antarctica from its former location 2,000 miles north to its current site at the South Pole. We must not confuse earth-crust displacement with continental drift or plate-tetonic theories.[20]

Hapgood's theory is most impressive. The outer crust of the Earth is less than 30 miles thick and rests on a lubricating layer that is termed the *asthenosphere.* This displacement would be accompanied by massive earthquakes, floods, massive extinction of animals and other phenomena, all of which appears to have happened.

Only those civilizations located near high mountains would be able to survive. They would have to abandon their technology and material possessions. It would be the sailors who would survive and search the globe in search of their lost homeland, or other places to colonize. This would explain a Lemurian or Atlantis origin to Egypt.

Applying this earth-crust displacement paradigm to Antarctica, its former location 2,000 miles north in the Atlantic between Europe and North America would have resulted in a stable climate for at least 10,000 years. Its climate would most likely have been a Mediterranean to sub-tropical one, due to the Gulf Stream. This 10,000 years of stability would have been long enough for an advanced civilization like Atlantis to have evolved.

---

[20] Charles H. Hapgood, *Earth's Shifting Crust: A Key to Some Basic Problems of Earth Science.* (New York: Pantheon Books, 1958).

This theory could also explain the glaciers in North America and Europe about 12,000 years ago. These continents were probably situated closer to the North Pole then. A displacement moving glaciated land masses into warmer climates would result in rapid melting of this ice causing floods. The land masses from the warmer climate (Antarctica), now relocated to polar zones, would be covered by quickly expanding ice-caps.

Einstein studied Hapgood's theory and wrote:

*The earth's rotation acts on these unsymmetrically deposited masses, and produces centrifugal momentum that is transmitted to the rigid crust of the earth. The constantly increasing centrifugal momentum produced this way will, when it reaches a certain point, produce a movement of the earth's crust over the earth's body, and **this will displace the polar regions towards the equator**.*[21]

Despite Einstein's backing, conventional geologists rejected Hapgood's theory. Later, John Wright, president of the American Geological Society, stated that Hapgood's thesis was worthy of further testing. None was initiated and no scientist has ever proved Hapgood wrong. Hapgood was professionally isolated by his peers until his death. Does this pattern by the establishment sound familiar?

A descendant of Noah named Peleg is described in *Genesis*.[22] This name means "in his day was the earth divided." If we interpret this as "in his day was the earth measured or surveyed," we may have a solution to this puzzle. One of Noah's grandsons, Mizraim, was the founder of Egypt, according to the *Old Testament*. His name means "to delineate, to draw up a plan, to make a representation," especially in association with measuring distances.

From this survey you can see then early man was no ape. He possessed a highly developed knowledge of mathematics, astronomy, architecture and other sciences. A strong organizational system was in place that efficiently built cities and established civilizations. These people surveyed and traveled throughout the World, mastered flight, developed atomic power and most probably were as technologically advanced as we are today.

It is now time to tear apart this orthodox historical and "scientific" view that states that we are the result of an evolutionary process that has brought us upward both intellectually and physically from a lower order of beings. Millions of years are involved in this hypothetical view of history, yet surprisingly the only evidence we have of civilization dates back 6,000 years. Now is the time to rethink this paradigm, open the closed doors to suppressed and forgotten evidence of advanced civilizations in prehistory and keep an open mind to other explanations for our

---

[21] Charles H. Hapgood, Earth's Shifting Crust: *A Key to Some Basic Problems of Earth Science*. (New York: Pantheon Books, 1958) pp. 1-2.
[22] Genesis 10:25

technological, cultural and spiritual development.

We can look to the work of Cremo and Thompson to see that there is evidence for being anatomically similar to modern man existing as long ago as the Miocene (25 million years ago), or even longer. Walking upright and using tools leads to the development of intelligence. The question we must ask is why didn't *Homo sapiens* develop earlier? My premise is that we did, but went through phases of annihilation and resurfacing throughout the last 200,000 to 400,000 years at least.

# CHAPTER 2 LEMURIA – THE TRUE GARDEN
## OF EDEN

It is truly amazing to consider the proposition supported by conventional Egyptology that the conventional Egyptology civilization arose spontaneously approximately 4,000 B.C. without any predecessors (other than nomads who were not more advanced than Stone Age man). Even more ridiculous is of the notion that this technologically superior and spiritually based civilization that dominated the Near East and Middle East for several thousands years is alleged to have come from nowhere.

Egypt actually arose from two very ancient and technologically advanced civilizations from well into prehistory. Prior to about 3000 B.C. Egypt was divided into Lower Egypt (northern Egypt) and Upper Egypt (southern Egypt), since the Nile River flows from south to north. The ancient continent of Atlantis settled Lower Egypt by way of the Mediterranean Sea, a white Upper Egypt was the result of explorations from Lemuria, or Mu, by way of India.

Throughout this chapter and the next one I will present evidence to show that these two prehistory continents with highly developed civilizations did exist.

My sources for depicting both Atlantis and Mu are from the occultist literature, archaeological finds, biblical and other writings of ancient civilizations and past life regressions conducted on several thousand patients from all over the world.

The main literature source for Mu comes from James Churchward. Churchward traveled to India and other parts of the world and after fifty years of gathering data on Mu wrote five books on this lost continent. *The Lost Continent of Mu, The Children of Mu, The Sacred Symbols of Mu, The Cosmic Forces of Mu,* and *The Second Book of the Cosmic Forces of Mu* were the result of his lifelong research. In 1935 James Churchward died as his last book was being released.

Churchward went to India during the latter part of the nineteenth century to supervise relief work during a famine. He befriended a Hindu priest, who later showed him a collection of ancient tablets written in a language called *Naacal*. Naacal was the language of Mu, and this Hindu priest taught Churchward how to decipher these tablets.

These tablets revealed a detailed history of Mu and their colonization of Upper Egypt. For those who do not believe that these tablets ever existed, Churchward was not permitted to remove these ancient tablets from the monastery that housed them. There are precedents for such ancient libraries.

For example, a Taoist monk in the early 1900s discovered a hidden library inside a series of caves located in a cliff in Dunhuang, China. Books, known as the *Lhasa Records*, were preserved by the desert air and kept in readable condition since the eleventh century. When the British archeologist Sir Avrel Stein traveled to Dunhuang in 1907, he convinced the monk to allow him to view these ancient writings.[23] We can also look to the Dead Sea Scrolls and their discovery in 1947 in the Qumran region northwest of the Dead Sea. Hebrew and Aramaic manuscript scrolls were found in eleven caves stored in jars. These 500 documents were well preserved and date back form 250 B.C. to 70 A.D. The Essenes are credited with storing these priceless records here.

From these ancient tablets Churchward learned that Mu was a continent in the Pacific Ocean stretching some 6,000 miles from east to west, and about 3,000 miles north to south. This great continent encompassed the Hawaiian Islands, Fiji, Easter Island, the Marianas and other South Pacific islands we find today. Originally these islands were part of this great continent.

Mu was the true Garden of Eden that produced modern man, and it was the seat of a rather advanced civilization. The population of this ancient continent was 64 million people, most of whom perished when gas-belts underlying much of the earth collapsed resulting in the sinking of both Atlantis and Mu approximately 11,000 B.C. We will discuss this cataclysm in detail later in this chapter.

The actual name of Lemuria is Mu. The origin of the name Lemuria can be traced back to the English zoologist Philip L. Sclater. Dr. Sclater suggested that the only way to explain how the lemur, a small mammal that resembles a cross between a monkey and a squirrel, could be found in India, the Malay Archipelago, Madagascar and Africa was by the previous existence of a continent that once was located in the Indian Ocean. Lemuria was chosen to acknowledge the widespread location of the lemur.

The Great naturalist Ernest Heinrich Haeckel was an ardent protagonist of this theory. It was his way of explaining the origin of man, as the lemur was assumed to be our ancestor. At that time no fossil linking man to apes had been uncovered. Haeckel's reasoning was that this fossil evidence disappeared when Lemuria sunk many thousands of years ago.

The inspiration for Churchward to write his five books on Mu came from an archeologist acquaintance named William Niven, who discovered 2,600 stone tablets in a Mexican village called Santiago Ahuzoctla. The figures and symbols on these ancient tablets were unrecognizable by scholars. However, Churchward identified the inscriptions as identical to the Naacal language he was translating in India.

---

[23] L. A. Waddell, *Lhasa and its mysteries with a record of the Expedition of 1903-1904.* (London: Methuen, 1929).

Churchward confirmed that these Mexican tablets also described the 200,000 year old Muvian civilization that sunk in the Pacific Ocean. The Mexican find was evidence of Mu's exploration and colonizing of Central America, especially in relation to setting up the Mayan culture.

It was difficult for scientists to accept Churchward's vague description of the temple where he claimed to have reproduced the Naacal tablets inscriptions. Niven had far more credibility, but critics still had a field day making fun of the archeologist's assertions.

Churchward spent two years studying the Naacal tablets under the tutorage of the temple's priest. The Naacal priests were originally sent from Mu to teach their sacred religion and sciences to each of their colonies, India and Central America being just two of these.

## THE MU CIVILIZATION

There were 64 million people in Mu when it submerged. A priest-emperor called Ra ruled this continent. Twelve (Churchward states ten) tribes were the origin of these people. Our five races originated on Mu, the true Garden of Eden. The white race dominated Mu and their religion was a monotheistic one. The Empire of the Sun is how the people referred to their homeland.

Churchward described Mu as being 6,000 miles from east to west and 3,000 miles from north to south. The Naacal tablets clearly show that our species was genetically created 200,000 years ago, even though we have no fossil evidence to confirm this theory. We will see in chapter 4 how several types of extraterrestrials assisted in this genetic manipulation in Mu.

There were ancient manuscripts that Churchward referenced that supported his translation of the Naacal tablets. These were the *Lhasa Record* of China,[24] the Mayan *Codex Cortesianus*[25] and, *Troano Manuscript*[26] I will be referring to these ancient writings throughout this chapter.

When Mu established colonies, the explorers from the Motherland were called *Maya*. The great civilizations of India, Babylonia, the Mayans and Egypt were the result of Mu's expansion. Mu even established Atlantis.

The French physician turned archeologist August Le Plongeon was the first to excavate the ruins of the Mayan civilization in Yucatan. He translated the *Troano Manuscript* and reported their story that clearly showed that Mu

---

[24] L. A. Waddell, op. cit.
[25] Jack Rau, *The Codex as a book form: three Maya Codices.* (New York: Pre-Columbian Press, 1976).
[26] Ibid.

established both the Mayan and Egyptian civilizations.[27]

Le Plongeon made the error of assuming that Mu and Atlantis were the same advanced civilizations. He described a romantic tragedy in which the land of Queen Moo was sought after by her two brothers, princes Coh ("Puma") and Aac ("Turtle"). Prince Coh won this quest, but was later murdered by his brother, Aac. Queen Moo later fled to Egypt to escape Mu's final destruction, changed her name to Isis and built the Sphinx as a memorial to her late brother-husband Coh (Osiris). She thus founded the Egyptian civilization under the direction of Thoth (Hermes).

It is interesting to note that this event was supposed to have taken place approximately 18,000 years ago in Sais, where Thoth built the first temple and taught the wisdom of his native Atlantis. Queen Moo's symbol was a macaw, while that of Coh was a leopard. The body of the sphinx is that of a lion or leopard.

Here is a section of Plongeon's translation of the Troano manuscript in which he describes Mu's destruction:

*In the year 6 Kan, on the 11th Muluc in the month Zac, there occurred terrible earthquakes, which continued without interruption until the 13th Chuen. The country of the hills of mud, the land of Mu was sacrificed; being twice upheaved it suddenly disappeared during the night, the basin being continually shaken by the volcanic forces. Being confined, these caused the land to sink and to rise several times in various places. At last the surface gave way and ten countries were torn asunder and scattered. Unable to stand the force of the convulsion, they sank with their 64,000,000 inhabitants 8,060 years before the writing of this book.*[28]

Le Plongeon also pointed out that certain high priests prophesized Mu's destruction and fled to several of their colonies prior to the continent's final submerging. We do not know the exact date the Troano Codex was written, so Le Plongeon could not confidently state when Mu disappeared.

We can find references to Mu in the Chinese Buddhist's *Lhasa Record*, the *Troano* and *Cortesianus Codices*, the cliff dweller writings from the western United States and hundreds of other ancient writings from Greece, Central America, Mexico, India and Egypt. Stone temples built by Muvian people still stand today in several South Sea Islands, notably Easter, Panape, Tonga-tabu and the Ladrone or Mariana Islands.

Mu was made up of three regions separated by narrow channels. This tropical paradise consisted of valleys, mountains and plains covered with fertile

---

[27] August Le Plongeon, *Sacred Mysteries Among the Mayas and the Quiches 11,500 Years Ago.* (New York: R. Macy, 1886).
[28] August Le Plongeon, op. cit.

fields and rich grazing grasses. Low rolling hill-lands supplied the tropical vegetation for this birthplace of modern man.

The number three is the most important digit in the universe. Modern technology is based on geometry, which in turn is based on the triangle. Egypt's pyramids are an excellent example of this concept. We see either threes, or multiple of threes throughout society.

There are three branches of government in America, the Christian and East Indian Trinity, Jesus was rumored to have died at 3:00 A.M., a jury is composed of twelve people (four times three) in the United States, the twelve signs of the Zodiac, the Twelve Tribes of the ancient Jews and Muvians, the twelve kings of Atlantis, three cataclysms of Atlantis and Mu and so on.

There were many slow-running rivers and streams curved around the wooded hills and fertile plains in Mu. Tall palm trees lined the river banks and ocean shores. Mu also had sacred lotus flowers that were used in meditation exercises for spiritual growth. Herds of mighty mastodons and elephants could be seen in their forests.

Mu had masons who built broad, smooth roads in all directions, constructed with such skill that not even grass could grown between them! Their people ranged in height from six to ten feet throughout their history, being tallest in the early years of their civilization.

The Empire of the Sun was the name Mu adopted when it began colonizing, at about 100,000 B.C. There were twelve tribes of distinct people all ruled by one high priest. The prefix Ra was added to his name, so the high priest was call Ra Mu. Everyone believed in reincarnation and the immortality of the soul, which eventually was reunited with the "great source," from which it came.

Nobody ever mentioned the name of the Deity. This God was addressed through a symbol, "Ra the Sun," and Ra Mu was the agent for this communication through prayer. Ra Mu was not worshipped as a god, but treated with reverence as a representative of God. We see this naming system used in ancient Egypt.

Prior to this time and up until Mu was victimized by its first cataclysm (there were *three*), savagery was unknown on our planet among our species. All of our races (white, red, brown, black and yellow) originated in Mu. The white race was the majority, but did not dominate the others. All lived in peace.

Mu had skilled architects and masons who built great stone palaces and temples. They also constructed great monoliths as monuments. Muvian sailors traveled all over the world and mapped every continent with extraordinary accuracy.

The Lemurians were, in the beginning, a successful experiment in human spiritual growth. From 200,000 years ago to about 100,000 years ago they were a spiritual people living in a Garden of Eden. Much of their time was spent in spiritual growth. The basic beliefs in a higher power, respect and love for each other and the planet and psychic empowerment were the foundation of this spirituality.

Inner wisdom was emphasized, more so than information or technology. Since each one of us has this potential for inner spirituality and inner wisdom, it was not necessary to verbalize this paradigm. Their religion wasn't a worship of a God as we do today, it was more of an appreciation and respect for a connection with the Higher Self (an extension of the God energy within and around us).[29]

Around 100,000 years ago changes occurred in the people of Mu. The Ra Mu priest and other highly evolved leaders expressed their concern about this development. Since the Lemurians were the keepers of the sacred history of the Earth, it was decided that this knowledge should be preserved in the form of crystals.

I earlier mentioned that the cause of this spiritual degeneration was the interference in our genetic development by extraterrestrials. We will cover this issue more thoroughly in the next chapter.

Some colonies were established 100,000 years ago, with the main settlement being Atlantis. Mu explorers (Mayas) moved in two main directions, east and west. The west coasts of North and Central America comprised Mu's eastern expansion. Atlantis was one of their main colonies.

Western Mayas initially established the east coast of Asia and eventually India in addition to the Empire of the Sun. The Atlanteans established settlements in Lower Egypt at about 16,000 B.C. The India route was utilized to set up their Upper Egyptian colony. Upper Egypt preceded the Atlantean Lower Egypt colony.

A colony that progressed to a level in which it could govern itself was converted into a Colonial Empire and a ruler was assigned. The Egyptian colony had two components prior to about 3000 B.C. The lower (northern) part originated from Atlantis, while the upper (southern) division came from Mu by way of the Naacal priests of India. Mu holy writings were called *The Seven Sacred Inspired Writings* and a copy of these were reportedly stored in the Temple of Sinai, where Moses copied them.

Unfortunately, the improper translations of these hieroglyphics by Ezra 800 years later led to the misinformation we have today about Mu. Moses used the Egyptian temple records when he wrote the *Pentateuch* (*The Five Books of Moses*) as part of the Old Testament in hieroglyphics.

Since hieroglyphics are merely symbols of a thought, they cannot be

---

[29] B. Goldberg, *Soul Healing*. (St. Paul: Llewellyn, 1996).

interpreted literally. Errors in Ezra's translations of Moses' hieroglyphics into Hebrew gave rise to many of the misconceptions we have today about God and the universe.

Moses correctly wrote that man was a special creation of God and lived in the Garden of Eden. The biblical location of Eden are impossible to discern from a careful reading of *Genesis*. I do not doubt that Moses accurately copied the Egyptian records, which were brought to Egypt by the Naacal priests from India as the *Seven Sacred Inspired Writings* from Mu.

Moses was a learned Master and his credibility as a scribe is beyond doubt. Since he wrote the holy scripture on clay tablets and papyrus in a pagan language at about 1315 B.C., the ancient Jews decided to assemble those documents in book form that eventually became known as the *Bible.*

Since Ezra and his colleagues 800 years later were neither Masters nor Egyptologists, many mistranslations resulted. Ezra simply embellished Moses' hieroglyphics when he didn't understand what Moses meant and added myths to the truth. The impossible boundaries of the Garden of Eden are but one example.

The *Old Testament* story of the Serpent and the Tree of Life is another illustration. Since Muvian theology taught that man was the only creature with a soul, man's soul was the only true life on earth. In Mu man was referred to as a fruit. As trees bear fruit, man was the first fruit of a tree and this fruit was life itself. The Tree of Life was the continent of Mu. Mu was the representation of this Tree of Life (Kabala in Jewish mysticism).

In Mu the Serpent was called Khan and it represented the waters (Pacific Ocean) surrounding this Garden of Eden. Naacal tablets illustrate the tree with a Serpent coiled around it. The Serpent was not the Devil. It was the Egyptian priests who invented the Devil and Hell at approximately 3000 B.C.[30]

One final example of Ezra's lack of understanding of hieroglyphics relates to the Bible's reference to angels preventing the reentry of Adam and Eve into Eden by wielding swords of fire. The Egyptian glyph reads: *Mu sinking into a fiery abyss. The flames of the fires of the underneath rose and enveloped her body as she went down.*

It was the sinking of Mu that prevented man from returning to the Garden of Eden, not those alleged angels. The word sacrifice did not exist in any language prior to the destruction of Mu. This term was applied to the manner in which the Motherland met its fate. A fire upon an altar symbolizes the memory of Mu. However, the burnt sacrifice took on quite a different meaning for the ancient

---

[30] Louis Herbert Gray, Editor, *The Mythology of All Races,* Volume 13 (New York: Cooper Square Publishers, Inc., 1964) pp. 179-180.

Hebrews and other cultures. It was a means to appease an angry and often cruel God.

We really don't know when the *Book of the Dead* was first written. Even conventional Egyptologists concede that its original form existed long before the First Dynasty. Hermes (Thoth) invented hieroglyphics and taught the Egyptians how to transcribe this sacred scripture sometime between 11,000 B.C. and 5500 B.C.

Initially this work contained only a few chapters, but more was added as time went on. Every part of the *Book of the Dead* refers to Mu. We know that Mu was destroyed first by earthquakes and sank into a fiery abyss.

Another section of the *Book of the Dead* titled "THE CHAPTER OF NOT BEING BOILED IN FIRE" states the following:

*Nu saith: I am the paddle which is equipped, wherewith Ra transported the Aged Gods, which raised up the emissions of Osiris from the Lake of blazing fire, and he was not burned. I sit down like the Light-god, and like Khnemu, the Governor of lions. Come, cut away the fetters from him that passeth by the side of this path, and let me come forth therefrom.*

Here we have another reference to Mu's destruction by sinking into a fiery abyss. We cannot place all of the blame on Ezra for these faulty translations of Moses' writings. Ezra undoubtedly made translation errors, but we must understand that Osirian religion was tampered with by Egyptian priests throughout its history.

The Osirian religion was originally taught by Thoth (Hermes) at Sais approximately 16,000 B.C. Unscrupulous Egyptian priests altered these teachings at a later period beginning with the second pharaoh of the Eleventh Dynasty (c.a. 2000 B.C.) through the Eighteenth Dynasty (c.a. 1570 B.C.). I have previously discussed how these manipulative priests invented the Devil and Hell to control their people when Egypt was united at about 3100 B.C.

There were *three* groups of prophets who wrote the *Old Testament*; (1) those who had the gift of prophesy, (2) those who had the office of prophet, and (3) those who had both the gift and the office. Moses is quite unique as a prophet and Master in that he possessed both the gift of prophecy and the office.

The period of the Sopherim (c.a. 458 to 300 B.C.) began with the return of the Jews from Babylonian captivity. Ezra functioned both as a priest and a scribe.

The Law had been handed to Moses by God at Mt. Sinai, and the writings of Moses, the *Pentateuch (Five Books of Moses)*, was the chief body of Scripture for the Jews after the exile. Very quickly, however, the inspired writings of the prophets and historians were added to the authoritative canon of scripture. At a still later period, a third collection of writings was begun which over many generations became for the Jews just as authoritative as the inspired writings. This body of work was the writings of the Scribes of decisions and interpretations of the Pentateuch, prophetical, and historical writings.

The Scribes main task was the theoretical development of the law. They assumed that it was their special task to improve what was already binding by developing more and more subtle sophistication in reasoning. To develop a system of law binding on everyone, it was necessary to come as near to a consensus as possible. So the whole process of systematizing the law was carried on by oral tradition. The Talmud was made up of the *Pentateuch* and the *Mishnah*. The *Mishnah* was the oral law, an amplification of the written law which was handed down by word of mouth by the scholarly priests (and Scribes) in each generation. Orthodox Jewish scholars believe that on Mt. Sinai, an oral law was given by God in addition to the written law. Both parts of the Talmud are sacred; both comprise what is referred to as the *Torah*. We can see how embellishments of Mu's *Seven Sacred Inspired Writings* could have been propagated.

Returning to Mu's civilization, Churchward reported that several of their cities were built along rivers for the purpose of trade and commerce. Mu was the center of the world's civilization, since all other countries were her colonies. Some colonies added the name "land of Kui" to Mu, so Mukai appears in other ancient writings referring to Mu.

Throughout Mu's long history each of its twelve tribes built its own cities and became somewhat isolated from the others. This led to changes in language and culture, so that when colonies were established a variety of cultural heritages became evident.

## THE DESTRUCTION OF MU

Three separate cataclysms spread over nearly 40,000 years resulted in the destruction of both Atlantis and Mu. Many legends depict both Atlantis and Mu being submerged in a single day. The earthquakes and fires that brought about the destruction of these continents took place in three stages (recall the significance of the number 3).

The first of these cataclysms occurred at about 50,000 B.C. during which time Mu was at the height of its civilization. Due to the flatness of the land at Mu, the lava accumulating as a result of volcanic eruptions formed the igneous rocks that are present today on some of the South Sea Islands, such as Easter Island.

Following this initial cataclysm, Mu began a rebuilding process and no further geophysical problems recurred. A second cataclysm took place at about 26,000 B.C. resulting in the submerging of this great continent and the death of most of its 64 million citizens. It has a combination of earthquakes, floods and fire that destroyed this great civilization.

Although until recently it was considered impossible for such a destruction to have taken place in a matter of days, modern tectonic plate theories affirm that such a destruction scenario could take place. Some scientists even concede that, at least theoretically, a single earthquake could result in the destruction of a large land mass, particularly if there were previous major tremors.

Churchward detailed the destruction of Mu and Atlantis as a result of pole shifts and enormous gas belts deep within the earth's crust below both now submerged continents. Every ten thousand years or so pole shifts do occur.

It is quite possible for such a pole shift to create tidal waves, volcanic eruptions and earthquakes through the generation of slippage of the earth's crust. This pole shift alone would not be enough to submerge a continent as large as Mu.

Churchward explained how the gas belts beneath Mu and Atlantis became overencompassed, split open, and this had the effect of buckling the continental arch of the Pacific causing Mu to sink. When Mu submerged other continents, South America for one, were forced up and mountain ranges were above sea level that previously were on the ocean floor. Modern day geologists agree that this could have taken place as recently as twelve to twenty-six thousand years ago.

The paradigm I just described is well within the 26,000 B.C. and 11,000 B.C. dates I presented for Mu's second and third cataclysms. Churchward's gas chamber theory was ridiculed during his time. Today, this is a leading trend in geology led by such eminent geologists as Cornell University's Thomas Gold. This is termed the Deep-Earth-Gas Hypothesis and has been discussed in *Scientific American*, *OMNI*, *Science News* and other publications and geological journals.

Gold believes that natural methane gas originates more from these gas belts than from fossil remains of dinosaurs and plants. Oil professionals sharply disagree with Gold, and state that oil is made *entirely* from decayed living matter.

Non-biological gas seeping up from giant gas belts deep within the earth's crust is what Gold feels is the true source of natural methane gas and oil. Not only does this theory explain our great natural energy reserves, but it also presents a workable paradigm that supports reports my patients give me in their past life regressions in both Mu and Atlantis during which they clearly state that both civilizations tapped into these gas belts as one source of energy for their advanced technology.

The Deep-Earth-Gas Hypothesis even explains the large amount of fossils we have uncovered during the past 200 years. When animals die they must be covered with earth or volcanic ash immediately to become fossilized, or simply decay to nothing. The displacement of millions of tons of organic matter that

41

occurs following a pole shift, superimposed upon entire jungles and forests buried under volcanic ash, create coal deposits or decay to produce organic oil in sedimentary rocks.

We can explain the massive creation of fossils with the Deep-Earth-Gas Hypothesis. If you think large amounts of fossils are created generally, consider the buffalo in America. During the 1800s hundreds of thousands of buffalo were slaughtered and left to die on the plains in the Mid-West. There was not one single fossil produced as a result. Certain events *must* transpire for a fossil to be created.

The only reason certain South Sea Islands and Hawaii survived the pole shifts that submerged the rest of Mu is that they were pivotal points in these pole shifts. As the earth's tectonic plates shifted downward during these past pole shifts, the South American Continent was raised and new land masses were created. This must have been between 50,000 B.C. and 11,000 B.C. prior to the Amazon Sea becoming the Amazon River of today.

The Mu priests and oracles knew about these destructions and took steps to preserve humankind's knowledge by disseminating it to their various colonies and storing this data in crystals. This mechanism was crucial to Atlantis and the preservation of both technology and spiritual principles so necessary for our civilization today. If not for these crystals and the role the Muvian survivors played as keepers of their sacred records, this data would be lost forever and our civilization's history would be quite different.

We can look to some examples of ancient peoples benefiting from this information and spreading it throughout history. The Atlanteans, Egyptian high priests, the Druids of England, the natives of the Pacific islands, the Naacal priests of India are but some examples.

## MU'S EGYPTIAN COLONY

Egypt's religion from the time of the unification of Upper and Lower Egypt (c.a. 3100 B.C.) to approximately 2700 B.C., according to Churchward, reflected two divergent views. Lower Egyptians of Atlantean origin taught that the soul traveled *west* following the physical death of the body to its destination in which it would eventually reincarnate. This soul plane was thought to be *east* by the Upper Egyptians from Mu.

Atlantis was west of Egypt. The Osiris cult in Lower Egypt always identified with gods from the west. Mu settled Upper Egypt by way of the Naacal priests from India and Myanmar (Burma). This was east of Egypt. We can see from these points of origin that they both were correct. To reach the soul plane where the soul selects its next lifetime, it would have to travel west to Atlantis or east to India or Burma. All ancient religions taught that the life force, or soul, was drawn to its source of creation for regeneration into a future life.

The principal symbol of the Upper Egyptian God was the Sun, as it was in Mu. Scholars disagree about who conquered whom at about 3100 B.C. Did Lower Egypt conquer Upper Egypt, or the reverse? Churchward clearly states (and many of my Egyptian past life regression confirm) that Upper Egypt (Mu) conquered Lower Egypt (Atlantis). One piece of evidence pointed out by Churchward was the introduction of the winged solar disk with its pair of serpents into Lower Egypt by Upper Egypt.

The Serpent was used by Mu to symbolize God as the Creator. The Sun is the central figure in their hieroglyphics. The pharaoh's crown included a serpent, but not the Sun, as the latter's addition would have been a sacrilege. The Sun, after all, represented the Almighty.

Conventional Egyptologists have tried to convince the world that Egypt was settled by people originating from the Euphrates Valley who crossed the Assyrian Desert and entered Lower Egypt. They then supposedly moved up to the White and Blue Niles and split up to create Upper and Lower Egypt.

There is no evidence whatsoever to support this hypothesis. These nomadic people would have had to cross a waterless desert twice the distance they would have had to travel by water. There were no obstructions in following the water route, and land was constantly in sight.

## THE REAL STORY BEHIND THE FLOOD

Among most cultures and civilizations we find stories of a great flood. Naturally, *Genesis* in the *Old Testament* dominates Western thought in this regard. Regarding a common paradigm to this flood scenario, we can observe four common features.
1.    A universal cataclysm took place in which water destroyed almost all of human life and other living things.
2.    A means of escape was provided by way of a boat or ark.
3.    Mankind was saved from complete extinction by a small group of survivors.
4.    It was the evil ways of man that led to this cataclysm.

Dr. Johannes Riem stated in his extensive book on flood legends *Die Sintflut in Sage and Wissenschaft*:

*Among all traditions there is none so general, so widespread on earth, and so apt to show what may develop from the same material according to the varying spiritual character of a people as the Flood traditions. Lengthy and thorough discussions with Dr. Kunnike have convinced me of the evident correctness of his position that the fact of the Deluge is granted, because at the basis of all myths, particularly natural myths, there is a real fact, but during a subsequent period the material was given its present mythical character and form.*[31]

The Scottish geologist Hugh Miller wrote during the nineteenth century:

*There is, however, one special tradition which seems to be more deeply impressed and more widely spread than any of the others. The destruction of well-nigh the whole human race, in an early age of the world's history, by a great deluge, appears to have impressed the minds of the few survivors, and seems to have been handed down to their children, in consequence, with such terror-struck impressiveness that their remote descendants of the present day have not even yet forgotten it. It appears in almost every mythology, and lives in the most distant countries and among the most barbarous tribes. . .*[32]

Churchward proposed a rather interesting theory to explain why both Mu and Atlantis submerged. He depicted a series of honey combed huge chambers and cavities beneath these continents filled with highly explosive volcanic gases. Each of these advanced civilizations actually tapped into these energy sources to supply power for their respective civilizations.

When these chambers somehow emptied their gases through volcanic eruptions, their supporting roofs collapsed and this led to the submerging of the land masses.

My research has confirmed that Mu and Atlantis were destroyed simultaneously. In addition to the disappearance of these two great civilizations, the ubiquitous stories of floods and the extinction of many species can be explained by these cataclysms. For example, scientists recorded the extinction of the following animals in North America at about 11,000 B.C.: the sloth, the camel, the giant bison, the sabre-toothed tiger, the mammoth and the horse.

The La Brea Tar Pits in Los Angeles and certain locations in Alaska and Siberia of sabre-toothed tigers, mammoths and other mammal's bones are jumbled into disorganized piles. Glacial forces from the last ice age alone would not create this phenomenon. It is possible that super cyclonic winds and firestorms from a sudden pole shift could explain this observation.

Donnelly points out that Hindu legends refer to four previous ages that ended in fire, water, wind or earthquakes. The most recent Hindu age and that of the Mexican-Guatemalan Mayan era ended by fire.[33] All ancient cultures mention a fiery cataclysm as being either the last or next to last cause of a major destruction of civilization.

---

[31] Johannes Riem, *Die Sintflut in Sage and Wissenschaft.* (Hamburg: Agentur des Rauhen Hauses, 1925) p. 7.

[32] Hugh Miller, *The Testimony of the Rocks.* (New York: John B. Alden, 18992) p.284.

[33] I. Donnelly, *Ragnarok.* (Blauvelt, N.Y.: Rudolf Steiner Pubs., 1971), p. 166.

The Carnegie Institution's Department of Terrestrial Magnetism reported that the north magnetic pole underwent a major shift sometime between 13,000 and 7,000 B.C. This conclusion was the result of studying the magnetism of various levels of clay in a New England lake.

The 1977 geologic findings of C. Warren Hunt showed that an "enormous tide" enveloped the Rocky Mountains and moved through the American Plains States "between 11,500 and 10,000 B.C.," as reported by Jon D. Singer.[34]

Another theory to explain these cataclysms relate to a large comet coming close to hitting the Earth. Velikovsky formulated such a hypothesis in which he stated that if a large comet approach the Earth, its gravitational field would slow the Earth's rotation. This would lead to a discrepancy between the speed of rotation of the solid outer crust and the plastic layer under it.

Since a point at the surface normally rotates faster than one inside the Earth or at the equator, a comet suddenly slowing the Earth's rotation would generate a tremendous amount of heat between the decelerating outer crust and the layer beneath it. Firestorms could result. Full thickness-crustal rifts would also open up. Another result would be a compression of the full-thickness Earth crust which could raise mountain ranges.[35]

One additional ancient culture we should consider is that of the Hopi Indians of Arizona. Their legends record *three* previous Suns, each culminating in a great annihilation followed by the gradual re-emergence of mankind. At least two different kinds of disaster may be portrayed as having occurred simultaneously (most frequently floods and earthquakes, but sometimes fire and a terrifying darkness). Here is an example:

*The first world was destroyed, as a punishment for human misdemeanours, by an all-consuming fire that came from above and below. The second world ended when the terrestrial globe toppled from it axis and everything was covered with ice. The third world ended in a universal flood. The present world is the fourth. Its fate will depend on whether or not its inhabitants behave in accordance with the Creator's plans.*[36]

## EVIDENCE OF MU

In the next chapter we will discuss a 1968 archaeological finding in the Bimini Islands that point to a possible Atlantean made building. The discovery of lime-mortar cylinders that appear to be man-made in the Southwest Pacific island

---

[34] John D. Singer, "The Origins of Lemuria." *Pursuit Magazine,* Fall 1982, p. 124.)
[35] Immanuel Velikovsky, *Worlds in Collision.* (Garden City, New York: Doubleday & Co., 1950).
[36] Frank Waters, *The book of the Hopi.* (London: Penguin Books, 1977).

of New Caledonia and the adjacent Isle of Pines carbon date back from 5,120 to 10,950 B.C. For comparison, these structures have not been found associated with Mediterranean civilizations before a few hundred years B.C.

L. Chevalier of the Museum of New Caledonia discovered these 40 to 75 inch diameter and from 40 to 100 inches in height cylinders. Over 400 of these tumuli (artificial mounds) have been found at both locations. Either very little or no vegetation was noted taking root in the sands in and around them. The cylinders were oriented in the center of the tumuli and set vertically.

Chevalier's opinion was that the mortar had been poured into the tops of the tumuli by way of narrow pits and allowed to set. Although no human bones or artifacts have been found in this region, it does suggest a possible Muvian building was once located here.[37]

Captain Louis-Claude de Freycinet in April of 1819 discovered strange capped stone pillars on Tinian Island in the Marianas, another South Pacific island chain part of the former Mu continent. A double row of pillars, about 15 feet high, each topped by a hemispherically shaped boulder, the rounded side resting on the pillar was observed. The sparseness of the grass around the pillars was most unusual, since the soil surrounding these pillars was just as fertile as that just a few feet away supporting lush vegetation.[38]

Cremo and Thompson report in their book *Forbidden Archaeology* a coin found at a depth of 114 feet from a well boring near Lawn Ridge, Illinois. The Illinois State Geological Survey estimated the age of the deposits containing the coin at between 200,000 and 400,000 years old!

J. W. Moffit discovered this coin in August of 1870 while drilling a well. William E. Dubois of the Smithsonian Institution described the coin as "polygonal approaching to circular." This object had crudely portrayed figures and inscriptions on both sides. Dubois could not decipher the language of these inscriptions.

Dubois did conclude that this coin was made in a machine shop. The problem conventional scientists have with this discovery is that only our species (*Homo sapiens sapiens*) are known to possess the intelligence to make and use coins. We have not been on this planet for more than 100,000 years, according to traditional paleontology. Metal coins were not used prior to the eighth century B.C., with Asia Minor being the site of the first man-made coins.

We have established that the citizens of Mu ranged from 6 to 10 feet tall. In the Kirabati and the Marshall Islands in the South Pacific, footprints have been

---

[37] Andrew Rothovius, "The Mysterious Cement Cylinders of New Caledonia" *INFO Journal. 1* (1967): 15-16.
[38] Louis-Claude de Freycinet, *Voyage autour du Monde plus Atlas Historique.* (Paris, 1825) pp. 279-280.

found in volcanic stone that depict a man ranging from ten to twelve feet tall. These footprints are very readable with the toes and heels outline rather distinct. They are naturally rounded and curved like the footprint of modern man.

Natural rock formations were quickly ruled out. Could these footprints be those of the tall, white navigators of pre-history reported by Phoenicians, Ethiopians, Greeks, Libyans and Egyptian scribes?[39]

I have stated earlier that the records of other cultures have referred to both the Naacal priests and Mu. The Hindu historian Valmiki obtained his records from the Rishi Temple at Ayhodia. He states:

*The Mayas from India established a colony in Egypt, giving it the name of Maioo.*[40] *And the Naacals first established themselves in the Deccan, India, and from there carried their religion and learning to the colonies of Babylonia and Egypt.*[41]

Schliemann discovered the *Lhasa Record* in a Buddhist temple in Tibet. This ancient document originates from a different source than the *Troano Manuscript* and the *Codex Cortesianus*. The *Lhasa Record* is not written in Maya symbols and is more recent in origin. Here is an important section:

*When the star of Bal fell on the place where now is only the sky and the sea, the seven cities with their golden gates and transparent temples, quivered and shook like the leaves in a storm; and, behold, a flood of fire and smoke arose from the palaces. Agonies and cries of the multitude filled the air. They sought refuge in their temples and citadels, and the wise Mu—the Hieratic Ra Mu—arose and said to them: "did I not predict all this?" And the women and the men in their precious stones and shining garments lamented "Mu, save us!" and Mu replied: "You shall all die together with your servants and your riches, and from your ashes new nations shall arise. If they forget they are superior not because of what they put on but what they put out the same will befall them." Flames and smoke choked the words of Mu: the land and its inhabitants were torn to pieces and swallowed up by the depths.*[42]

Le Plongeon's research in the Yucatan revealed other references to Mu:

*The Hieratic head of the Land of Mu prophesied its destruction, and that some, heeding the prophecy, left and went to the colonies where they were saved.*[43]

In addition, at Uxmal in the Yucatan, Le Plongeon found a temple with the

---

[39] I. G. Turbott, "The Footprints of Tarawa," *Journal of the Polynesian Society.* 58 (4), December 1949.

[40] Valmiki, *Ramayana: The concise Ramayana of Valmiki*, trans. by Swami Venkatesananda. Albany: State University of New York Press, 1988).
[41] Ibid.
[42] L. A. Waddell, *Lhasa and its mysteries with a record of the Expedition of 1903-1904*, op. cit.
[43] A. Le Plongeon, *Sacred Mysteries Among the Mayas and the Quiches 11,500 Years Ago*, op. cit.

following inscriptions on its walls:

*This edifice is a commemorative monument dedicated to the memory of Mu—the Lands of the West—the That Land of Kui—the birthplace of our sacred mysteries.*[44]

What is most interesting is that this temple faced west, the location of Mu in the Pacific. We must also recognize the fact that Le Plongeon's work preceded that of Schliemann. The land of departed souls is what Kui represented. The Egyptians used the word *Ka* to express *Kui*.

The *Codex Cortesianus* are as follows:

*By his strong arm Homen caused the earth to tremble after sunset and during the night* **Mu, the country of the hills of earth, was submerged**.

*Mu, the life of the basin (seas), was submerged by Homen during the night.*

*The place of the dead ruler is now lifeless, it moves no more, after having twice jumped from its foundations: the king of the deep, while forcing his way out, has shaken it up and down, has killed it, has submerged it.*

*Twice Mu jumped from her foundations; it was then sacrificed by fire. It burst while being shaken up and down violently by earthquakes. By kicking it, the wizard that makes all things move like a mass of worms, sacrificed it that very night.*[45]

Today we can see remnants of Mu. Japan is known as the "Land of the Rising Sun." Its history reflects a metaphysical base (Muvian) and militaristic component (Atlantean).

Other countries representing strong spiritual basis, with an emphasis on reincarnation and other metaphysical beliefs, reflect Muvian influence. India, China, Australian Aborigines, the South Sea Islands, Native Americans to name a few are some examples. Egypt illustrated both Muvian and Atlantean influences.

Any reference to the sun is indicative of the Muvian influence, in which the sun was the dominant theme.

One last piece of evidence needs to be presented is the origin of the occultist Great White Brotherhood. The whole purpose of the Mu culture was to create "Masters" to assist the population in their spiritual growth, so that they may ascend and no longer have to reincarnate. The ultimate goal of ascension is to reunite with God.

The Masters became known as Essenes and were often called Elders. These Elders were wise, loving, kind and did their very best to assist others in their ascension. Although moderately successful, they could not get through to the

---

[44] Ibid.

[45] J. Rau, *The Codex as a book form: three Maya Codices.* New York: Pre-Columbian Press, 1970).

Atlantes, who experimented with dark forces of the universe and created the Black Brotherhood, specializing in malicious uses of magic.

To counteract this effect, the Elders formed the White Brotherhood. Personal and spiritual growth, rather than the acquisition of power or material possessions, was emphasized by the White Brotherhood. Occasionally strong occult forces had to be accessed to offer protection to those attacked by the Black Brotherhood. This battle is still going on today. My book *Protected by the Light*[46] details this ongoing struggle.

The number thirteen was most important to Mu. The last cataclysm and final submerging was supposed to have taken place on a Friday the thirteenth at about 11,000 B.C. The Elders of Mu were referred to as the "Thirteenth School" and moved their headquarters to Tibet prior to the final destruction of Mu.

We can find references to these "Ancient Masters" in the writings of the Chinese philosopher Lao Tzu. In his *Tao Te Ching* he described a trip to the west to the legendary land
of His Wang *Mu*. This represented the headquarters of the Ancient Ones. It is possible that this land was the home of the "Thirteenth School." Notice the name Mu appears in this legendary land. Lao Tzu writes:

> The Ancient Masters were subtle,
> mysterious, profound, responsive.
> The depth of their knowledge is unfathomable.
> Because it is unfathomable,
> All we can do is describe their appearance;
> Watchful, like men crossing a winter stream.
> Alert, like men aware of danger.
> Courteous, like visiting guests.
> Yielding, like ice about to melt.
> Simple, like uncarved blocks of wood.
> —Lao Tzu, Tao Te Ching, Chapter 15.

## PAST LIFE REGRESSIONS

This section will explore life in ancient Egypt as a result of past life regressions conducted through hypnosis with many of my patients over a span of twenty years. From this data we will get a bird's eye view of life in ancient Egypt from about 16,000 B.C. to 11,000 B.C.

---

[46] B. Goldberg, *Protected by the Light: The Complete Book of Psychic Self Defense. Tucson, AZ: Hats Off Books, 2000).*

During the first 100,000 years of its existence, Mu was a fairly successful experiment in civilization. My definition of success does not refer to technological achievements or colonization. It specifically refers to our spiritual growth.

Although millions of people lived on this Pacific continent divided into twelve tribes (Churchward incorrectly stated ten) and separated by rivers into *three* lands, they all got along and mastered the art of spirituality.

Mu had learning centers called Temples of Wisdom, in which all citizens underwent extensive training in spiritual development. Citizenship had to be earned through completion of a rigorous course of instruction.

Science and technology had advanced to such a stage that the average life expectancy was between 500 and 1,000 years. Since Mu was the true Garden of Eden, this may explain the long life reported for several *Old Testament* figures, Adam, Noah, Methusaleh, etc.

My research has also pointed out that Muvian people were taller in the early phase of their civilization, ranging between 8 to 10 feet in height. Later their height was reduced to between 6 to 8 feet. Many ancient legends report giants and these Muvians most definitely fit this profile.

The language of Mu was called Sansar and their writing was based on glyphs. We see this pattern reflected in Egyptian hieroglyphics. Another similarity between Mu and Egypt is that both were Sun worshippers.

Muvians were expert in out-of-body techniques and spent most of their time exploring our planet and other dimensions through this method. We can look to Mu for the origin of the concept of soulmates (an original, perfect soul split in two occupying two different physical bodies and will eventually reunite when perfection is again achieved).

Early in its development Mu was a perfect civilization. Disease, pollution and crime were nonexistent and life was characterized by spirituality and luxurious living. Two separate groups appeared in Mu around 125,000 B.C. The Essenes comprised this first group and functioned as "keeper of the records." These spiritual practitioners had long blond hair, piercing blue eyes and always wore white robes.

Far less spiritually evolved were the Atlantes, who represented the second group of Muvians. Unfortunately, these Atlantes exhibited warlike and materialistic traits so characteristic of civilization today. Mu's overpopulation combined with the problems brought on by these Atlantes resulted in Mu enacting a program of colonization at about 100,000 B.C.

Mu's explorers were called *Maya* and the initial colonies founded were located in Atlantis, North and South America and Australia. Since the Muvian elders could not trust the Atlantes to completely control Atlantis, Essenes were sent along to the maintain Muvian spiritual practices and to assist in keeping the peace.

Colonies in which the Atlantes group dominated were located in Mexico, the Mediterranean, Peru and Atlantis. The Essene group was dominant in colonies established in North and South America, China, India, Tibet and Australia.

## AN EGYPTIAN PAST LIFE IN 15,000 B.C.

Eva's past life regression gives us further insights into Egyptian life at 15,000 B.C. At that time her name was Meru and she was born in Mu, where she spent the first 275 years of her life.

Meru was dark skinned and had been thoroughly indoctrinated in Muvian spirituality as a result of the rigorous training she received in Mu's Temple of Wisdom. She never married and was so impressed by the architecture, as well as the philosophy, behind this massive temple that she decided to become an architect and design these temples for Mu's Egyptian colony.

By this time Mu was very much politically weakened by persistent attacks from Atlantis. It was too dangerous for Meru to go to Egypt and complete her plans so she had to remain in Mu. Finally, a the age of 275 the government of Mu allowed her to make the trip directly to Upper Egypt to design these temples.

Meru flew on a large propeller driven plane that was powered by a rear engine. This was an unusual trip in that most Muvians came to Egypt by way of India. Meru flew directly to Egypt by way of Central America and Atlantis.

Upon her arrival in Upper Egypt, Meru spent many years working with the local Muvian elders being oriented to Egyptian customs and received further instructions on how to deal with the locals so as not to cause political problems.

By the time she was 375 years old, Meru had designed and witnessed the completion of several small Temples of Wisdom. Unfortunately, local uprisings were common and she was killed during one such rebellion, along with several hundred of her fellow Muvians. The fruits of her labor were destroyed following the Flood of 11,000 B.C.

## EXAMPLES OF ANCIENT FLYING CRAFTS

We can look to the South Sea island of Panape, whose legends talk of learned men with light skin who traveled from the west (Mu) long before the European explorers. The "shining boats" they traveled in "flew above the sea." A "flying canoe" is reported by the Mangareva aborigines of the Gambora Islands. Priests who operated these flying machines were able to fly nearly 2,500 miles away to Hawaii.

An artist's depiction of one of these ancient flying canoes had wings that looked like the winged solar disc of the Egyptian god Horus. Dr. Kalil Messiha, an Egyptologist and archeologist at the Cairo Museum of Antiquities, in 1969 discovered a model of a plane dating back to 200 B.C. This plane was originally uncovered in a tomb near Saqqara, Egypt. It was catalogued as Special Register No. 6347, Room 22.

The model's wings are straight and aerodynamically shaped, with a span of 7.2 inches. The pointed nose is 1.3 inches long, and the body of the craft measures 5.6 inches long, tapered and terminating in a vertical tail fin. A separate slotted piece on the tail is precisely like the back stabilizer section of a modern plane. The small craft is made of very light sycamore wood and weighs 1.11 ounces. Experts have concluded that this craft in full size could carry large amounts of freight at speeds below 60 miles an hour.

This model made a perfect glider, and when engineers tested it, it soared considerable distances with only slight effort. Since all of its highly accurate integral proportions were present in ratios of 2:1 or 3:1, these experts deducted that this plane was not a toy, but the result of sophisticated computation and experimentation. The ancient Egyptians were known to construct scale models of everything they made from ships to temples. This suggests that there were life-sized gliders in ancient Egypt.

One of the most interesting aspects of this model plane concerns both the shape and proportions of the wings. They curve downward in what is called "reverse dihedral" by engineers. The result is a maximum lift without detracting from its speed. This design was used in the European Concorde super-jet. Experts predicted that even a tiny engine would keep it flying at speeds of 45 to 65 m.p.h. At least thirteen other model planes have been discovered from other Egyptian tombs.[47]

The pre-Aryan Indian Epic *Ramayana*[48] by the poet Valmiki depicts a tale of Prince Rama of Ayodhya, who searches for his kidnapped wife Sita. An evil king Ravana abducted her in his *Vimana* (a flying machine) to Sri Lanka. These Vimana were mentioned many times in Indian literature.

One final note about the Essenes is that we find many references to these "keepers of the knowledge." The writings of the ancient Roman historian Josephus tells of a devoutly religious Jewish community flourishing at about 150 B.C. Although not mentioned directly in the Bible, the Essenes are alluded to in Mathew 19:11, 12 and Col. 2:8 and 18. This group disappeared from history after

---

[47] Anonymous, "The Little Wooden Airplane." *Pursuit*, 5:88, 1972.
[48] Valmiki, op. cit.

Jerusalem was destroyed in 70 A.D.

The extremely ascetic Essenes lived in Palestine and Syria with their main colonies near the northern end of the Dead Sea around the town of Engedi. They produced the *Dead Sea Scrolls* as an example of their keeper of the knowledge function.

Essenes all wore a white garment at all times and were sworn to secrecy concerning the doctrines of their order. They did not marry, but trained children sent by outsiders to become assimilated in their order, which was focused on agriculture and theology.

We can see in the Essenes an absolute reverence to God (monotheism) and the lawgiver Moses. They believed in angels and had compulsory bathing in cold water before meals, after bowel movements and following contact with strangers. This ritual reflects their respect for the Motherland, an island with its three rivers. A strong belief in an afterlife of the soul was part of their theology.

A strong respect for the sun (representing their Muvian heritage) was exhibited by facing it during prayer. The Jewish custom was to turn toward the temple (representing the learning temples of Mu) during prayer.[49]

---

[49] W. H. Brownlee, "A Comparison of the Covenanters of the Dead Sea Scrolls with Pre-Christian Jewish Sects." *The Biblical Archeologist*, Vol. XIII, Sept. 1950, pp. 50-72.

# CHAPTER 3 ATLANTIS – EGYPT'S IMMEDIATE PREDECESSOR

In the last chapter I pointed out how Egypt was originally a colony of both Atlantis and Mu. Mu settled Upper Egypt by way of India and the Naacal priests, while Atlantis lay claim to Lower Egypt from the Mediterranean.

Atlantis was the most important colony established by Mu, but became an uncontrollable antagonist. The Atlantes from Mu degenerated into a materialistic and warlike people. The Essenes represented the opposite traits and were sent along to Atlantis to share Muvian technology and function as a source of spiritual growth for this new land.

The Essenes were also sent to India, Tibet and other surrounding lands where they formed the main Asian colonies of Mu. As a military power, Mu and her colonies were far superior to Atlantis in the beginning. As time went on and the final destruction of both continents neared, Atlantis became the dominant power.

There have been between two and ten thousand books written about Atlantis. Plato's *Timaeus and Critias* is the first documentation we have concerning Atlantis. This story is in the form of two dialogues during which *Timaeus*, Critias, Socrates and others are conversing about various topics.[50] According to Plato's *Timaeus*, when the Greek statesman Solon visited Egypt around 600 B.C., Egyptian priests told him the story of the destruction of Atlantis, about nine thousand years earlier.

These two dialogues were reportedly designed as the first parts of a trilogy, the third of which was to be called Hermocrates. This third dialogue was never written and even the *Critias* is incomplete, breaking off in the middle of an explanation of why it was necessary for the Atlanteans to attack Athens. In both dialogues all the description of Atlantis comes from Critias.

We do know that Critias was a real person, the grandson of Critias the Elder, who died in 403 B.C. Solon was also a real figure in antiquity. He was Plato's ancestor, a prominent Athenian statesman, lawgiver and considered one of the wisest of the ancient Greeks. Plato's descriptions of Atlantis' gods begins with Poseidon, the god of the sea, who has ten sons with his mortal wife Cleito. Atlas is the eldest and hence the name Atlantis for this continent in the Atlantic Ocean.

Although critics have dismissed Plato's account as fiction or political propaganda, at no time does Plato appear to be advancing political theories. His account is rather matter of fact, as if reiterating a history and devoid of judgments.

---

[50] Plato, *Timaeus and Critias*. (New York: Penguin Classics, 1977).

While we may view Plato's *Timaeus and Critias*, as Atlantis' *Old Testament*, Ignatius Donnelly's *Atlantis: An Antediluvian World*[51] is its New Testament. Donnelly goes well beyond Plato in declaring that Atlantis was the source of all civilization. He was either not familiar nor convinced of Mu's status in this regard.

Donnelly attempts to illustrate resemblance between many species of American and European plants and animals to show that Atlantis was the true source of them. For example, certain plants like tobacco, guava, and cotton were not, as was generally thought confined to one hemisphere before Columbus, but were grown in both the New and Old Worlds.

Egypt, Donnelly deduced, blossomed all at once, rather than the slow evolution would expect in such a civilization. This showed that it had to have originated somewhere else, in Atlantis. How else can we explain the growth of Egyptian culture from the Neolithic Merimda people living in mud houses and wearing animal skins to the sophisticated civilization of the Fourth Dynasty?

Donnelly also pointed out that the gods and goddesses of the ancient Greeks, the Phoenicians, the Hindus, and the Scandinavians were simply the kings, queens, and heroes of Atlantis. Egypt was one of Atlantis' first colonies and many components of Egypt were merely a reproduction of Atlantis itself. The Phoenician alphabet that was the source of all European languages originated in Atlantis. Atlantis also represented the Gardens of the Hesperides, the Elysian Fields, the Gardens of Alcinous, the Mesomphalos and Mount Olympis.

Plato describes Atlantis as being situated in front of the Pillars of Hercules (the Straights of Gibraltar) and being larger than Libya (Mediterranean Africa in Plato's time) and Asia (actually Asia Minor) combined. This would place this lost continent at least to the 45th parallel of longitude and from the 45th parallel of latitude to about the 22nd parallel of latitude. The Sargasso Sea, the Azores and Canary Islands would be rough landmarks for Plato's Atlantis.

Plato describes in detail the capital city. The general architectural plan of the city of Atlantis, as described by Plato, appears to have been copied far and wide. We see it duplicated in Carthage, the Aztec city of Mexico – Tenochtilan and others.

The design of a citadel hill encircled by zones of land and water, a canal to the sea, and bridges over the zones, fortified by towers is part of this design. This island within an island design in which the docks were roofed in, the cities were encircled by *three* walls, great cisterns for the supply of drinking water and baths were present. The city was guarded by a great seawall, masking the entrance to the

---

[51] Ignatius Donnelly, *Atlantis: An Antediluvian World.* (New York: Harper & Brothers, 1882).

harbour was noted in the ancient city of Carthage, being a replica of Atlantis' main city.

Many scholars look upon Plato's Atlantis as a mere myth. But the fact is that King Poseidon of Atlantis, a sacred hill and the Flood dominate Plato's and other legends throughout the world at or before his time. Mythologists call this the "test of recurrence." Since overlapping components of the same myth were found in various parts of the world, and since this data could not have been available to Plato, these fragments must have been part of a once homogeneous myth. The parts of these myths which do not correspond are supplementary to each other, linked together by those which do correspond.

The pyramid in Egypt and America is merely a later reminiscence of the sacred hill of Atlantis. In early Egypt, Mexico and Peru certain hills were regarded as especially sacred, as the homes of powerful supernatural beings. We can see a common ancestor to both the Egyptian and American pyramids, the sacred hill of Atlantis. It is interesting to note that the Antilles and Canary Islands also have pyramids. Mu did not build pyramids, but Atlantis most certainly did.

Donnelly further points out that the early Egyptians depicted themselves as *red* men on their monuments. They were brown-skinned people, but worshipped the Atlanteans (some of whom were members of the red race). These ancient Egyptians recognized four races of men as shown (red, yellow, black and white).

The ancient Egyptians, according to the scientific establishment, stemmed from the Nubian tribes, the Berbers of Algiers and Tunis, and had to have brown skin according to the scientific establishment. Egyptian artists even exaggerated their supposed red complexion by representing themselves as a crimson hue. Red was a sacred color in antiquity. The gods of the ancients were always painted red.

It is of interest that the Egyptians were the only people of antiquity who were well versed about Atlantis. Plato received his information about Atlantis from his ancestor Solon who visited Egypt at about 600 B.C. Since Egypt was never a maritime power, the Atlanteans must have come to Egypt and not vice versa.

The fact that Egypt claimed descent from the twelve great gods is considered by Donnelly a reference to Poseidon and his wife Cleito and their ten sons. These were the twelve gods of Atlantis.

The Egyptian belief in the "underworld" as the land of the dead located West (for Lower Egypt) and that this underworld was beyond the water is interpreted as referring to the submerged continent of Atlantis, which lies West of Egypt. Only by crossing the water in an ark (the symbol of Atlantis in all cultures) could an Egyptian reach the land of the dead (Elysian Fields) from which his soul would reincarnate.

Donnelly is quick to note the fact that the Basques of the Spanish Pyrenees differ from all their neighbors in appearance and language. The Basque tongue is the only non-Aryan tongue of Western Europe. In addition, inhabitants of the Canary Islands practice mummification techniques and look nothing like any African group. 626 reference sources were utilized by Donnelly in his classic book.

A rather impressive piece of evidence to Egypt's heritage being from an advanced civilization in pre-history is their cult of Osiris. Pyramid texts prove that this religion had a far more ancient history than the First Dynasty. Budge, the Egyptian scholar, clearly stated that the *Book of the Dead*, which describes the Osirian religion, was edited and re-edited many times. The scribes who copied them could hardly follow their general meaning because of their antiquity. Budge states:

*We are in any case justified in estimating the earliest form of the work to be contemporaneous with the foundation of the civilisation which we call "Egyptian" in the Valley of the Nile. One of these texts was indeed "discovered" in the First Dynasty (c.a. 3,000 B.C.), and was then referred to a date which equates with 4,266 B.C. When, then, was it first reduced to writing, or to literary shape?*[52]

We can distinguish Atlantis and its colonies by certain key traits. These are the practice of mummification, magical practices, cataclysm legends and the presence of the pyramid. Egypt most certainly fulfills these criteria. From the western coasts of Europe to the eastern shores of America, including the western European islands and the Antilles, this cultural evidence is manifested. Other than in Egypt, these common cultural traits are not to be found associated with each other in any other part of the world.

It is also interesting to note that Atlantis would have received the warm weather benefits of the Gulf Stream, which would have given it a climate favorable to the growth of tropical and subtropical fruit such as coconuts, pineapples, and bananas. The warm waters of the Gulf Stream would also have been cut off from Europe by the existence of a great Atlantic island, and most of Europe, in turn, would be cold and glacial. As we now know, this was exactly the case during the period of the last glaciation, at the end of which Atlantis sank into the ocean and freed the Gulf Stream to furnish a warmer climate to Europe.

## ATLANTEAN INVENTIONS

Before we discuss Atlantis' influence on Egypt's civilization, let us consider

---

[52] E. A. W. Budge, Book of the Dead, op. cit.

the wonders created by this civilization from prehistory. As did Mu, Atlantis had airships. The difference being those of Atlantis were used for war.

An Atlantean airship was powered by forces not yet discovered by science. They were made of metal and appeared seamless and perfectly smooth. Their maximum speed was about 100 miles per hour, and they could be seen in the dark. These crafts were shaped like a boat, contained a ramming nose and could carry up to 100 men. A fireball-type weapon from this craft could destroy an entire city. It was most likely a nuclear device.

Atlantis fought a terrible war with Mu's colony called Rama in India. This war probably took place before 2,600 B.C. Both combatants had airships, being known as Vimanas in India and Vailix in Atlantis. From the ancient Indian poem Ramayana a Vimana was described as a double-deck, circular (or cylindrical) aircraft containing a dome and portholes. It flew with the "speed of the wind."

Some form of anti-gravity device may have been present on the Vimana, as it took off vertically and could hover in the sky in a manner like a modern helicopter. The Atlanteans invaded India to make the Rama Empire its colony. After the Rama Priest-King refused to surrender to the Atlantean army, an invasion was carried out by Atlantis.

At dawn the Rama Priest-King raised his arms upward and applied a technique known only to certain Himalayan yogis. The result was a massive display of Atlantean officers dying of heart attacks. Devoid of their leaders, the Atlantean force retreated to their airships and returned home defeated and confused. Not one soldier from the Rama Empire was lost.

However, this was not the end of the story. The vengeful Atlanteans under the leadership of Gurkha dropped a nuclear bomb on the Rama people. This is described in the 5,000 year old Indian epic *Mahabharata* we discussed in chapter 1.

The Atlanteans mastered atomic power and built power plants to produce electricity. Radio and television existed in Atlantis. A structure known as the Great Crystal somehow tapped into the gas belts and other sources of energy beneath the continent of Atlantis and converted it into electrical and nuclear energy.

Other Atlantean technology included:
- printing presses
- telepathy machines that could both read and alter thoughts
- guns using electricity to kill opponents
- high tension electrical lamps that were used in the construction of Egyptian pyramids

- monorail transportation systems
- a generator that condensed water from the atmosphere
- air conditioners

## THE DESTRUCTION OF ATLANTIS

Atlantis met its end at the same time Mu was submerged, approximately 11,000 B.C. Both continents were located above isolated gas chambers as part of a gas belt. The blowing out of these gas chambers led to the submerging of both continents, as I described in the previous chapter.

Instead of these isolated gas chambers, had there been a great depth of rock free of chambers between these chambers which comprised the belt, mountain ranges would have been raised and no submerging would have occurred.

Before we discuss the precise details of the destruction of Atlantis, let us recall that there were three phases to these cataclysms. The first phase took place at about 50,000 B.C. In Atlantis' case the large island continent of Atlantis was split into two land masses called Antilla and Poseidon. Oxygia or Og was the name several Greek and Roman writers used to describe Antilla.

At about 26,000 B.C. Antilla sunk leaving only Poseidon, which was now simply referred to as Atlantis. The lost remnant of Atlantis went down around 11,000 B.C. Many Atlanteans left for Egypt and other colonies prior to its final demise. Atlanteans either came directly to Egypt or went first to Spain (Basque people) and Portugal, focusing on the Pyrenees Mountain region. From this area they migrated to Egypt.

Atlantis' final destruction was the basis of the Biblical and Sumerian Floods, as well as those reported by just about every culture throughout our planet. We must not forget Mu's submerging, which occurred concurrently with that of Atlantis.

The earlier breakup of Atlantis and Mu at about 50,000 B.C. and 26,000 B.C. may explain the cavemen referred to as Cro-Magnon men who were first reported in Europe at about 40,000 B.C. and became extinct at about 25,000 B.C.

What is interesting to note is that makes it practically impossible for Cro-Magnon man to be our ancestor. I pointed out in chapter one how recent DNA tests eliminate, for all practical purposes, Neanderthal Man as our ancestor. Our species has been documented to have lived on this planet for at least 117,000 years. Cro-Magnon Man was just another failed experiment, and may have lived on Atlantis before being exiled to Europe just prior to Atlantis' destruction. We have no evidence of Cro-Magnon man existing prior to 40,000 B.C. It can't be our ancestor, since our species has been around at least 117,000 years.

A new type of geological equilibrium was established in both the Atlantic and Pacific oceans after Mu and Atlantis submerged. But this equilibrium is far from perfect. There have been several breaks in this equilibrium causing islands to sink or be severely compromised. Consider the following recorded cataclysms:

- An earthquake in 1622 created tidal waves on the capital of the Azorian island of São Miguel.
- Port Royal, Jamaica submerged in 1692 without warning.
- Over 60,000 people died in a 1755 earthquake in Lisbon, Portugal that occurred in a matter of minutes.
- One quarter of the population of Iceland died during the mid 1700s from a single earthquake.
- Mt. Pélee on Martinique exploded in 1902 and killed everyone in St. Pierre, its capital. The only survivors were a convict and a psychiatric patient in a protective prison cell. Nearly 30,000 people died in this event.
- In 1811 a large volcanic island appeared in the Azores and was named Sambrina. This new island then submerged as suddenly as it appeared.
- A similar fate occurred in 1931 to two islands that appeared in the vicinity of the Fernando de Noronha group off the coast of Brazil.
- In the midst of flame and smoke a new island arose in 1963 off the southwest coast of Iceland. It was named Surtsey, aptly for the Norse god of fire. Soon, two other islands joined it.
- These land-sea inversions have taken place for centuries, characterized by sections of existing islands (or entire islands) submerging and new land masses appearing. This is particularly common in the Azores, Canaries and Madeira, representing the location of Atlantis.

Perhaps the mysterious forces tapped into by the Atlanteans, coupled with their malicious use of Unseen Forces, created some form of energy vortex that have resulted in the mysterious disappearances and other events reported in the Bermuda Triangle and the Devil Sea (a Pacific Ocean equivalent to the Bermuda Triangle). The latter would have resulted from Mu's actions.

## TECTONIC-PLATES

Tectonic-plate boundaries between North America, Europe and Africa are marked by the Mid-Atlantic Ridge. This is the world's largest and most active seismic area, in which a triple junction of tectonic plates occurs at the Azores. These tectonic plates are masses of land on the ocean floor that move both horizontally and vertically in a manner similar to being pushed under each other.

The fiery interior mantle of the Earth would be exposed and result in lava being spewed out by way of volcanic eruptions when movements of these tectonic-plates take place. This movement can occur in a matter of minutes. This mechanism explains how the islands of Japan were formed.

Tectonic-plate movements could easily explain both the submerging of Atlantis and Mu. Instead of a continental drift theory dating back millions of years, a more recent time frame (11,000 B.C.) is quite possible.

## COMETS AND ASTEROIDS DESTROYING ATLANTIS

Our planet is blessed with a magnetic field that protects us from being bombarded by meteors, comets and asteroids. This magnetic field deflects these potential attackers, while our atmosphere and ozone layer function to burn them up or considerably reduce their size should they enter our airspace.

Some rather huge asteroids have struck the Earth, leaving large craters on its surface as evidence. Examples of this past activity are the Meteor Crater in Arizona, the Curswell, Deep Bay, and Manicouagan craters in Canada. Turtle Mountains between North Dakota and Manitoba, the Siljan in Sweden, the Ashanti in West Africa, the Araguainha in Brazil, and the Korla in Siberia, north of the Arctic Circle.

The late Otto Muck, a German rocket scientist, hypothesized that a huge meteor struck part of Atlantis in its western region. This has been called the Carolina Meteorite, and was accompanied by a great number of smaller ones. When this incident occurred, Atlantis was crushed and volcanic eruptions, tidal waves and tectonic-plate movement resulted.

If this meteorite were ten kilometers in diameter it would weigh 200,000 megatons. Such an explosion would be equivalent to 30,000 H-bombs hitting Atlantis, more than enough to submerge it. This could easily explain the origin of the crater field of Carolina, two deep sea holes in the southwest North Atlantic and the shallower trough in the eastern Caribbean. The Biblical and other Flood legends would also be explained by this phenomenon.

Muck was an authority on oceanography and geology. He noted that the present pock holes are distributed in a wedge-shaped area extending to the Carolina coast. The direction of the wedge as well as the compass-angulation of the individual holes point directly toward the two seafloor depressions north of Puerto Rico. Theoretically, they could have arisen from a trailer stream of asteroid material, as he theorized.

We must not forget the possibility of this meteorite's magnetic shield being responsible in part for unusual events associated with the Bermuda Triangle. Such

61

unusual phenomena as magnetic fogs, the interference with radio signals, spinning compasses, and the malfunction of navigational equipment so often noticed by crew members on air or surface craft crossing the area.

## EVIDENCE OF ATLANTIS

In June of 1940 the American psychic Edgar Cayce made the following prediction:

*Poseidia will be among the first portions of Atlantis to rise again. Expect it in '68 and '69 not so far away![53]*

In 1968 an underwater road (or a series of foundations of a building) was discovered off north Bimini on the ocean floor. This "Bimini road" was dismissed by skeptics as naturally formed beach rock.

Dr. Manson Valentine, the American oceanographer and archeologist who discovered the rock formation, emphasized that beach rock does not form such blocks which fit together as discovered, nor does it make 90-degree turns or have regularly positioned passageways running between its sections. Finally, the stone pillars discovered precisely beneath these beach rocks have never before been observed as a result of natural rock formations.

Vertical walls, bases for pyramids and a great arch were found with 100 miles from the shore. Pilots have photographed formations on the ocean floor that appear similar to the Stonehenge standing stone blocks at Andros Island.

Several interesting conclusions have been drawn from this find. Sections of pillars appear "to have been carved from natural stone." "Pavement-like stones" or blocks form single or double lines roughly parallel to the present shoreline. The blocks here are between 60 and 90 cm thick, somewhat pillow-shaped in cross section. Their originally right-angled corners have been trimmed back, chiefly by boring molluscs and sea urchins. All of the blocks are of coarse-grained limestone lying on a stratum of denser limestone of finer grain. At no place are blocks found to rest on a similar set beneath.

The field of blocks appear to have been fitted together. Two of the cylinders are composed of marble and have flute-like marks parallel to the long axis. Analysis of one of the marble samples showed that its composition was calcite (90 percent) and quartz (8 percent) along with muscante, pyrite and sphene. This marble is not found in the Bahamas. It could not have come from Georgia either. The material from the cylinders also was not indigenous to the Bahamas.

---

[53] Edgar Evans Cayce, *Edgar Cayce on Atlantis*. (Virginia Beach: Association For Research and Enlightenment, 1968).

Valentine believed that the pillars may have formed one continuous portico originally, since they appear at regular intervals along the sunken wall. The Andros Island submerged rectangle find is almost an exact duplicate in size and design of the Temple of the Turtles, an ancient Mayan sanctuary found at Uxmal in Yucatán, indicating that the survivors of this Caribbean civilization center may have influenced the development of the early Central American cultures and the culture of the Mound Builders.[54]

Other Bahama finds of note are underwater limestone caves known as the famous Blue Holes. These caves contain stalagmites and stalactites and connect through caves to deep water. This is evidence that they were formed above sea level. Some of these formations are tilted and broken, as though they were suddenly thrown into the ocean.

Finally, a find near Vero, Florida dating back to about 15,000 B.C. consisted of bones of the extinct sabre-toothed tiger mixed with human artifacts. The most unusual aspect of this find was the astonishingly fine workmanship displayed in the artifacts, which comprised bone tools and pottery. The find's chronology and the workmanship seemed totally incongruous with existing ideas about prehistoric man in the Americas.

Mainstream archeologists do not like to consider dates prior to 11,000 B.C. for man's habitation in the Americas. That is the date given to primitive Asian man crossing the Alaskan land bridge that existed at that time. Florida archeologist E. H. Sellards confirmed the 15,000 B.C. date. Other maverick scientists have demonstrated that modern man lived in the Americas as early as 70,000 B.C.[55]

When both Atlantis and Mu were submerged in 11,000 B.C., several geological events transpired. They may be summarized as follows:

- The Amazon Sea was closed off forming the present Amazon River.
- The Mississippi Valley and St. Lawrence Valley dried out.
- Florida arose.
- South America and countless other land masses and mountains arose.
- A huge flood took place that was felt around the world.

We cannot ignore the tales of nearly all civilized people of Europe, Asia and America that talk of Antediluvians, of Cyclopean builders and a superior race or races of navigators travelling around the world in ships and flying machines.

Whereas the Greeks regarded the gods and Titans as having originated in the West (Atlantis), the American races spoke of them as coming to their shores from

---

[54] W. Harrison, "Atlantis Undiscovered–Bimini, Bahamas." *Nature*, 230 (1971): 287-289.
[55] Jeffrey Goodman, *American Genesis*. (New York: Summit, 1981).

the East (Atlantis) and West (Mu). This advanced ancient world was regarded as ending in ruin and cataclysm, induced by the wickedness of its rulers, and it is invariably spoken of as having existed at a period so remote that only the broad outlines of its history were, through tradition, available to the writer.

One final comment before I present data from my patient's past life regressions in Atlantean Egypt concerns the often reported Atlantean League. This group of superior sailors traveled the world building the great monuments we see today. They controlled all the oceans that lay beyond the Straits of Gibraltar and were made up of the Phoenicians, Carthaginians and "Mediterranean Sea Peoples."

The Phoenicians were the best ancient seamen. This group founded Carthage prior to 800 B.C., which became their greatest colony. Carthage not only was built on the Atlantean model, but became the greatest maritime power of the world at its time. The Western Mediterranean was totally controlled by her. Alexander the Great devised a plan for her conquest, but died before he could carry it out. Rome eventually destroyed Carthage in 146 B.C. as a result of the Third Punic War.

## PAST LIFE REGRESSIONS

According to the past life data I obtained from my patients, the most important person in the history of Egypt was the Greek Hermes. In Egypt Hermes was known as Tehuti, Thoth, Taat, Tuti and other names. His Atlantean name was Taatos. According to Churchward, the archeologist Henry Schliemann discovered an inscription in Maycarne, Crete that stated: *The Egyptians descended from Misor. Misor was the child of Thoth, the god of history. Thoth was the emigrated son of a priest of Atlantis, who having fallen in love with the daughter of King Chronos, escaped, and after many wanderings landed in Egypt. He built the first temple at Sais and there taught the wisdom of his native land.*[56]

There is some truth to this inscription, but as we shall see Thoth is far more significant to the history and development of humankind than is reflected in Schliemann's find. Before we can effectively discuss Thoth's role in the Egyptian experiment, a little background about his Atlantean life is necessary.

Thoth or Taatos, lived in Atlantis during the time of Osiris at approximately 20,000 B.C. Atlantis at that time consisted solely of one island, as it had survived two major cataclysms. The Antilla (Og) island submerged at around 26,000 B.C. This had an enormous effect on the citizens of Atlantis. They reached their height of power and technology just prior to the second cataclysm (26,000 B.C.), but their

---

[56] J. Churchward, *The Children of Mu*. (New York: Ives Washburn, 1931) p. 107.

arrogance, cruelty and moral degeneration seemed to coincide with this last destruction.

Religion became critical to the Atlanteans. Two main groups dominated this island continent. The Atlantes were materialistic and can be compared to the citizens of Ancient Rome. We have previously discussed the Essenes as being spiritual and the complete opposite of the Atlantes.

Although both the Essenes and Atlantes were represented in Atlantis, the latter dominated and set the tone for Atlantis. The majority of Atlantis' population were now frightened by the two previous cataclysms and decided to follow the Atlantes religious and political paradigms.

The dominant religion of Atlantis was that of bull worship, a theology that found its way into Egypt. The most spiritually evolved citizens of Atlantis were two individuals named Osiris and Isis, representatives of the Essene group. Although Isis the Atlanteans proposed making Osiris and Isis their rulers, this couple declined political involvement.

Both Osiris and Isis were Caucasian, tall and had piercing blue eyes. They also possessed blond hair and always could be seen in white robes. It was Taatos who was responsible for keeping the following legend of Osiris and Isis as common knowledge in both Atlantis and ancient Egypt.

Petty politics was the rule in Atlantis. The fact that Atlantis was ruled by kings did not eliminate the paranoia of royal advisors and those next in line to the throne from being threatened by the popularity of Osiris and Isis.

Osiris and Isis functioned as spiritual missionaries teaching spirituality and universal laws. This couple had no interest in politics, but nonetheless an advisor to the current king named Seth attempted to kill Osiris one evening.

Seth stabbed Osiris and mortally wounded the latter. Although Isis appeared helpless to save her colleague, Taatos came onto this scene and with Isis' assistance somehow saved Osiris' life. When this crime was made public, Seth was caught and executed for this attempted murder.

This became part of the Osirian religion of Egypt taught at Sais by Taatos when he was known as Thoth. Taatos altered some of the facts and setting of this story so the masses would easily accept it. For example, Osiris and Iris were portrayed as brother and sister and joint rulers of Egypt, opposed by Osiris' brother Seth.

Taatos depicted Seth as an evil god of darkness murdering Osiris, dismembering this king and scattering his body parts abroad. Thoth supposedly assisted Isis in finding those remnants of Osiris' body and reassembling them so that Isis could impale herself on Osiris' penis long enough to become pregnant with her son Horus.

Horus would later banish Seth to the desert where Seth would now become the evil desert winds. Geb was portrayed as the father of Osiris and Isis who bequeathed half of Egypt's land to both Seth and Horus. Upper and Lower Egypt would represent this divided kingdom. It was not until later that Geb would reverse this strategy and make Horus the sole ruler of a united Egypt.

The era during which Osiris and Isis ruled Egypt was called *Zep Tepi*, or First Time, by Taatos. The cities of Heliopolis and Memphis were the sites of these ancient capitals.

This particular detailed account was reported to me by two different patients who lived as priests in ancient Egypt at about 14,000 B.C. They described Thoth as a tall, blond, blue-eyed Caucasian male who also wore a white robe most of the time. We can see that Thoth's influence on ancient Egypt persisted for at least 2,000 years. I will show how this occurred without Thoth being a 2,000 year old human.

Thoth (Taatos) was called Hermes by the Greeks. My patients past life regressions revealed the presence of Taatos from 16,000 B.C. to 10,500 B.C. He simply couldn't have been over 5,500 years old! We shall see how Taatos could indeed have lived in ancient Egypt during these years without having to be several thousand years old.

The relatively small numbers of Atlanteans that survived the destruction of Atlantis and settled in Lower Egypt at about 11,000 B.C. are known as "Companions of Osiris." No pyramids or Sphinx existed in Egypt at this time. Taatos is responsible for both designing and initiating the construction of the Sphinx and the three pyramids at Giza at about 10,500 B.C.

These Companions of Osiris that fled to Lower Egypt numbered about 5,000 people. There were about 10,000 Muvians in Upper Egypt at this time. Considering the total population of ancient Egypt at its height has been estimated at about four million people, these Atlantean and Muvian emigrants were a minority component of its population.

The survivors of Atlantis and Mu functioned as kings, high priests, astrologers and royal advisors. Their chief concern was their own survival, which meant they could not afford to bring about an uprising of the local primitive inhabitants. This did occur several times in prehistory and only a handful of Atlanteans and Muvians survived.

Most of the Sphinx was completed by 10,500 B.C., but only about one third of the pyramids at Giza were constructed. Taatos made sure that the primitive local inhabitants of Egypt were never eligible to become either pharaohs or priests. Local inhabitants were trained in medical techniques and other functions.

Both Essenes and Atlantes were represented in Lower Egypt, whereas Upper

Egypt was dominated by the Essenes. Following the transfer of these refuges from Atlantis and Mu to prehistorical Egypt, the ships that brought them were sent to other locations and formed the basis of the Phoenicians, Carthaginians and other seafarers of antiquity. From about 9000 B.C. to 5500 B.C. many uprisings took place in both Lower and Upper Egypt that resulted in mass killings of both Atlantes and Essenes.

It appeared that the Atlantes didn't learn from their experiences in Atlantis and continued to exhibit materialistic and arrogant behavior patterns in the Egypt of prehistory. Their lack of understanding and poor treatment of the indigenous population resulted in many rebellions and mass execution of these Atlanteans and Essenes. Although neither the Atlantes nor Essences were completely eliminated, their numbers were significantly reduced.

From 9000 B.C. to 5500 B.C. my patients reported the names of Tehuti, Taat, Tuti and Thoth for the kings of Egypt. Taatos obviously became pharaoh of Lower Egypt during this time. Although Muvians lived to between 500 and 1,000 years of age, they most certainly did not live to be 10,000 years old. I will explain how this occurred in chapter 5.

From the many past life regressions that took place during this time and reported to me by my patients reports surfaced of strange beings and UFO in ancient Egypt, especially during the time of the Sphinx construction at about 10,500 B.C. In addition, there were abduction incidents throughout Egypt's history, as we will explore in great detail in chapter 4.

Some of my patients described past lives during which they were either astrologers or priests when Taatos was either king or a high priest in both Atlantis and Egypt. This is the main source of my statements concerning Taatos' influence and presence in these two civilizations.

The main method the Atlantes living in Egypt controlled the masses was by their theology. The Mystery Schools were the main form Egypt's religion took through the application of secret rites the Mystery Schools instructed the initiate to both improve their present life and their afterlife.

The Mysteries were divided into the Lesser Mysteries (which included reincarnation and the Osirian and Isis legends and were taught to the general population) and the Greater Mysteries (which dealt with the true origin of civilization and ascension techniques). The general population were excluded from receiving the Greater Mysteries. Initiates were carefully selected by the high priests and had to undergo a rigorous initiation process. The ultimate goal was ascension back to God, the One.

Hypnosis was commonly taught and most of these mysteries were transmitted through oral teachings. Although Taatos was against the secrecy so characteristic of the mysteries, he was outvoted by the Atlantes and would have risked his own life had he continued his objections.

Taatos' history is vividly depicted in the Egyptian *Book of the Dead*, also known as the Per-em-Hru and *Book of Coming Forth into the Day*. This is considered by many to be the oldest book in the world as we have records. If you accept the authenticity of Churchward and Niven's tablets and other Mayan Codices, these would have to be considered as predating the *Book of the Dead*.

Plato originally received information concerning Atlantis when he went to Sais and spoke to an Egyptian priest Patenit, as reported by Proclus. In the temple of Neith at Sais secret halls contained historical records that were over 9,000 years old. In 560 B.C. these records were reported to Plato's ancestor Solon. Another noteworthy point is that Pythagoras' teacher, the Egyptian high priest Psonchis, also alluded to sacred records dating back thousands of years. This priest even made reference to a giant asteroid colliding with the Earth in a remote past![57]

Several different patients have reported the existence of these sacred writings. Egyptologists have used the term *Emerald Tablet* to depict Egyptian magic and philosophy originating directly from Hermes. The famous expression "as above, so below" is attributed to this work. This expression specifically refers to whatever is taking place on the astral plane (above) is also manifesting on the physical plane (below).

## THE EMERALD TABLET OF HERMES

*True, without falsehood, certain and most true,* **that which is above is as that which is below, and that which is below is that which is above,** *for the performance of the miracles of the One Thing. And as all things are from One, by the mediation of One, so all things have their birth from this One Thing by adaptation. The Sun is its father, the Moon its mother, and the Wind carries it in its belly, its nurse is the Earth. This is the father of all perfection, or consummation of the whole world. Its power is integrating, if it be turned into earth.*

*Thou shalt separate the earth from the fire, the subtle from the gross, suavely, and with great ingenuity. It ascends from earth to heaven and descends again to earth, and receives the power of the superiors and of the inferiors. So thou hast the glory of the whole world; therefore let all obscurity flee before thee. This is the strong force of all forces, overcoming every subtle and penetrating every solid thing. So the world was created. Hence were all wonderful*

---

[57] Herodotus, *The History* (translated by David Grene). (Chicago: University of Chicago Press, 1987).

*adaptations, of which this is the manner. Therefore am I called Hermes*
*Trismegistus, having the three parts of the philosophy of the whole world. What I*
*have to tell is completed, concerning the Operation of the Sun.*[58]

This version of the tablet came from the Arabic *Kitab Sirr al-Asar*, which is
dated at about 800 A.D. This book of advice to king was translated into Latin by
Johannes Hispalensic around 1140 A.D. and by Philip of Tripoli at about 1243.

According to the ancient Egyptian priests who wrote the *Book of the Dead*,
Hermes invented writing, medicine, religion, astronomy, music, exercises,
mathematics, metal working, and most of the things necessary for life as we know
it. It was Hermes who selected a certain select number of people to reveal the
Greater Mysteries and train them in science and the arts.

Hermetic writing dealt with the key to immortality. This was then the most
important of the Greater Mysteries. Another of Hermes' sacred books is called
*Book of Thoth*. This work is the key to his other writings. Its pages were covered
with unusual hieroglyphic (Muvian?) figures and symbols. Anyone who
understood their meaning would have unlimited power over spirits of the air (Sky
World to the shamans) and subterranean entities (the Lower World or underworld
in shamanic jargon).

The *Book of Thoth* described in detail how to stimulate certain regions of our
brain by secret methods (Greater Mysteries) to expand our consciousness so that
we may be in the presence of the far superior gods. This is the basis of Egyptian
magic. Unfortunately, this book has not survived.

The *Book of Thoth* was housed in a golden box located in a temple in Sais.
The highest initiate of the Hermetic Arcanum alone knew its contents.
Supposedly, certain initiates transported it sealed (hence the origin of the term
hermetically sealed)[59] to another land, possibly the Himalayas. This work is
reportedly still in existence and continues to lead other initiates to have an
audience with the gods.

The *Book of the Dead* describes Hermes wandering in a rocky and desolate
place in meditation and practicing his consciousness expansion technique. While
out of his body he was in the presence of the Great Dragon. The Mysteries taught
that a dragon represented the symbol of Universal Life.

When Hermes asked the Great Dragon to identify itself, this terrifying figure
declared that its name was *Poimandres*, the Absolute. In reality, Poimandres was
the god Osiris, according to many scholars.

Suddenly the image of Poimandres was transformed into a glorious and

---

[58] Garth Fowden, *The Egyptian Hermes*. (Boston: Cambridge University Press, 1978).
[59] I also feel the term "hermetically sealed" refers to the precise Egyptian mummification procedures that prevented
gases from leaving the body following death.

pulsating radiance. When Hermes was in the presence of this Light, all material connections with the universe ended. Next, a great darkness descended and swallowed up this Light. A smokelike vapor resulted, which represented materialism, whereas the Light signified the spiritual universe.

Following this a Voice of the Light rose out of this darkness as a great pillar. The fire and air followed it, but the Earth remain behind. Now the waters of Light were divided from those of darkness. The former created the worlds above, while the worlds below were a result of the latter's creation.

Although not revealing his form, Poimandres now declared:

*I Thy God am the Light and the Mind which were before substance was divided from spirit and darkness from Light. And the Word which appeared as a pillar of flame out of the darkness is the Son of God, born of the mystery of the Mind. The name of that Word is Reason. Reason is the offspring of Thought [Thoth] and Reason shall divide the Light from the darkness and establish truth in the midst of the waters.*[60]

Hermes taught that man had taken on a mortal body to commune with nature. We are a divine and creative spirit at heart and represent an immortal essence. We do not die, we merely dissolve and transform into another form in a new dimension. This re-becoming a god is part of gnosis.

The Greeks referred to Thoth as Hermes Trismegistus (thrice greatest). Today we have what is called the *Corpus Hermeticum*. This is a fusion of Greek philosophy and ancient Egyptian theology. The *Corpus Hermeticum* is written in the form of dialogues between Trismegistus, Thoth, Isis and several other Egyptian gods.

Although this work claims to be the actual writing of Hermes and depicts him living at the time of Moses and long before, scholars have shown that much of the material contained herein reflected the Greek style of Plotinus (a Neoplatonist who lived during the second and third century A.D.).[61] That may be true, but it does not nullify the data my patients have presented to me as a result of their hypnotic regressions.

Furthermore, we must not forget Hermes' Atlantean life as Taatos and the evidence I have already presented demonstrating the existence of that continent in prehistory. Throughout my work with hypnotic past life regressions to ancient Egypt, Taatos has always portrayed himself as a human being. It was others who deified him.

You will never see Taatos depicted wearing a white robe by the Egyptians.

---

[60] Garth Fowden, op. cit.
[61] A. J. Festugiere and A. D. Nock, op. cit.

70

Yet he did and the significance of that trait will be discussed in chapter 5. Taatos always refers to himself as a philosopher, priest and king.

There is a legend concerning Alexander the Great who, when he visited Egypt, after adding it to his empire, discovered the Emerald Tablet clenched in the mummified hands of Hermes (Taatos) himself. I cannot verify this particular story, but I can state with absolute certainty that Hermes did live and was single handedly responsible for Egypt's development.

Returning to additional past life regressions, an interesting pattern emerged. The Atlantean and Muvian influence in Egypt's civilization began to decline significantly from about 7500 B.C. to around 5000 B.C. The original Atlanteans, few in number, did keep their genetic line potent in the early days following the final submerging of that continent.

There was a tendency for those who lived in Atlantis (and Mu for that matter) to reincarnate in Egypt. A karmic Atlantean and Muvian bloodline (soulline would be a more accurate term) was maintained. As time went on the Atlantean influence was focused on the Egyptian priesthood and prehistory kings.

The presence of extraterrestrials and abductions also waned during this time. We will discuss these aliens in greater detail in the next chapter. A significant struggle developed between Lower and Upper Egypt. It was the militant and power hungry Atlantes descendents that initiated raids and wars on Upper Egypt.

In Upper Egypt the Essenes and their successors dominated early on. Later the Atlantes factions mingled with these people and began to exhibit warlike tendencies.

Taatos appeared on and off during these years. He became king several times, but was not heard of for several hundred years at a time. Whenever he did make an appearance it always had a positive influence on Egypt's development. I should point out at this time that Hermes became king in both Lower and Upper Egypt during this transition period of 7500 to 5000 B.C.

Osiris and Isis also functioned as king and queen at various times, but only in Lower Egypt. At about 3500 B.C. a strong movement towards unification of Egypt under one crown emerged.

One would assume Lower Egypt, with its statistically greater Atlantes population, would easily defeat Upper Egypt, still dominated by the spiritual and peaceful Essenes. That did not occur.

Many of my patients' past life regressions reported that the civil war went on for several hundred years, until finally Upper Egypt won out. Interestingly enough, the culture and customs of the north were assimilated into the now victorious Upper Egypt.

This new unified Egypt more closely resembled Lower Egypt than Upper

Egypt.  Hermes was a priest and advisor to the early kings.  Menes was not the first king of this united Egypt.  He did appear later on.  Yes, there was a Menes (It was in reality Osiris).

The hieroglyphics that were passed down from many centuries before became eventually a part of the *Pyramid Texts* and still exist today in the form we call the *Book of the Dead*.  Hermes is reported time and time again as the orchestrator of this first civilization that our conventional historians recognize as Egypt.  In reality it had many predecessors, with Atlantis being the most fascinating to Westerners.

## CHAPTER 4  EXRATERRESTRIAL ORIGINS OF EGYPT

If you carefully assess both society and history you will observe a pattern of polarities. Up-down, black-white, left-right, good-evil, pacifist-militant and so on become dominant themes. We see this pattern with Upper and Lower Egypt also.

One of the most controversial aspects of my work concerns itself with the presence of extraterrestrials (ETs)and UFOs in abduction cases. No matter how many documented cases of videotapes, cattle mutations, crop circles and other such evidence, most people consider ETs science fiction, at least publicly.

We ascribe the term "flying saucer" to a pilot named Kenneth Arnold who on June 24, 1947, viewed strange airborne crafts. Arnold used flying saucer to depict his sighting to a reporter. In January 1878 a Texas farmer described the dark flying object he saw as a "large saucer." An "earthenware vessel" was reported on October 27, 1180 in ancient Japan as flying from a mountain in the Ki province beyond the northeast mountain of Fukuharal, leaving a luminous trail.

Close encounters with alien crafts were reported on November 25, 1896 by Colonel H. G. Shaw and his companion Camille Spooner, in 1901 in Bournebrook, England; in 1910 in Baltimore, Maryland; in 1919 in western Australia; in 1925 in La Mancha, Spain; in 1944 in Rochester, Pennsylvania.

It wasn't until November 1957 that twenty-three year old Brazilian farmer Antonio Villas-Boas reported being abducted aboard a 35 feet long and 23 feet wide alien craft and having sexual intercourse with a naked blonde, blue-eyed four feet five inches tall female extraterrestrial (ET) with a strange nose, high cheekbones, a pointed chin and wide face, that the world was exposed to scientific experimentation of our species by aliens.

The main ET influence on Egypt's development can be traced to two main classes of alien beings. These were the Sirians and Lyrans. Although many ET groups have visited our planet, it is these two groups that have exerted the greatest influence on Egypt's development.

## THE LYRANS

The Lyrans came to Earth several million years ago and preceded the Sirians. Although physically smaller than humans, they increased their height to between 6 and 9 feet as a result of genetic manipulation. They exhibited light eyes, light hair and light skin and constituted some of the giants reported in the Bible and the mythology of the ancients.

Dogmatism, authoritarianism, materialism, selfishness and power hungry traits were exhibited by these ETs. Bird and cat symbols represented this group. Certain components of Lyrans possessed red hair, were smaller in size and were well known for their aggressive, rebellious, violent and passionate traits.

Other subgroups of Lyrans had dark skin and brown eyes and functioned to protect our species from the more violent and aggressive ones. We can find references to thin, birdlike and even catlike Lyrans in ancient Egypt.

The arrogance of the Lyrans can be seen in the myth of the Phoenix bird dying and rising up from its own ashes. This myth was perpetrated by the Lyrans and was supposed to demonstrate their indestructibility.

The Pleidians are another subgroup of Lyrans who are Caucasian and stand between 5 and 7 feet tall. In addition to being dimensional travelers, they have acted as our guardians since the first Lyrans came to our planet.

Other noteworthy examples of Lyrans are representatives from the Orion belt and the Zeta Reticuli (the classic gray ETs). The Lyrans had to utilize a form of suspended animation when they came to Earth, since only the Pleidians were dimensional travelers. They trained primitive humans to awaken them from this hibernation.

This explains why primitive man always viewed heaven as being above the sky, rather than within (which is the predominant metaphysical view). Since ETs have looked upon us as being gods, their coming from the sky must indicate the location of heaven.

In addition, the devices used for hibernation would like coffins to primitive man. In order to get to Heaven the body must be placed in a coffin and preserved by following an intricate series of steps. The ancient Egyptians would use the mummification procedures (obtained from Atlantis) to achieve this end.

## THE SIRIANS

Compared to the Lyrans, Sirians possessed darker eyes, hair and skin and are shorter. The Sirians have always functioned as our protectors and have represented their race with dog and serpent symbols.

Since the Lyrans came to Earth first and attempted to enslave us, the Sirians have spent most of their time correcting Lyran mistakes and shielding us from Lyran enslavement. A small component of the Essenes from Mu, Atlantis and Egypt were the result of interbreeding between Sirians and primitive humans.

This genetic picture became even more complex as interbreeding also took place between the Lyrans and Sirians. Eventually it became impossible to separate these ETs. This leads us to the legend of the Flood.

The Flood story is actually the submerging of Atlantis and Mu at about

11,000 B.C. In reality there were several Noahs preserving mankind, with Egypt being the most important location for a new civilization.

## EVIDENCE OF ETs

The earlier Egyptian temples at Annu and Heliopolis were oriented to northern stars at the summer solstice. When the Giza pyramids were completed (remember, they were begun at about 10,500 B.C.) they used both the eastern and northern stars.

Sirius's star became the most significant star by 3200 B.C. because it rose at dawn at the beginning of the Egyptian New Year. This was the time the Nile began to rise. In addition, Sirius was the home of Osiris, the god who presided over life and death. This is the Sirian influence in Lower Egypt at about the time of its unification with Upper Egypt, when Sirians dominated. The Lyrans controlled Lower Egypt prior to the unification.

The ancient Egyptians considered Sirius sacred after 3200 B.C., and referred to it as Sothis. It was associated with Isis, who is often portrayed in boat paintings accompanied by two other goddesses Anukis and Satis. This strongly suggests that the ancient Egyptians knew that Sirius consisted of a three star system.

We know that the pyramids at Giza lack hieroglyphics. Those at Saqqara (5th Dynasty c.a. (2300 B.C.) contain a plethora of inscriptions and form the basis of the *Pyramid Texts*. Rituals for the pharaoh's journey to the afterlife are contained in five of these pyramids.

In one of the Pyramid Texts the pharaoh Unas states that his soul is a star: *Oh king, you are this great star, the companion of Orion, who traverses the sky with Orion . . .* Other fragments declare: *In your name of Dweller in Orion, with a season in the sky and a season on earth. O Osiris, turn your face and look on this King, for our seed which issued from you is effective.* And another states: *The sky conceiveth thee together with Orion, the dawn beareth thee together with Orion. Live the one who liveth at the order of the gods and so will thou live.*[62]

These passages are significant in that the Orion constellation was the sacred home of Osiris, their ascended Master. Slightly below Orion and to the left is located Sirius, Isis' star. Experts feel that these texts were copies of far older documents (this is confirmed by my past life regressions with several patients). I previously pointed out that the scribes did not comprehend what they were writing.

Robert Bauval, a Belgian construction engineer, wondered why the third

---

[62] James Henry Breasted, *Ancient Records of Egypt: Historical Documents from the Earliest Times to the Persian Conquest.* (London: Histories and Mysteries of Man Ltd., 1988).

pyramid at Giza, built by King Menkaura, was so much smaller than the other two. It was also set off to the east. He arrived at the conclusion that this arrangement was intended to depict the three stars of the Orion belt with the Nile River symbolizing the Milky Way.[63]

Bauval didn't know at that time that an American astronomer named Virginia Trimble in 1964 demonstrated that the southern "air shaft" in the King's Chamber of the Great Pyramid pointed straight at Orion at the time the Great Pyramid was built, at about 2450 B.C. This verified a theory proposed by the Egyptologist Alexander Badawy.

The premise Badawy was working on was that the southern shaft of the King's Chamber was not an air vent, but a channel to direct the dead pharaoh's soul to Orion, where he would become a god along with Osiris. This mechanism was reminiscent of a gun shooting the pharaoh's soul from his body to Orion. It was a most unusual ascension technique, and one that would be a component of the Greater Mysteries.

Bauval then calculated that the Queen's Chamber of the Great Pyramid pointed toward Sirius, the star of Isis, during the same time frame. This demonstrates that the Great Pyramid was not built as a tomb, but an ascension vehicle for King Cheops to ascend to Zeta Orionis (called Al-Nitak by the Egyptians) to live forever as Osiris.

Since the three Giza pyramids represent the three stars of Orion's Belt (Zeta, Epsilon and Delta), the design of these structures had to have been made long before the Great Pyramid was completed. We have established that date as about 10,500 B.C. when the Sphinx was built.

The precession of the equinoxes is a term applied to the wobble on earth's axis that causes its position in relation to the stars to change – one degree over 72 years, and a complete circle every 26,000 years. This results in the Orion Belt appearing to travel upwards, in the sky for 13,000 years and downward again for another 13,000 years.

Additional calculations showed that the only time the positions of the three pyramids on the ground reflect the positions of the three stars of Orion's Belt is 10,450 B.C., when Orion is at its closest to the southern horizon in the processional cycle, which takes 25,920 years. Zep Tepi, or the "First Time," is what the ancient Egyptians called this earlier epoch. 10,450 B.C. is when the Sphinx was built, just after Atlantis and Mu submerged and immediately following the Flood. This First Time was a new era in many ways for ancient Egypt.

Another interesting piece of evidence relating to UFO contactees was

---

[63] Robert Bauval and Adrian Gilbert, *The Orion Mystery*. (London: William Heineman, 1994).

reported by Berlitz in *Without a Trace*. Venturo Maceiras was an Argentine farmer who described an episode during which he was enveloped by a ray, directed at him, by a hovering UFO. This had a rejuvenational effect on Maceiras, resulting in tissue healing, growing new teeth and a reversion to a much younger and healthier man.[64]

The *Book of the Dead* relates a battle between the god Horus and Seth (the god of darkness and death), which depicts an aerial dog fight of two UFOs over water. Seth murdered Osiris, who was Horus' father and Horus set out to avenge his father's death. Recall my earlier comments concerning Taatos and the origin of this story.

## UFO COVER-UPS

Before I present the results of past life regressions from some of my patients reflecting their experiences with ETs in ancient Egypt, a summary of UFO cover-ups is necessary. The main reason UFOs and ETs are such a controversial issue, with low credibility among many people, arises from the manner all governments have treated this issue. They are all guilty of cover-ups.

When the U.S. Air Force is contacted about a UFO their standard response is, "In view of the time which has elapsed since the sighting, it would be difficult to obtain additional data today." That line may have worked in days past when the American public was gullible enough to accept the "I'm from the government and I'm here to help you" mentality, but today things are quite different.

We see a double standard with the military. On the one hand they state with absolute certainty that these UFOs do not pose a threat to the security of the United States. They feign complete knowledge of this phenomenon, but in reality they know very little. How come witnesses report a scrambling of jet fighters in the air every time a massive UFO sighting is reported?

There are no regulations requiring military personnel to report UFOs to the public, and careers would be destroyed if certain information was released without going "through channels." They can attempt to explain flying saucers as swamp gas, cognitive dissonance, temporary lobe epilepsy, plasma discharges, refraction effects, weather balloons, etc. all they want. The metaphysical bottom line is that ETs and UFOs are real, and have been on this planet for millions of years.

It is rather difficult to get credible scientists to become involved with validating this phenomenon. Ridicule, from peers, especially in respected "scientific" publications, deters scientists from coming forward. One solution to

---

[64] Charles Berlitz, *Without a Trace*. (New York: Ballantine Books, 1985).

this problem has been the establishment of the "Invisible College," consisting of a network of scientists privately researching this issue.[65]

Many reports around the world from credible witnesses and other evidence have established that the government has made pacts with ETs. UFOs are spotted near military bases all over this planet. The disturbing hum reported in the southwestern part of the United States is most likely attributed to some massive underground project in Nevada and New Mexico.

For example, there are many reports of a CIA-alien underground installation in Dulce, New Mexico. This facility has been described as massive in size and contains huge vats filled with amber fluid in which animal and human body parts are suspended. A "Section B" in the Dulce center contains above ground ventilation shafts for the base on the top of Mount Archeleta. These ducts were described as rectangular and about thirty feet wide.[66]

Groom Lake, Nevada is the reported site of recovered alien crafts and comes under the auspices of NSA's Project Snowbird. The goal of this project is to test fly these UFOs. Other locations are the YY-II base at Los Alamos, New Mexico and an underground base in the western part of the Antelope Valley in southern California, known as the "Tehachapi Ranch." This latter installation is reportedly manufacturing a saucer-like craft.

Historically, General James H. Doolittle in 1946 investigated reports of "ghost rocket" UFOs in Sweden. Thousands of sightings of these crafts were reported. Praying mantis-like creatures were reported who must have been far more advanced than our race. Several of the people in the loop at that time committed suicide, the most prominent of which was Defense Secretary James V. Forrestal who jumped to his death from a 16 story hospital window. His medical records are sealed to this day.

In 1947 then President Truman established a group of twelve (note the multiple of that universal number three) top military and scientific personnel to keep this truth hidden from the public. MJ-12 was the name given to this elite group of those behind the UFO and ET cover-up. This group is still in existence, although none of the original team is alive.

Several more UFO crashes occurred in the late 1940s. Some of these locations were Roswell, New Mexico, Aztec, New Mexico and Laredo, Texas. The MJ-12 cut a deal with various ETs (now called EBE's or extra-terrestrial biological entities).

In exchange for advanced technology the EBEs would provide us, the

---

[65] Jacques Valee, *The Invisible College: What a Group of Scientists Has Discovered about UFO Influences on the Human Race.* (New York: Dutton, 1975).
[66] John Lear, *Flying Saucers: Government Cover Up.* VHS. Lightworks Audio & Video, 1996.

government would ignore the abductions and suppress information related to such activities as cattle mutilations. These EBEs specifically assured the MJ-12 that they would provide a list of those to be abducted (for one to two hours at a time), and that these abductions would be kept to a minimum and were done for the purpose of monitoring our civilization.

The problem with the Zetas is reproductive, so their genetic disorder required many more unannounced abductions than the MJ-12 was led to believe. This may have been the result of a nuclear war on Mars one million or so years ago, or on their home planet.

In any event, these ETs required an enzyme or hormone obtained from either human or cattle tissues to survive. Cows and humans are genetically quite similar. Cattle mutilations have been prevalent since at least the early 1970s. Extreme surgical skills were involved in removing cattle genitals, rectums, eyes, tongue and throat parts.

No blood was present on the animal carcasses, and in certain cases intercellular incisions were made, which is a technique our field scientists have not mastered as of yet. A human mutilation took place in 1956 when a Sgt. Jonathan P. Lovotte at the White Sands Missile Test Range was found devoid of his genitals, rectum, eyes and all blood. His abduction was witnessed by an Air Force Major, who reported a UFO while on a missile debris search.

There are reportedly several alien crafts and three EBEs being held in the YY-11 Los Alamos, New Mexico installation. These ETs are supposed to possess a recording device that has logged in all of our planet's history and can display it in the form of a hologram. Remember my earlier comments concerning the Sirian time energy points.

There were over 4,000 UFO sightings reported in October and November of 1987 alone. These included such regions as the Hudson Valley in New York, Wytheville, Virginia, Lake Superior and Gulf Breeze, Florida to name a few.

One may ponder as to why these reports don't make it to the evening news. No reporter or news organization is willing to risk their reputation on such an event. Regardless of the number of credible witnesses, these news people are in the same Egyptian boat as scientists.

Consider the instance of the Wytheville, Virginia sightings in which 900 foot objects ran witnesses off the road. Dozens of NASA vans arrived, but this failed to attract the attention of the newsmen. NASA spokespeople stated that they were there to do a "weather survey."[67]

---

[67] Richard Hall, *Uninvited guests: a documented history of UFO sightings, alien encounters & coverups.* (Santa Fe, N.M.: Aurora Press, 1988).

Not all EBEs are trying to regenerate their own species at our expenses. The ones that are have atrophied digestive and reproductive systems, along with other medical problems. The increase in the number of missing children and cattle mutilations have gotten the MJ-12 and NASA quite alarmed. Although these abductions are officially considered a "hoax," we citizens are just not that easily brainwashed by miscalculating and repressive military types who refuse to tell the public the whole truth.

It appears that many of these military industrial complex types are reincarnates of ancient Egyptian priests, still trying to preserve the Greater Mysteries. We must never forget that our spiritual evolution has been guided since the beginning by nonhuman intelligences whose agenda has been to infiltrate, and even instigate, religious traditions in all cultures. The similarities between many distinct culture's mythology have been the subject of speculation of "racial memory" by such notables as Carl Jung and Joseph Campbell.

We can look to the legends of various cultures ranging from Babylonia to Hindu to Native American that are with beings who possess superior technology, who are spiritual beings enjoying worship and reverence in exchange for distributing wisdom. These god-like beings appearing in dreams, trances and who are seen traveling in the sky may very well be the result of alien technology. This does not justify the American government, or any other nation, from truthfully informing its citizens of exactly what is going on up there and out there, in some cases underground.

One of the most interesting aspect of the U.S. government's cover-up policy relates to a Federal law known as Title 14, Section 1211 of the Code of Federal Regulations (14 CFR Part 1211) adopted on July 16, 1969. Contact between U.S. citizens and ETs or their vehicles was illegal! Punishment for this offense was a prison term for one year and a $5,000 fine.[68]

This ridiculous law gave NASA the power to quarantine under armed guard anyone suspected of ET exposure, without even a hearing! Whatever happened to the American Constitution? NASA's excuse for this law was to protect American citizens from alien viruses that could wipe out the human race.

We don't have to look for Men In Black to silence witnesses of UFOs and ETs, just refer to Congress' passage of this dangerous law with its habeas corpus interruptus provision. Interestingly enough, this law coincided with the Condon Report that closed Project Bluebook of the Air Force. According to that "report" there were no UFOs or ETs and investigating such claims was a waste of the

---

[68] The complete text of this law may be found in my book *Time Travelers from Our Future: A Fifth Dimension Odyssey*.

taxpayer's money.

Fortunately, there were no sections of the U.S. Federal ET Law that applied to past life exposure to ETs. If there were we would all be in jail. On April 26, 1991 Congress, in its infinite wisdom, repealed this section of 14 CFR Part 1211. For twenty-two years this fascist law was on the books.

## PAST LIFE REGRESSIONS

I began this chapter with an overview of the basic groups of ETs, focusing mostly on the Lyrans and the Sirians. Much of that data was obtained as a result of hypnotic past life regressions I conducted with several hundred patients.

This section will continue that premise. Before we can properly discuss ancient Egypt's ET innervation, we must trace the history of ETs in previous civilizations in prehistory.

Our search takes us back over five million years ago when the Lyrans first arrived on Earth. Apparently they were the first ETs to visit our planet. These Lyrans are the more aggressive aliens that eventually became the Atlantes of Mu, Atlantis and Lower Egypt.

Originally this group was around five to six feet tall, but grew to become giants reaching heights of nine feet. They attempted to genetically manipulate apes into man. Spiritual growth was not their aim. Their motive was to reign as our masters.

Fortunately for us their technology was still relatively primitive. Since they couldn't return to their home planet in one lifetime, they had to make do as best they could. These Lyrans were still quite skillful with their genetic engineering in guiding our evolution.

Our progress was also being monitored by the peaceful and spiritual Sirians. They came on the scene well after the Lyrans, but functioned as our protectors. At around 500,000 B.C. their genetic experiments were showing the fruits of their alien labors. Our brain capacity increased dramatically and we were well on our way to becoming truly humans.

Still this experiment required more and more adjustments and variations in procedures. The Lyrans, Sirians and other ETs began carving up our planet and fighting among themselves for the right to control certain regions of our planet.

Mu represented a true victory for the Sirians. They dominated this Pacific continent from about 200,000 B.C. to 100,000 B.C. Lyrans were also present, and eventually evolved into the Atlantes, while the Sirians were some of the Essenes we have previously discussed.

The Elders of Mu couldn't allow the Atlantes to settle Atlantis by themselves. Sirian ETs were constantly monitoring Atlantis' progress and their hybrid offspring took up residence as Essenes in both continents.

Temples of healing have been reported on both Mu and Atlantis by my patients. These places were more like ET clinics and laboratories in which DNA experiments were conducted and various laser beams were used to bring about both medical and psychological healing.

Energy balancing techniques involving chakras (Indian) and meridians (China) originated first in Mu and then Atlantis as an offshoot of these ET technologies. As time went on the Lyran influence dominated our planet, even Mu.

Many occultists make the correlation that both Mu and Atlantis were destroyed due to their respective degenerations morally, spiritually and ethnically. That is only partly true. The gas belts comets and pole shift were the chief factors that destroyed both continents geophysically.

This destruction and legendary Flood would not have occurred if there wasn't a conscious shift downward of prehistory man. The ETs, like it or not, were greatly responsible for our decay in spirituality.

I suspect that our spiritual growth would have been greatly accelerated if the Sirians were the only ETs on this planet to the extent that we would all have perfected our souls and ascended by now. This attainment of a state of Grace was undoubtedly the Sirian goal, but not that of the selfish and militant Lyrans.

My purpose is not to blame these ETs for our current state of affairs, merely present the mechanism for its solution. We chose karmically this mess. It was our consciousness, even if it was trapped in the mindless body of Austropithecus, that chose to invite these ETs to our planet and play out this drama.

Atlantis was a complete spiritual failure as an ET experiment. As with Mu, it started out fine. This happened only because the Sirians managed to sway the masses to spiritual pursuits.

Unfortunately, the Atlanteans allowed themselves to be corrupted by the Lyrans, a pattern also noted in Egypt, Greece, China, Rome and throughout civilization today. The prejudice, materialism, arrogance and other negative Lyran traits so common to industrialized nations witnesses this point only too well.

The ETs directed their efforts mostly in Egypt following the submerging of Atlantis and Mu. India, China, Mexico and South American were also seeded with civilization, but Egypt was considered the pet colony of the ETs.

It was the white robed, tall, blond, blue-eyed leaders of Mu, Atlantis and Egypt that the ETs feared. These spiritually evolved humans functioned to protect mankind even more so than the Sirians. The main efforts toward establishing a civilization in Egypt took place from about 16,000 B.C., which was 5,000 years before the final destruction of Atlantis and Mu. Some activity began several thousands years before this, but the main efforts were manifested about 18,000 years ago. Egypt was originally colonized by Mu (Upper Egypt) first and later by Atlantis (Lower Egypt) under the specific guidance of the Sirians and Lyrans respectively.

Although Taatos designed and began the construction of the Sphinx, the Lyrans were responsible for most of its construction. This design was a concession by Taatos to the cat symbol that signified the Lyran race, in addition to the body of a lion representing the Leo constellation. The Sirians assisted the Lyrans in designing the three pyramids at Giza for the reasons I have previously discussed. There were many examples of sophisticated technology in the Egypt of prehistory that was lost due to the Flood of 11,000 B.C.

We must recall that while the rest of the world was recovering from the last Ice Age at about 11,000 B.C. and living the life of the cave dwellers, Egypt was technologically advanced as a result of these ETs.

The ETs were advocates of God and reincarnation. They deduced from their experience with Mu and Atlantis that humankind needed to be led and could not be trusted. The purest religion ever created on the Earth was that of Mu in the earliest years of its civilization. This paradigm was never to be seen again.

Many ET wars occurred between 16,000 B.C. to 11,000 B.C. Competition among these beings resulted in numerous turf battles characterized by aerial dogfights, along with ground attacks. One can visualize how the primitive local inhabitants must have responded to these assaults. Running for cover and praying to their gods for salvation undoubtedly became a full-time job.

The Flood following the submerging of Mu and Atlantis changed everything. The number of ETs visiting our planet dropped off considerably. That left Egypt in the guiding hands of the high priests, whose goal was to control the masses.

The Lesser Mysteries were taught to anyone who passed the initiation and they consisted of basic laws of karma and metaphysics. Gods were used to control the masses. Esoteric meanings of exactly what these Gods were and other matters of the Greater Mysteries were withheld from the public at all costs.

In order to increase their control over the recently unified Upper and Lower Egypt at about 3000 B.C., the Egyptian high priests created the concept of Hell and Devil to inject fear into the masses. These depictions were the result of out-of-body experiences. Trips to the upper astral planet were depicted as heaven, while those to the lower astral plane represented Hell. The being in charge of the lower astral plane would now be called the Devil.[69]

These techniques have been documented throughout prehistory. Shamans dating back 15,000 to 20,000 years used astral projection methods, as depicted on cave paintings in Las Caux, France.[70]

My purpose is not to portray these ETs as mean and evil entities. If they wanted to enslave the human race they most certainly could have done that hundreds of thousands of years ago. What they did do was manipulate us with false paradigms to control our evolution.

With all of the destroyed civilizations resulting from ET "guidance," I must conclude that we are far better off without their help. Our own Higher Self can be accessed and this simple technique properly applied leads to unlimited spiritual growth. Chapter 7 presents self-hypnosis exercises to illustrate this method.

Throughout the transition period beginning around 9000 B.C. to 5500 B.C., the ET influence began to lessen. Their numbers were few and their attention span even lower. My research has revealed that ETs found more desirable planets to visit and those that were left here were assimilated into the Egyptian communities.

That is not to say that other UFOs didn't arrive, merely that the massive manipulation and interference so characteristic of Mu and Atlantis weren't duplicated on that same scale. This was a form of Dark Ages for Egypt.

At about 5500 B.C. Egypt became more interesting to the ETs. This Renaissance in interest brought new ET blood into Egypt. The hunting-gathering mentality of the primitive locals was now carefully molded into a true civilization.

The ETs introduced life after death beliefs like never before to those primitives. An artistic and scientific community was now established that would result in tremendous advances in medicine, with many specialties created.

City planning began to become manifest around 4500 B.C., as the ETs decided to make Egypt their prized possession again. The Cult of Osiris became the chief religion and now there was no turning back.

We must now consider the three pyramids at Giza. They were designed and begun back around 10,450 B.C. when the Sphinx was constructed. Following the unification of Egypt these pyramids were completed at about 2500 B.C.

Both the Sirians and Lyrans had specific timetables, as I have previously discussed. The Giza pyramids represented a permanent truce between these two groups and a monument to their home planet. It was an expression of who they were and where they came from. As a result of interbreeding with our race, many ETs had more human blood than their other worldly DNA.

---

[69] B. Goldberg, *Time Travelers from Our Future: A Fifth Dimension Odyssey*, op. cit., pp 165-166.
[70] B. Goldberg, *Astral Voyages: Mastering the Art of Interdimensional Soul Travel*. (St. Paul: Llewellyn, 1999).

The Osirian religion was incorporated in their megalith construction, as I have detailed earlier in this chapter. These pyramids were completed rather quickly, comparatively. Details of their construction bring out another mystery.

You will often read about the use of anti-gravity devices in the construction of the pyramids. In order to complete their construction in a short time some form of anti-gravity device had to have been used.

My research has shown that no anti-gravity devices were used by the ETs in reference to any megalith construction in Egypt. All of the past life regressions I have conducted revealed some form of tractor and crane-like apparatus involved in the pyramid construction.

My first book *Past Lives-Future Lives* specifically details such a case. Injuries did occur during the pyramid building and these were often treated by the use of the lasers and energy beams I discussed previously.

To make matters even more complicated, other ET groups directed certain phases of the pyramid construction. I still don't know why the Sirian and Lyran attention span was so short, considering they had a specific astronomical timetable to deal with, but it was.

At no time did the ETs use anti-gravity devices on the pyramids at Giza, yet these scientific marvels were used to build these pyramids. Herein lies the mystery. If the ETs did not use anti-gravity devices, who did? The answer to this enigma will be dealt with in the next chapter.

Following the completion of the pyramids at Giza, the ET influence began to wane again. Now Egypt was civilized, scientific, artistic and dominant in the ancient world. It wasn't that she no longer needed or wanted the ETs, it was simply a matter of abandonment by them.

Many ETs returned to their home planet within 200 years following the completion of the Giza pyramids. Those that remained on Earth focused their attention on the other civilizations throughout the world.

With so many other developing cultures (Babylonia, India, China, etc.) and so little manpower, the ETs had to reorient their priorities. They decided to pretty much leave Egypt to its own devices and concentrate on other nations.

We must always remember that the ET influence was never entirely abandoned. There were always representatives in ancient Egypt whose origins were from another planet. These were the priests and pharaohs, for the most part.

## AN ET WAR IN ANCIENT EGYPT

I have previously discussed the many problems between the various ET groups when they came to our planet. There have been many wars between ET groups resulting from their attempts to carve up our planet.

Bernie's past life in ancient Egypt at about 9500 B.C. relates such a scenario. This male patient lived in Sais in Lower Egypt and worked as a carpenter. He described several instances during which his work was interrupted by loud noises and flashes of light.

What was taking place was an ET war between the Lyrans and a reptilian race. Laser beam devices were used on flying saucer ships to destroy buildings and kill hundreds of people.

Bernie described the completed Sphinx and the Great Pyramid at Giza being about one third constructed at this time. This corroborated reports I received from many other patients.

Certain ETs attempted to bring about peace, notably the Pleidians, but they failed. Suddenly, another series of highly advanced ships entered the scene and the ETs were outnumbered.

In addition, these new ships had more technologically advanced weapons. The representatives from these advanced ships finally were able to negotiate a peace treaty. The ETs appeared to be frightened by these white-robed, blond, blue-eyed Caucasian humans who piloted these advanced ships.

We will explore in detail in chapter 5 just who these white-robed people were and why they so intimidated the ETs. Following this incident Bernie observed what we would term Men in Black entering the city and debriefing the local inhabitants.

## A SUMMARY OF THE ET PHENOMENON

ETs and UFOs have been with us throughout our history and had a great effect on Egypt's civilization. They are quite real and unexplainable in terms of contemporary science. We may view these aliens as a guiding intelligence shaping the development of human consciousness throughout the history of this planet.

Some of this guidance has been destructive (the Lyrans), while others (the Sirians) have accelerated our spiritual awareness and growth. Their technology is based on and generates quite a bit of radiation. We still don't know the ultimate effects of this radiation on our nervous system.

The universe is large enough to sustain other forms of life than us. They are undoubtedly much more advanced technologically, and in some cases spiritually. Several options present themselves in reference to ETs and UFOs. These can be listed as follows:

- ETs have attempted direct communication with us, but we have failed either to detect or notice it.

- Our civilization is the most advanced in the universe, so it is up to us to go and find them.
- ETs simply refuse to interface in our affairs.
- We are under ET introspection, but it is being carried out in such a manner as to escape our attention.
- We are alone in the universe.
- ETs have seeded life on Earth in the distant past and we are the result of their genetic experiments.
- Our governments know exactly what is going on with ETs, but prefer to lie and cover-up the truth.

I wholeheartedly feel the last two options represent the past and current ET scenario. Our species is not the result of random evolution. It has been controlled by beings of far greater intelligence that have their own agenda.

We can look the word Elohim in Genesis to a partial answer to the true origin of Egypt's civilization. Elohim in Hebrew translates as "God" in the singular, but in its plural form it means "those who came from the sky."

Museum storerooms and warehouses contain vast stores of boxes, drawers and crates whose contents have been buried for decades. Much physical evidence have been discarded by curators and bureaucrats as "fakes" or "hoaxes" simply because they didn't fit into contemporary paradigms. I have presented several examples of this forbidden archaeology already. Does this remind you of the ending of the feature film *Raiders Of The Lost Ark?*

We all carry the memories within our very cells and time energy points of all of the ancient civilizations (Mu, Atlantis, etc.) and our ET heritage. If you look within yourself and access your Higher Self you will always find your ultimate truth. My superconscious mind tap technique to do just that will be presented in chapter 7.

But are these ETs the ultimate answer to the architects of ancient Egypt? What about those occasional reports of gods wearing white robes, tall, with blond hair and blue eyes? What about Hermes? For the true designer of Egypt's past we must take a dimensional leap forward into the future and discuss time travelers.

# CHAPTER 5  TIME TRAVELERS – THE MAIN SOURCE OF EGYPT'S DEVELOPMENT

Up until now I have been unfolding the true history of Egypt's civilization little by little. We can look to Atlantis as predecessors to this great civilization. But Mu came before Atlantis in establishing an advanced culture in the land of the Nile. The ETs were responsible for speeding up our evolution and creating the Garden of Eden in Mu.

Is this the complete picture? Thankfully it isn't. I do not want to play the blame game, but the ETs used Egypt and our entire planet as an experiment. They blew it. Egypt was a technological success for a time, but a spiritual failure.

The Mystery Schools were an insult to spirituality. The secrecy, selfishness and control they represented just doesn't measure up to my definition of spirituality. Killing people who openly discuss the Greater Mysteries is not going to get you to Heaven. Most of the patients I have regressed to ancient Egyptian priests had other lives in the Catholic Church hierarchy, the Inquisition, and other examples of less than open minded theologians. Some reincarnated in ancient Greece, Rome, the Dark Ages and so on. The point is that they reincarnated. If they were so spiritual and following the Greater Mysteries cookbook to Heaven, then why didn't they ascend?

The answer is simple. These souls just didn't earn the right to enter Nirvana. ETs have caused more problems than they are worth. Yet, some of them have greatly assisted us. This only took place after they, or their colleagues, brought havoc into our primitive lives.

So what is the answer? Who is really responsible for Egypt's civilization? What group acted as overseers, corrected the mistakes of ETs and truly desired our species to purify our souls? Remember those white robed, tall, blonde, blue-eyed mysterious beings, such as Taatos? These were and are time travelers, and herein lies the answer to Egypt's enigma.

Egypt as an experiment failed on many levels, the most important being spiritual growth. These time travelers originate from 1,000 to 3,000 years in our future and are responsible for who we are today, including Egypt's development. This chapter will discuss these *chrononauts*, or time travelers, in detail.

Space does not permit more than a brief summary of these time travelers and the precise mechanism of how they are able to travel back in time to our century, as well as millions of years into prehistory. A thorough presentation of this concept is given in my book *Time Travelers From Our Future: A Fifth Dimension*

*Odyssey.*[71]

Most of the information I have been able to obtain concerning these time travelers is a direct result of past life regression during which these chrononauts abducted my patients. In some cases these time travelers abducted the very same person in several of their past lives.

When on board a space craft, or in a military installation (these time travelers have also made pacts with the various governments), abductees are eventually brought into a conference room and showed holograms of their past and future, including other lifetimes. These time travelers also depict various eras in history via holograms, and this is how I have been able to piece together the true origin of Egypt, Mu and Atlantis.

First let us discuss the makeup of these time travelers. There are four main groups of these chrononauts. The first group consists of pure humans. These represent about twenty-five percent of these voyagers. Human chrononauts are between six and seven feet tall, blond, blue-eyed, clean shaven and always appear dressed in white robes.

Zeta ETs comprise the second group. These time travelers have large black eyes, stand about three to five feet tall, have no ear lobes, four fingers and toes and usually grayish skin. Some of this group have white or blue skin.

Hybrid ETs represent the third group. These time travelers are the result of interbreeding between the Zetas and other ETs and our race. Their height ranges from five to six feet, and from a distance they appear completely human.

A mixture of various other ETs comprise the fourth class of chrononauts. These may be Sirians, Lyrans, Pleidians or any other of the myriad of ETs that have been referenced in UFO reports.

Each group of time travelers wear either jumpsuits or robes, with the pure humans favoring the latter. A team may consist of all humans or a combination of the four groups I described. A pure human is always in charge of a time traveler team.

What is interesting about our future is the fact that while today we view ETs as superior to our race intellectually and technologically, in the future our human race is the more advanced one.

Abductions are conducted by time travelers and genetic experiments are most definitely carried out, but the main purpose of these chrononauts is to assist our spiritual growth. They are us in the future and their ability to ascend is tied in somehow to our level of spirituality. It is to their advantage to see to our spiritual maturation.

---

[71] B. Goldberg, *Time Travelers From Our Future: A Fifth Dimension Odyssey*, op. cit.

The time traveler ETs and hybrids I described are not really ETs, since they live on Earth in our future. Their genetic base is extraterrestrial, but so is ours. By the 31st century they are no more ETs than we are.

Additional characteristics of these time travelers are:

- They can travel through hyperspace and move interdimensionally (we will discuss this shortly), as well as move through solid objects.
- These beings can remain *invisible* by functioning at a frequency vibrational rate far beyond our level.
- They use holograms to show us our past and future.
- Whenever they choose a chrononaut can induce a state of suspended animation on us and telepathically communicate with our subconscious.
- Time travelers can enter our dreams and function as spirit guides and angelic beings helping us in time of need.
- Chrononauts have mastered advanced medical techniques called *quantum medicine*, in which they can replace lost limbs and literally resuscitate the dead.
- The time travelers from 1,000 to 2,000 years in our future make many mistakes and come to our century in spaceships. Those from 2,000 to 3,000 years ahead in time are far superior in their manipulation of time and space and can beam themselves anywhere instantly. They do not require any type of craft.

As I stated earlier, the main purpose of these time travelers is to speed up our spiritual evolution. This is accomplished through a rather complex mechanism of altering our soul's energy by a form of frequency modulation that I explain in detail in *Time Travelers From Our Future*.

## HYPERSPACE

We are most familiar with the three dimensions of length, width and depth. Time is the fourth dimension and anything beyond the four-dimensional universe, in which time is the fourth-dimension of the space-time continuum, is known as hyperspace.

Most of you by now have heard of the concept of parallel universe. These alternate worlds exist side by side with ours, only we are not aware of them. Parallel universes are connected to each other by a blackhole-wormhole-whitehole mechanism and represent hyperspace.

Any space that contains all of the parallel universes that exist is known as hyperspace. Hyperspace is composed of an infinite number of hyper-universes from their future into our century, or at anytime in the past.

As strange as this theory sounds, it is backed up by solid mathematical models and supported by such eminent scientists as Caltech Astrophysicist Kip Thorne, Cambridge University Professor Stephen Hawking, Princeton University's Edward Witten and many others around the world.

These scientists have established that traveling back in time will not violate causality principles (going back in time and killing your ancestor so that you cannot exist today) and that physical time machines per se are not required if a time traveler moves through hyper-universes.

In the example of someone traveling back in time and killing their ancestor, this individual would cease to exist in only that parallel universe. He or she would be alive on all the others. It is physically impossible to eliminate every ancestor on each of the parallel universes to make a violation of causality possible.

We only experience the parallel universe that is in harmony with our present consciousness. Any lack of harmony among these universe layers results in us not experiencing that particular reality. The term *time loop* is applied to journeying from the future to our present and back to the future. One nice conclusion from this concept is that there is no death per se, merely a change of awareness from one dimension to another.

Blackholes represent a type of time machine. When we enter a blackhole in our future, we move through a wormhole and exit a whitehole in the past. In the future technology is capable of enlarging a blackhole (which is usually microscopic to us here on Earth) and allowing a chrononaut to enter into it with or without the need of a spaceship!

One advantage of the hyperspace theory is that it unifies all known physical phenomena in a simple paradigm. This is what Einstein tried unsuccessfully to accomplish during the last thirty years of his life.

Miguel Alcubierre's classic paper discusses the concept of hyper fast space travel. He develops the principle of Alcubierre Warp Drive (AWD) as a consequence of Einstein's General Theory of Relativity. In it Alcubierre states that spacetime can be twisted, deformed, and possibly even engineered by concentrations (random or selective) of mass/energy.

Spacetime is changed in such a manner by AWD that the region directly in front of the ship contracts, while the region directly behind the ship expands. The net effect of this is that the ship is propelled on a weightless path through spacetime. Alcubierre states: *The previous example shows how one can use an expansion of spacetime to move away from some object at an arbitrarily large speed. In the same way, one can use a contraction of spacetime to approach an object at any speed. This is the basis of the model of hyper fast space travel that I wish to present here: create a local distortion of spacetime that will produce an expansion behind the spaceship, and an opposite contraction ahead of it. In this way, the spaceship will be pushed away from the earth and pulled towards a distant star by spacetime itself. One can then invert the process to come back to earth, taking an arbitrarily small time to complete the trip.[72]*

As with Thorne's time travel model, Alcubierre's mechanism requires "exotic matter," not available today. Exotic matter has negative energy propagating forward in time. This is exactly the opposite of what ordinary antimatter does. Scientists predict that future technology will be able to manufacture such matter and make time travel possible. NASA is working on exotic matter research today at the University of Alabama in Huntsville.

This AWD would go a long way in making interstellar travel to other planets possible, as well as time travel, by eliminating the time dilation problem. For example, you could leave on a Monday morning and travel on a 1000 light year journey and return the following Monday to find everyone else including yourself) has aged no more than one week.

Alcubierre's work is one of the first theoretical realizations of "metric engineering," an idea first advanced by Russian Nobel Laureate, Andre Sakharov and American Nobel Laureate, T. D. Lee, and further developed by physicist Hal Puthoff and others.

Puthoff is a graduate of Stanford University and the author of over thirty scientific articles in the areas of electron-beam devices, lasers and quantum zero-point energy fields, and is co-author of a textbook, *Fundamentals of Quantum Electronics*. As a theoretical and experimental physicist specializing in fundamental electrodynamics, and Director of the Institute for Advanced Studies at Austin, his research ranges from the study of quantum vacuum states as they apply to the stability of matter, gravitation, cosmology and energy research, to laboratory studies of innovative approaches to energy generation.

Puthoff states in one of his papers:

*Alcubierre's result is a particular case of a broad, general approach that might loosely be called "metric engineering," the details of which provide further support for the concept that reduced time interstellar travel, either by advanced extraterrestrial civilizations at present, or ourselves in the future, is not, as naïve consideration might hold, fundamentally constrained by physical principles.[73]*

John Archibald Wheeler's "delayed choice experiment", now confirmed in

---

[72] M. Alcubierre, "The Warp Drive: Hyper fast travel within General Relativity." *Classic and Quantum Gravity, 11* (1994): 73.
[73] H. Puthoff, "SETI, the Velocity-of-Light Limitation, and the Alcubierre Warp Drive: An Integrating Overview." *Physics Essays, 9* (1), 1996.

the laboratory, shows that, if we use the traditional Bohr Copenhagen interpretation of quantum theory, then whether a photon acts as a wave or a particle in the past depends on the future freewill choice of a conscious observer. This conscious choice acts backward in time. If there is free will, then it has to act backward in time for about one second. In other words, our conscious intention seems to depend on Wheeler's quantum delayed choice effect. The consciousness paradigm implies that through hypnosis and other alpha brain wave states, avenues exist that would allow the shaping of the spacetime metric using controlled quantum action at a distance.

The only disadvantage from time traveling through hyper-universes is that the fabric of spacetime is stretched until a tear is created. This tear produces a wormhole that allows the chrononaut to travel back in time. Unusual and negative phenomena have been created by these tears in spacetime. This may very well be one of the reasons why the Earth's poles shift every so often. Remember, these pole shifts represent one explanation for the submerging of Mu and Atlantis.

As far as these time travelers are concerned, I have no data of any such chrononauts beyond the year 5000 A.D. Either they have completely abandoned the Earth or have ascended. Being an external optimist I prefer the latter possibility.

## TIME TRAVEL — A "GROOVY" THEORY

Since we know that the space-time continuum in which we live is made up of many dimensions, let me describe a paradigm of how events in our time may be altered. The three-dimensional universe of length, width and depth that our physical plane eyes can see are common to us all.

When we factor in time as the fourth dimension of the space-time continuum, scientists label this as a *worm line*. This worm line is a space-time line that stretches form the Big Bang (the creation of our universe) to the time the universe ceases exist.

A time traveler residing in the fifth dimension of hyperspace can manipulate the fourth dimension (time) and subsequently our easily observed three-dimensional universe in a manner similar to how a record player operates. Our three dimensions are guided by time very much like the way in which a record player's needle is guided by the groves on the record's surface.

Our time traveler can easily see your worm line just as you can see a two-dimensional character in a cartoon strip. If a three-dimensional object were to fall into this two-dimensional cartoon strip, the cartoon character would only see shapes appearing and disappearing. We, on the other hand, can view the entire scene simply by existing in our three-dimensional world.

The universe is made up of an infinite number of worm lines. The very instant a time traveler exceeds the speed of light, as in entering a blackhole, a gap in the worm line is created. In the very same way we can poke a two-dimensional carton character without it knowing the source of this poke, a time traveler can manipulate our worm line without our being aware of the process. Every dimension is connected to ours in the same way and a time traveler can easily alter events in our past, present or future.

## TIME TRAVELERS IN EGYPT

Before we trace these time travelers to their role in Egypt's development, let us consider the part they played in history. These chrononauts have traveled back in time to correct the mistakes made by ETs. They were around during the genetic experiments several million years ago (and those that are still going on), and made their presence known in Mu and Atlantis.

Some of the original Muvian Elders were time travelers. Most of the time these chrononauts came on the scene to monitor our development and keep the ETs in line. The ETs were always fearful of the time travelers, since the advanced technology of these chrononauts were far superior to that of the ETs.

You will recall that I stated in the last chapter that the ETs observed these white robed, tall, blond, blue-eyed humans and often did not like their presence. This was especially true of the power-hungry Lyrans.

## THE DOGON OF AFRICA

One of the patterns of behavior I have noted from my communications with time travelers is their specific desire to both inform us of our universe and plant seeds for us to unravel these chrononauts origin and involvement in these time travel expeditions. Of the best examples is the Dogon of Africa.

Chrononauts have frequent contact with ETs from various time periods, and indeed many team members are from ET origins genetically. The Dogon tribe of Mali in Northwestern Africa possesses an uncanny body of knowledge in the field of astrology. The time travelers have informed me that they have educated the Dogon as to a star system known as Sirius.

The Dogon word for star is *tolo* while *po* is the name given for one of their grains. Their religion centers around the star Sirius and its invisible companion they refer to as *po tolo*. This knowledge of the star Sirius is not unusual, as it is rather bright and easy to see. What is unexplainable is their identification of its companion, which is undetectable by the naked eye. Astronomers refer to the visible star as Sirius A and its invisible companion as Sirius B.

In addition to po tolo (Sirius B), the Dogon also identify a second invisible companion star they call *emme ya*. This latter star (not yet confirmed by astronomers) is supposed to be larger than po Tolo, yet weighs about one fourth as much as po tolo. The Dogon assert that each of these invisible companion stars revolves around Sirius A once every fifty years. The material that constitutes po tolo, called *sagaha* by the Dogon, is not found on Earth!

The Dogon priests are also aware of the rings surrounding Saturn, which they describe as a "permanent halo."[74] They know Jupiter has four moons (each of which can only be seen with the aid of a telescope); the planets revolve around our Sun in *elliptical* orbits; the Earth revolves on its own axis; they describe the Milky Way as "spiraling words that fill the universe—infinite and yet measurable[75]; and that our planet is part of a larger galaxy. The main point here is that it is impossible for such a primitive tribe as the Dogon to be aware of these facts.

*Amma* is the name the Dogon give to their chief god and creator of the universe. The Dogon most definitely believe life exists on other planets. In the 1950s the French anthropologists Marcel Griaule and Germaine Dieterhen first studied the Dogon. These investigators reported the following summary of the Dogon's belief in life on other planets:

*The worlds of spiraling stars were populated universes, for as he created things, Amma gave the world its shape and its movement and created living creatures. There are creatures living on other "Earths" as well as our own; this proliferation of life is illustrated by an explanation of the myth in which it is said: man is on the 4th earth, but on the 3rd there are "men with horns", inneu gammurugu, on the 5th, "men with tails" inneu dullogo, on the 6th, "men with wings" inneu bummo, etc. This emphasizes the ignorance of what life is on the other worlds but also the certainty that it exists.[76]*

Might these "men with horns," "men with tails" and "men with wings" refer to reptilian ETs? The first two could be time travelers, as futuristic reptilians never exhibit wings.

## THE FIRST TIME TRAVELER

We have discussed Taatos several times already. His origin is from the thirty-first century and he has the honor of being the very first time traveler or

---

[74] Robert Temple, *The Sirius Mystery*. (Rochester, VT: Destiny Books, 1987) p. 28.
[75] Ibid., p. 30.
[76] Ibid., p. 30.

chrononaut. Taatos is his true futuristic name and he discovered the specific mechanism for time travel.

It is an understatement to depict Taatos as the world's greatest mind. His skills extended to science, art, writing, archaeology and many other disciplines. Following his discovery of time travel, Taatos eventually headed the first time traveler team comprised of Geb, Isis, Osiris and Horus. Sound familiar? These names were retained when this team worked in Mu, Atlantis and ancient Egypt.

We have previously discussed the Osirian legend spread by Taatos in ancient Egypt. The events were supposed to have occurred in Atlantis, but in reality they took place in Mu.

Seth was a power-hungry Atlantes representatives in Mu who became envious of the popularity of Osiris and Isis. The latter couple functioned as religious teachers instructing the Muvians in spirituality.

Neither Osiris nor Isis had political ambitions. They were, after all, time travelers on a mission. Seth was paranoid and stabbed Osiris one evening following a spiritual training session conducted by Osiris and Isis. Osiris would have perished if not for the medical skill of Taatos, with Isis serving as his nurse.

Osiris' life was saved and he returned to the thirty-first century to recuperate. Atlantis would be his next assignment. Taatos, Geb, Isis and Horus remained in Mu, later joining Osiris in Atlantis. Now we have a solution as to how Taatos and his team could live in Mu 200,000 years ago and be in Atlantis in 20,000 B.C. and finally in Egypt from 16,000 B.C. and finally Egypt from 16,000 B.C. to at least 300 B.C. without being 200,000 years old.

Horus was much younger than either Isis or Osiris, so he was portrayed as their son in the legend formulated by Hermes and taught as Sais in Lower Egypt from 16,000 B.C. on. This legend was taught as the Osirian Cult to the primitive Egyptians. The Osirian legend depicts the young Horus as having avenged his father's death by exiling Seth into the desert. In reality, Osiris did not die at that time and Seth was murdered by an angry mob following his attack on Osiris in Mu. It is interesting to note here that statutes of Osiris from ancient Egypt depict him as having fair skin and blue eyes.

The *Troano Manuscript* is one of the four known books on ancient Mayan history that survived the book burning at the hands of the fanatical Catholic monk Bishop Landa, who accompanied the Spanish soldiers when they colonized Mexico. This manuscript, along with the sculptures and mural paintings at Chichen-Itza and Uxmal in Mexico, describe a tale quite similar to the Osirian legend.

In the "Lands of the West" (Mu) the king Can (represented by a Serpent) founded a dynasty and had three sons, Cay (fish), Aac (Turtle) and Coh (Leopard).

The serpent was the symbol used by the Sirians. Can's two daughters were Moo (Macaw) and Nicté (Flower). The youngest son by law had to marry the oldest daughter. Egypt retained his principle of princes marrying their sisters.

Prince Coh was a brave soldier and was to wed his eldest sister Moo. She loved Coh, but her brother Aac was also in love with her. Aac spent his life in luxury and accomplished nothing. He was jealous of Coh's fame and engagement to Moo.

Aac murders Coh by stabbing Coh three times in the back. Three was a very significant number in Mu, as we have discussed. Now a civil war breaks out. Aac proposes to Moo, but she rejects him. Finally, after her soldiers are defeated Aac imprisons her and his other brother Cay.

Later Aac has Moo and his brother Cay (who sided with Moo) put to death. We find this same theme in many other cultures. In Atlantis Hermes substituted Osiris for Coh, Isis for Moo and Seth for Aac. Isis had a sister (Nephthys), according to the *Pyramid Texts*. Nephthys represents Moo's sister Nicte. Other legends told of Queen Moo coming to Egypt and studying with Hermes at Sais. It is at Giza that Moo builds the Sphinx in dedication to her slain brother/lover Coh. The lion's body of the Sphinx is supposed to represent Coh's leopard symbol.[77]

We find leopard skins nearly always near the depictions of Osiris in Egypt. These skins were a component of the ceremonial dress of Osirian priests. A crouching leopard with the eye of Horus over it symbolized Osiris and was used in the Mystery Schools rituals.

The ancient Egyptians referred to Kneph as the creative power and represented it as a serpent or dragon. The serpent was the founder of Mu's dynasty by Can. Here we have an identical symbol for two creators, illustrating Egypt's and the Mayan's tie to Mu.

Taatos used this story in Atlantis to spread the Osirian religion and continued this story in Egypt. We can see this theme reflected in *Genesis*, in which Cain (Aac) murders his brother Abel (Coh). Osiris would be Adam and Isis Eve in this depiction.

In my book, *Time Travelers from Our Future: A Fifth Dimension Odyssey* I depicted the ancient Egyptian version of the Osirian legend spread by Taatos. Here is this legend:

The ancient Egyptian mysteries honored Osiris by the following story of his murder and resurrection. Osiris became a culture hero of Egypt. After he became king and instructed his subjects in the arts of civilization, he went to other lands to do the same.

---

[77] Jack Rau, op. cit.

Osiris left his wife and sister Isis in charge of the affairs of the kingdom which she administered aided by the counsels of her friend and preceptor Thoth. Isis, being extremely vigilant, Seth, her older brother, had no innovations in the government. Still he desired to sit on the throne. After the return of Osiris, he conspired against him and persuaded seventy-two other persons to join with him in the conspiracy, together with a certain queen of Ethiopia named Aso, who happened to be in Egypt at that time.

Seth invited his unsuspecting brother to a banquet, and caused a beautiful chest to be brought into the banqueting-room. It was much admired by all. He then, as if in jest, offered to give it to the person it fitted best. All tried getting into it one after another, but it did not fit any as well as Osiris when he in turn laid himself down in it. Then Seth, aided by the conspirators, closed the lid and fastened it on the outside with nails.

Following this act of murder by Seth, he dismembers Osiris' body and cuts off the latter's penis. Isis reassembles Osiris' body and sits on his reattached penis becoming pregnant with Horus, who later avenges his father's death by castrating Seth and exiling him into the desert. This makes Horus' birth a divine one, not unlike that of Jesus.[78]

Taatos has the same place with the chrononauts that Osiris had with the ancient Egyptians. Nobody refers to him as the "old man," although he lived to be at least 1000 years old. He is more like a professor emeritus. In the beginning he was a pioneer, the only time traveler in existence from our planet for at least several years.

As I stated earlier, Taatos was a man of many talents. He can be likened to a DaVinci, Edison, Einstein and Teddy Roosevelt all rolled into one. Although a modest man who liked to remain in the background, he led the ancient Egyptians as king several times when they needed him the most. This was during what I refer to as Egypt's Dark Ages from about 9000 B.C. to 5500 B.C.

Scholars today more often than not consider Taatos a mere legend. There were several Hermes in history, but only one time traveler. Let us first follow his role in the construction of the Step Pyramid at Saqqara.

I previously mentioned that Taatos and his team were not very involved with the building of pyramids. The Step Pyramid was one exception. Taatos saw this as an attempt to improve upon Egypt's technological growth and hopefully their spiritual one as well.

Taatos functioned now as Imhotep, the Grand Vizier and High Priest to pharaoh Zoser. Imhotep (Taatos) was a renowned architect who designed and built

---

[78] B. Goldberg, *Time Travelers from Our Future: A Fifth Dimension Odyssey*, op. cit., pp. 182-183.

the funeral complex and Step Pyramid at Saqqara. He was also a talented physician and later the Greeks called him Aesclepius the god of Medicine. In addition this historical figure was an astronomer, writer and sage. Sound familiar?

The Step Pyramid was six stories high and laid the framework for many other pyramids. Remember, Taatos designed the Giza pyramids in 10,450 B.C. Unfortunately, this failed to keep the excellence achieved at Saqqara going. A subsequent pyramid at Meidum appears today as a huge square tower on top of a hill. It is unfinished because it collapsed prior to its completion, with undoubtedly a great loss of life.

It is assumed that poor workmanship was responsible for one of the casting stones being squeezed out of place. A collapse followed. Never again would Egypt experience the excellence following the construction of the Giza pyramids. Taatos was not involved with the pyramid at Meidum, that was an ET fiasco. The artistic beauty depicted by the Pyramid Texts would also never appear again. Another failed experiment.

An attempt was made by Taatos to change the polytheistic religion of ancient Egypt to one of monotheism, a belief in one god. He failed to convince the Egyptian priests to mend their ways. He couldn't talk them out of the Mystery School mentality, nor could he influence them to forego their creation of the Devil and Hell in 3000 B.C. (See chapter 2). Taatos didn't always fail, but these were some of his frustrations.

We must always remember that the single purpose of the time travelers is to promote our spiritual growth so that we may eventually ascend. Their assistance in this goal, along with a carryover effect throughout the next 1,000 to 3,000 years, allows them to ascend. Whenever a time traveler reaches his level of perfection, they most often choose to ascend.

Such was the case with Osiris and Geb at about 6000 B.C. Horus, Isis and Hermes remained and were joined by many other time travelers. Isis became Taatos' wife (consort) Ma'at. Her name meant "truth" and "justice." Some authorities equate her with the Chinese Tao.

Horus ascended before the First Dynasty. Isis stayed around until about 400 A.D. and she also ascended. The Hermetic literature refers to three grades in the Egyptian mysteries. These were:

- Mortals. Those who were instructed but who had not yet gained inner vision.
- Intelligences. Those whose vision enabled them to tune into other life forms within the universe.
- Beings of light. Those who had become one with the light.

Taatos later appeared as the third century B.C. Egyptian High Priest and historian Manetho. During his time he lived in Heliopolis and kept the memory of Egypt's distant past alive, as well as the Atlantean experience in the minds of Egyptians.

The first time traveler functioned as an advisor to many important figures in antiquity. Taatos advised Moses. We know from the *Old Testament* that, "Moses was learned in the wisdom of the Egyptians."[79] He most certainly was, as Taatos was his main teacher, as we shall explore in the next chapter.

Taatos communicated with Herodotus in the 5th century B.C., and the Jewish historian Josephus. He advised Socrates in his waking and dream states and was later referred to by the philosopher as his daemon (advisor).

When Octavian became Emperor of Rome and changed his name to Augustus, Taatos was there to assist him in Rome's greatest era. Many historical events were either precipitated by Taatos, or not completed without his input. He truly was a master time traveler.

These experiments, including that of Egypt, may have failed but we cannot blame Taatos for this. He was always playing "catch up ball" with the ETs. Our materialistic, selfish and cruel tendencies that has fostered society's problems have their origins with ETs and our basic human nature, not time travelers.

The ancient Egyptians regarded Taatos as the god of wisdom, letters and the recording of time. It was Taatos who taught the Egyptians hieroglyphics, astronomy, astrology, medicine, architecture, music and so on. He advised Claudius Ptolemy on rather significant advances in astrology, but Ptolemy couldn't incorporate them for fear of his own life.

We find in the *Pyramid Texts* many references to Taatos:

*He who reckons the heavens, the counter of the stars and the measurer of the Earth.*

*The inventor of arts and sciences, scribe of the gods, the One who made calculations concerning the heavens, the stars and the Earth. The Reckoner of times and of seasons.*

*The personification of the mind of god, the author of every work on every branch of knowledge, both human and divine, and as the inventory of astronomy and astrology, the science of numbers and mathematics, geometry and land surveying, medicine and botany.*

*The Lord of the Divine body" and "Scribe of the Company of the Gods.*

*The god of the equilibrium" and Master of the Balance (to indicate that he was associated with the equinoxes – the time when the day and the night were balanced).*

---

[79] Acts 7:22.

*The master of wisdom and teacher of mankind.*

*Thoth ordained measure, number and order in the universe; was master architect.*[80]

Taatos' wife was known as Sophia to the Gnostics and as Nehemaut or Ma'at to the Egyptians. A white feather was his symbol. He was depicted with a symbol combining the Suns disk and the Moon's crescent upon his head. Taatos was also the Moon God.

According to Graham Hancock:. . .*Copernicus, the Renaissance astronomer whose theory of a heliocentric universe had overturned the earth-centered complacency of the Middle Ages, had said quite openly that he had arrived at his revolutionary insight by studying the secret writings of the ancient Egyptians, including the hidden works of Thoth himself. Likewise the seventeenth-century mathematician Kepler . . . admitted that in formulating his laws of the planetary orbits he was merely 'stealing the golden vessels of the Egyptians'.*[81]

In a later work, Hancock states that, Hermes, was also regarded as a deity who understood the mysteries of "all that is hidden under the heavenly vault", and who had the ability to bestow wisdom on selected individuals. It was said that he had inscribed his knowledge in secret books and hidden these about the earth, intending that they should be sought for by future generations but found "only by the worthy" – who were to use their discoveries for the benefit of mankind.[82]

In Chapter 125 of the *Book of the Dead* a "Judgement Scene" is depicted in which the scribe Ani's heart (the seat of the intellect and will and well as the life-giving center of the physical body) is weighed against the symbol of ma'at [truth and justice] (usually depicted as a feather), which serves as an ethical standard. Anubis, who has become an attendant of Osiris, lord of the nether world, is master of the balance, and is in control of the pointer; the scribe Thoth records the verdict and announces it. If the verdict should be unfavorable, the sinner falls victim to "the devourer", a hybrid monster with the head and jaws of a crocodile. If the verdict should be favorable, the deceased in invested with the attribute of ma'at and as "one who has been vindicated" is brought before Osiris, seated upon his throne.

According to the ancient Egyptians, the heart recorded all of the good and bad deeds of an individual's life. That is the reason it is weighed against the feather of Maat. Anubis is the god of embalming. The ibis-headed Thoth (Taatos) records these events and makes known Osiris' decision. A negative judgment resulted in the departed soul being devoured by the "Eater of the Dead." If Osiris

---

[80] E.A.W. Budge, *Book of the Dead*, op. cit.

[81] Graham Hancock, *The Sign and the Seal*. (London: Mandarin, 1993).

[82] Graham Hancock, *Fingerprints of the Gods*.(London: William Heinemann, 1995).

approved of the departed, this soul would now live forever in paradise with Osiris and the other gods.

Taatos was the god of learning and of healing; judge of celestial disputes and secretary of the gods; weigher of the souls of the dead. It was he who spoke the incantations that knit the severed members of Osiris' body back together. He invented numbers; measured time; was a god of transitions; from chaos to cosmos, strife to friendship, death to rebirth, causes to effects. Taatos was seen by the people as a god of magic spells and astrology, folk-medicine, and the lore of plants and minerals.

In the *Corpus Hermeticum* Thoth became Hermes Trismegistus ("thrice-greatest") and now was looked upon as a philosopher-king. The significance of the number three has already been discussed in relation to Mu and Egypt (pyramids, etc.). Plato was to adopt this philosopher king model. After all, Taatos tutored Plato.

We find the *Corpus Hermeticum* reflecting the absolute goodness of God, who is both One and All; the self-revelation of the Divine Mind in the cosmos; the universe as an emanation of living beings in hierarchical order; the unique constitution of the human being as microcosm; the way to regeneration and the direct knowledge of God (Gnosis).

The development of the ancient science alchemy, the forerunner of modern chemistry, is attributed to Taatos, along with Isis. This ancient discipline was an art of transmutation. We also see the doctrine of correspondences in the *Corpus Hermeticum*. Each planet corresponds to specific powers of the soul; Mercury to the intelligence, Venus to desire, Mars to anger, etc. The human soul is a microcosm of the universe.

Our soul has acquired various energies form the universe on its downward (or inward )journey from the celestial regions through the planetary spheres. It emerges into earth life through the womb, full of potentials and tendencies that are represented by its natal horoscope.

As the soul goes through life on Earth it hopefully learns its karmic lessons, so that when it leaves the body at death it merges with its Higher Self (conscious dying)[83] and ascends to God. Failure to do this results in being held back by the disorienting forces of the karmic cycle (Purgatory, Bardo or the Lower Astral Plane) and a subsequent encumbered future life.

In order to achieve this ascension, the initiate must develop a "radiant body" as a vehicle. The techniques to accomplish this were taught in the Mystery

---

[83] B. Goldberg, *Peaceful Transition: The Art of Conscious Dying and the Liberation of the Soul.* (St. Paul: Llewellyn, 1997).

Schools. Taatos was more concerned with useful knowledge: arts and sciences that improve the quality of life, such as music and mathematics and writing. His goal was to enlighten the masses so they became aware of the divine Mind through the works of Nature.

Following the fall of the Roman Empire, the *Corpus Hermeticum* expanded into a broader Hermeticism. This embraces much of the Western tradition we see today. The ancient Jews incorporated Hermetic principles in their *Kabbalah*. This discipline was represented by the *Sepher Yetzirah*, and expounds a cosmology based on the doctrine of correspondences, notably the sevenfold one of the planets, days of the week, openings in the head, etc., and the twelvefold one of the zodiac, directions of space, months, organs of the body, etc. It describes a cosmos organized by positive and negative energies, not through good and evil. Enlightenment is obtained by becoming aware of oneself as a microcosm, seating the "King on his Throne" (the divine presence) in the center of life.

The Hermetic paradigm of science, self-purification and contemplation does not conflict with any religion. It is simply an analysis of our relationship within the cosmos and a suggested regimen for spiritual growth and eventual ascension.

We even see its influence on Freemasonry. The Masonic symbolism of the Great Architect of the Universe, forming humans as rough stones to be worked into perfect blocks for the cosmic Temple, involves various stages of initiation and are like the steps on the Hermetic ascent, complete with their planetary symbolism.

Masons refrained from religious discussions in the Lodge itself to avoid persecution. They were nonetheless harassed throughout history by the Catholic Church and others. Egypt developed most of what we know as Freemasonry. Its true source comes form Mu first and then Atlantis.

Taatos was a truly great time traveler. His effect on Egypt and the history of the world form Mu to the present cannot possibly be appreciated or estimated. Yes he did exist, but he is not with us now.

The last assignment Taatos took was advising George Washington throughout his life. It was Taatos who suggested Washington visit New York in 1780. Here the future first president of the soon to be United States of America discovered that General Benedict Arnold was about to turn over West Point to the British. This could have cost the colonists the war.

Taatos guided Washington through his eight years as President and then ascended himself. With all of the problems humankind has experienced, I would hate to think of a world without this time traveler, the noblest chrononaut of them all.

We will discuss Taatos again in chapter 6 when he worked with Moses. For a more comprehensive discussion of Taatos and the technology of the time travelers I refer you to my book, *Time Travelers from Our Future: A Fifth Dimension Odyssey.*[84]

The history of civilization is characterized by many dark ages. Humankind, assisted by ETs and time travelers, had to begin all over again following the destruction of Mu and Atlantis. The Egyptian *Book of the Dead* referred to this prehistorical era as the Zep Tep, or first time, actually named by Taatos.

Although they tried to remain in the background as advisors, time travelers did become pharaohs and high priests in ancient Egypt to repair the damage caused by ETs and the personality failings of our ancestors. Let us not forget the statues of Osiris and Isis discovered in Egyptian tombs depicting both of them as Caucasian with blue eyes and blond hair!

## THE BUILDING OF THE PYRAMIDS

The time travelers were responsible for the majority of the construction done on the various pyramids, especially those at Giza. It was the ETs that initiated these megaliths. They did not have anti-gravity devices back in 10,450 B.C. I have never received data showing these anti-gravity machines were utilized by the ETs.

We must turn to the time travelers for these technological devices. Many different groups of ETs had their hand in the pyramid construction, especially at Giza. Their attention span was short and we have already discussed how they left Egypt to shape other civilizations during the time these pyramids were completed.

The pyramids were designed and begun in 10,450 B.C. About half of them were finished by the time the Sphinx was built. Anti-gravity devices were used at both periods of times. This only further annoyed the ETs, who felt intimidated by the time travelers.

There were two types of anti-gravity devices in use. To transport the large stones the entire ship of the chrononauts were used to float these blocks from quarries to Giza. In order to manipulate them into place on the pyramid site itself, a smaller craft was used.

My patients have described an *anti-gravity flying craft* as a pyramid-shaped flying car that hovered from six to nine feet above the ground. Three small circular anti-gravity generators were located on the underside of this craft. A constant air stream was created from an air cushion generator on the underside that assisted in this hovering capacity.

The time travelers had at least three of these crafts present at all times. They

---

[84] B. Goldberg, *Time Travelers from Our Future: A Fifth Dimension Odyssey,* op. cit.

were stored on the mother ship when not in use. A form of multidimensional effect was created that allowed these crafts to function as anti-gravity vehicles.

A cockpit that sat two time travelers was present, with a Zeta usually driving it. Eight small circular lights on the underside allowed for night work. There were five lights situated by the angles of the triangle. Finally, there was a triangular shaped insignia on the hood of this vehicle, between the apex of the triangle and the cockpit.

I do not mean to imply that Taatos and his team were the only time travelers visiting and living in ancient Egypt. Taatos was the very first time traveler, and he was later joined by Osiris, Isis, Geb and Horus as a team. Other teams eventually made their way back to ancient Egypt.

Taatos and his team had very little to do with the actual construction of the pyramids. Other time traveler teams, composed of Zeta and hybrid ETs handled that chore. I have noted that Taatos' team was one of the few consisting entirely of pure humans.

One of the main reasons why ETs and hybrids were permitted on time travel away team was a commitment from these futuristic genetic aliens living on Earth to correct the wrongs and errors made by their ancestors.

Healing temples were used throughout ancient Egypt. Metallic devices that shined multicolored light down to the top of the head of an Egyptian would cure them of many ailments. These devices were located on board the main time traveler ship, so they would have to abduct a patient in order to work with them. The ETs had similar, but far less effective devices.

Another type of device used by the time travelers was a helmet that tapped into and recorded the memories of a subject. This was one method used by the chrononauts to correctly record our history.

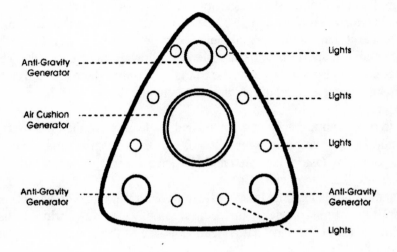

**Fig. 2**     **Underside -- Anti-Gravity Flying Craft**

Anti-Gravity Generator

Air Cushion Generator

Anti-Gravity Generator

Lights

Lights

Lights

Anti-Gravity Generator

Lights

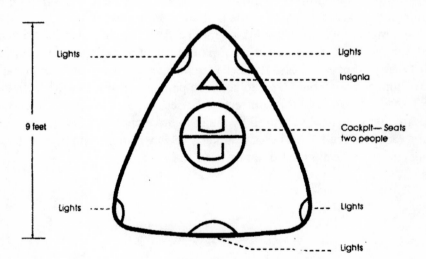

**Fig. 2A**     **Top View of Anti-Gravity Flying Craft**

Lights

Lights

9 feet

Lights

Lights

Lights

Insignia

Cockpit— Seats two people

Lights

Lights

# AN ANCIENT EGYPTIAN HEALER

The past life of one of my patients whom I shall refer to as Cora illustrates the advanced types of healing available in the Egypt of prehistory. Cora's past life began in Atlantis at about 16,000 B.C. She was a healer named Saqi. During that time the King of Atlantis was a man named Gadeiros.

Gadeiros was a ruthless tyrant, so Saqi decided to escape to Lower Egypt, Atlantis' chief colony. Saqi, along with several other Atlanteans, flew from Atlantis to Lower Egypt in a cigar-shaped flying craft called a Vailixi.

It was not difficult for Saqi to continue her profession as a healer in Lower Egypt, specifically Sais. She was bilingual, being proficient in both the Vril language of Atlantis and the Egyptian dialect of Sais.

Saqi mastered telepathy, could see auras and was an expert in out-of-body techniques. She worked at a healing temple in Sais that was run by a man named Tehuti. This was one of the names Taatos used, so it is evident that Saqi knew the first chrononaut.

The healing temple Saqi worked in was a large white building powered by crystals. She was 185 years old at this time and used various methods to bring about healing. Flower essences, crystals and color therapies were utilized, along with laying on hands approaches. In addition to various forms of healing, this temple also assisted the citizens of Sais in both psychic and spiritual development.

One very interesting technique utilized by Saqi was something known as etheric plane surgery. Saqi would train the patient to leave their body and travel to another dimension known as the etheric plane.[85] Then Saqi herself would join the patient in this dimension and perform a color and sound based form of surgery on the patient's etheric body.

Since the etheric body is identical to the physical body, any healing applied to this etheric body would manifest itself on the physical body as well. I use a similar approach with my patients, as I described in *Astral Voyages*.

Saqi did not have much contact with Tehuti and reported living out the rest of her life (another 150 years) as a healer, totally fulfilled with her karmic purpose. What is significant about this life is the degeneration Atlantis underwent and the presence of Taatos.

Although no Men in Black were reported by Saqi, she did describe many instances of white-robed time travelers arriving in ships, some even teleporting into the Egypt of prehistory. During the 35th century time travelers perfected

---

[85] For a comprehensive treatment of the other dimensions I refer you to my book *Astral Voyages*.

teleportation as a means of traveling back in time, so ships were no longer required. A comprehensive treatment of this technology can be found in my book *Time Travelers from Our Future: A Fifth Dimension Odyssey*.

## ANGELIC ENCOUNTERS

The time travelers had the ability to enter our very thoughts through their hyperspace travel techniques. It was common for them to appear in a dream of an ancient Egyptian and inspire that person to aspire to greater heights. Free will of the recipient prevented this approach from working much of the time. This dream effect gave rise to the dream incubation temples of Egypt, Greece and Rome.

Despite these repeated failures, the chrononauts kept assisting our ancestors. These time travelers have been the unknown power behind many of the "lucky breaks" and life saving situations that resulted in exactly the right information or circumstances being present at exactly the right moment.

Not only have these time travelers assisted the ancient Egyptians in this regard, but they have done this in all cultures throughout history. They sometimes are the "glowing beings of light" that assist people in times of need.

Many of the insights we receive that somehow positively affect our lives can be attributed to a time traveler. Only some of these may actually be the work of these chrononauts. It is usually the ones that have significant influences in our lives. I do not mean to imply that there are no spirit guides or angels. My previous books clearly depict these highly evolved beings. It is imply that time travelers have the ability to function as angels, due to their advanced technology.

## THE ESSENES

We have discussed the Essenes in the chapters on Mu and Atlantis. These Essenes were always the spiritual leaders, often recluses, in these cultures. Sirian ETs and their followers functioned as these Essenes throughout history. The time travelers themselves either advised or actually were the most important of these Essenes.

We find these Essenes in Upper Egypt in the beginning. Following Egypt's unification they moved to Lower Egypt in greater numbers. They always represented a balance against materialism and Lyran ET influence. Let us not forget that these time travelers were also capable of influencing the ETs, to a small degree.

The ancient Jewish Essenes were another expression of this class of dedicated and spiritually evolved souls. Many time travelers stayed in our past to mold our growth. These time travelers were represented by the Essenes more often than not.

We can thank the fanatical ancient Egyptian priests for the concept of the Devil and Hell, as I previously discussed. The time travelers tried their very best to block this control mechanism in 3000 B.C., but they failed to win their case. Here is another example of how the Egyptian experiment failed.

## TIME TRAVELING —— TEXAS STYLE

I had the pleasure of meeting Josi Galante while in Dallas on January 21, 2000. Josi is an artist who reported two incidents of contacts with time travelers.

During each of these experiences Josi meditated precisely four days before the event and received communication that she would meet these time travelers.

The first incident took place during the summer of 1997 in Austin, Texas on a college campus. Josi, her husband and her daughter were walking down the main street of the campus when her eyes were drawn to a tall man (at least six and a half feet) walking about 50 feet ahead and towards her.

This time traveler locked eyes with Josi and established a telepathic communication. He said to her telepathically. "I came in answer to your call. Observe and remember. Do not raise the alarm. Observe and remember."

Despite his height, this time traveler appeared to blend in with the other students. Josi sensed his incredible energy. He wore a plaid shirt and jeans, and had an athlete's physique.

Another encounter took place in Palmer Auditorium in Austin during a convention in early 1998. In the crowded building Josi felt an electric tingle on her neck and suddenly noticed two rather tall people (a man and a woman) about three feet from her. This couple telepathically advised Josi not to identify them to anyone else. When Josi asked them mentally if they were from a different time, they said "Yes."

Shortly thereafter, Josi turned away to call her friend over who had wandered away. When Josi turned back quickly, the couple had disappeared. Their height would have made it impossible to leave unnoticed in that crowd of people. They were nearly seven feet tall!

These two time travelers either dematerialized or entered a tear in the fabric of space-time to "disappear." This means they teleported and my research clearly states that these chrononauts (time travelers) had to be from at least the 35th century, where teleportation is the accepted mode of time travel.

Fig. 3  Josi Galante's time travelers

# JOSI'S ANCIENT EGYPTIAN ENCOUNTER

Tracing the origins of Josi's encounters with time travelers requires us to explore her childhood and adolescence. Here are her three trips to ancient Egypt in her own words compliments of chrononauts:

*The time travels began when I was a child of about 8 years of age. My parents, sister and I lived in a small rather isolated town in the eastern part of north Texas. My first time travel took place in early summer, and began when I awoke in the middle of the night, feeling a strong sense of being "called" to go somewhere. I was barefoot and wearing light cotton pajamas and the night was warm with little wind. Our street was unpaved, just a dirt road which curved at a 90 degree angle and continued on out of town between grassy fields. I hurried down this road about half a city block, following the pull of some strong vibration. Ahead was a dark oval shaped mound, a hump in the road that shouldn't have been there, that wavered and seemed to shimmer like a mirage in the moonlight. There was an opening in the side, and I could see something brightly colored inside.*

*There was no one visible, so I climbed a short ramp and went through the opening. Immediately I blacked out, and only awoke later, to find myself lying on the floor of what later proved to be a craft of some kind. A slender boy, probably thirteen years of age, was sitting beside me, cross-legged, and I was very surprised by his hair and clothing. He wore a short kilt or skirt of pleated white cloth, a wide tightly cinched belt decorated with symbols, and leather strap sandals.*

*He smiled shyly and talked to me in my mind [telepathy]. He replied that his name was "Kinofer" (or Kinofir) and wore the clothing and hairstyle of a culture from an island I would later recognize in my schoolbooks as Crete. He was not from that island though. He said he was to serve as a guide for a trip I was taking, to show me a place where I had lived, a very long time ago.*

*After what seemed to be a long time, the door opened and a blast of hot dry wind gusted into the room. Kinofer offered me a hand up and went to the doorway, with me close behind. It was blindly bright outside, with golden sand a jumble of stone blocks everywhere. Men dressed in skirts similar to Kinofer's were shouting and crowding around crude ladders propped up against some of the huge stones, where other men worked with chisels and carving tools. It was a dazzling sight. I heard a language I didn't understand, but Kinofer gave me mental descriptions and explanations. We were in ancient Egypt, he told me, in a place where building stones were cut and prepared for use in the cities and tombs.*

*There were mud houses, where people worked at making bricks with what* looked like straw and mud, packing it into wooden forms and slapping them out to dry in the sun. There were palm trees everywhere, with skinny trunks bending under the weight of fruit and bunched fronds. We walked for a long way towards a large square structure, which Kinofer said was a temple. We would not be allowed inside, but could watch to see the procession of priests, who were dressed in snowy white garments and were bald.

We watched the priest's solemn march, and then slipped in through a side door of another building that I think was the royal palace, and mingled with a crowd of people. Kinofer pointed out the king, or Pharaoh, who wore what I later came to know as the double crown, of white and red. A regal woman stood near him, and I thought this was the queen. He then left me in the crowd and joined the ranks of people who went forward, one by one, to pay respect to Pharaoh by lying face down, arms outstretched and forehead on the stone floor. There was such a clatter with the unfamiliar language, and pushing and crowding, and the strange sound of their music——stringed lutes or harps, cymbals, and an instrument they shook with little pieces of metal, not unlike a tambourine.

In late afternoon he gently pressed my eyes closed with his fingertips, and I blacked out. I awoke in my bed the next morning and thought at first that it had been a wonderful dream. When I went down for breakfast, my mom (a registered nurse very fixated on personal cleanliness) immediately asked why I was so dirty. My pajamas were smeared with brown dirt stains, my feet were grimy and dusty, and my hair was a wind-tangled mess. This was odd, since I had bathed before going to bed and had put on clean pajamas.

My time travel guide
KINOFER
GALANTE
© '99

Fig. 4

Josi's artwork that her time traveler had dark hair. Not all chrononauts are blond. Also, note the reference to the pharaoh's "double" crown. This took place after the unification of ancient Egypt (c.a. 3100 B.C.).

Josi's second trip to ancient Egypt with her time traveler Kinofer as her guide was as follows:

*Kinofer had grown older, as had I, so was now a youth of perhaps fifteen years of age. The night before I had gone to bed as usual, with no sense that anything was going to happen, and now assumed it was still in the middle of the night. It appeared to be night as we stepped out of the craft. I turned and looked at it curiously, but it was just a large oval shape in the darkness, looking like a dull metallic gray. Kinofer took my hand and pulled me along a rocky path between boulders, under a starry sky with a half full moon. I recall these details because the stars were so much brighter in those ancient skies.*

*We were met by several bare chested men wearing the same simple kilts that Kinofer wore, and they carried torches which cast spooky shadows on the rocks as we wound through a canyon and into a rubble strewn valley. After about a quarter of a mile, we came to a slot in the rocks, and the torchbearers led the way into a passageway, which descended down a rough-hewn stairway. It wound down and down, ending at a square cut entrance to a dark chamber. As we stepped into this huge room, I was astounded by the bright, new looking frescoes painted on the high stone walls. There were animal headed beings depicted in various ways, usually posed in the stylized manner that ancient Egyptian artists used. I saw a hippo, cat, dog or coyote, a water bird, an alligator, and many other animal types. The strangest was a beetle head god. I especially noticed a figure colored leaf green with a head shaped like that of my Mantis people, who had been in my life for so long. I have never seen this figure since that experience, so wonder if this underground room is an undiscovered or unpublicized tomb of some kind.*

*Kinofer pointed out the various animal deities, explaining their role in the religious beliefs of Egypt at that time. There was one figure arching across the top of one wall, whose name he pronounced as "Noot" (Nut – phonetic) and said represented the night. Her body was dark cobalt (lapis) blue and studded with stars. I've never forgotten how she looked, stretched over everything and protecting the world with her body.*

A trip to a pyramid was the highlight of Josi's third time travel experience in ancient Egypt:

*When I was about twelve years old my third time travel trip to ancient Egypt occurred. This time Kinofer appeared after I had come to consciousness on a riverbank. As I sat up and rubbed my eyes, Kinofer walked towards me from the shade of the trees. He was taller now, probably seventeen years of age, and smiled as he told me that we were scheduled to go hunting in a boat moored nearby.*

*The men were dressed in the usual short-skirted garments worn in Egypt in those times, and were happily singing as they loaded supplies on a sloped deck. There was no sail, just half a dozen rowers equipped with broad bladed wooden oars. There were several cages which contained tawny, yellow-eyed cats, who meowed continuously.*

*Two bejeweled young men were holding ornate hunting bows, and boys stood ready nearby with a supply of arrows. To my horror, these men quickly shot several squawking water birds, and astonishingly, three of the cats leaped into the water and swam after the birds, which they grasped in their teeth as they swam back to the boat. The laughing men scooped the cats up and deposited them, dripping and squirming on the deck, where a short struggle ensued as they took the birds away from the poor, wet animals. Kinofer explained that certain cats were trained from kittens to be retrievers, and even learned to enjoy swimming in the warm river water. It was hard to believe, but I saw it happen several times before we pulled the boat about to return to shore.*

*I asked Kinofer if we could see a pyramid before we left, because that was my dearest wish. Smiling, he asked me to close my eyes, touched my lids and I was out. Looking back this seems very silly to me, but I assume these precautions were to keep me from seeing what the exterior of the travel craft looked like.*

*Whatever the reason, he woke me later aboard the ship and I eagerly followed him to the doorway, where I saw a very odd pyramid a short distance ahead of us. It was in stair step layers with three levels, and a rounded sort of knob on top. I was expecting the flat-sided pyramids I had seen pictures of, but was excited nonetheless. He explained that it was old even in those ancient times, and was an experiment that had been abandoned in favor of the more triangular style.*

*We left soon after that, and as before, he pressed his fingertips to my eyelids and I was immediately unconscious, awaking in my bed at home the next morning. Sadly, this was the last trip to Egypt that I recall; though I did experience time travels to other locals.*

# CHAPTER 6  HERMES MEETS MOSES

Throughout this book I have been presenting the results of hypnotic regressions that literally rewrite the history of civilization. The time travelers role is by far the most important in this respect, as well as facilitating our spiritual development.

This case I am about to present illustrates the complete antithesis of any type of imagination or confabulation by a patient in relating their experience with the time travelers. Ben heard me give a talk on past life therapy at the Beth Jacob Congregation in Beverly Hills in the fall of 1996.

As an orthodox Jew, Ben was initially quite offended by the information he related to me in trance, as it went completely against his religious upbringing. In addition to a close relationship between Hermes and Moses and Moses' role as an Egyptian high priest, this case reveals a totally different Exodus story.

Ben reported missing time episodes throughout his life, but never sought previous therapy. He most certainly did not believe in UFOs, least of all time travelers. I was able to obtain a tremendous amount of data concerning Hermes and his relationship to the history of civilization from my work with Ben. Fortunately, there were several other sources for this data, and much of this information was corroborated by other patients who lived in other countries and did not know Ben. But no other patient has ever depicted Moses as did Ben.

In chapter 5 I related the scenario of a time traveler abduction with Charles' case. The basic components were similar in Ben's case, only the revelations Ben revealed were quite different.

The time travelers revealed the following information concerning the relationship between Moses and Hermes. I must point out at this time that some occultists have equated Hermes and Moses. Other patients have reported that Hermes was one of Moses' tutors and a close advisor. Hermes was not Moses. Although the time travelers would refer to Moses' tutor and chief advisor as Hermes (not Thoth or Tehuti), they would state repeatedly, "You would know this man as Hermes."

Ben was both shown holographic scenes and informed that Moses was a native Egyptian who was tutored by Hermes, among others. Both Moses and the young son of the king were advised by Hermes, educated by the same people and used the same libraries for research. A close friendship grew between Moses and the pharaoh's son. Ben could not get a close view of Moses or Hermes, but the advisor and tutor to Moses always wore a white robe, was tall and blond.

Moses became an Egyptian high priest who appeared to be the chief priest of the young pharaoh when the latter assumed the throne. Much of Moses' responsibilities seemed to revolve around establishing a new religion in Egypt. He ordered and supervised the alteration of inscriptions in temples and other references to previous gods. All of these actions appeared to have been influenced by Hermes.

What was unusual about this scenario was that Moses was portrayed as an Egyptian and not a Jew. This bothered Ben greatly. Moses appeared to be heavily involved with Egyptian politics. He made many trips to other lands and appeared to consider Egypt his home. At all times Hermes was his close advisor. The time travelers never revealed the precise name Hermes was called then, nor Moses! They simply referred to Moses as the deliverer of the Hebrew Law.

Ben was assertive enough to question the time travelers during the conference room hologram phase of his missing time episodes. These chrononauts explained that Moses was a religious/political figure attempting to both establish monotheism in Egypt and rule as pharaoh after his king died. Moses' king died after a relatively short reign. The precise dates were not mentioned.

This political intrigue became complicated as Moses was forced to flee Egypt to save his life due to some political factors. Hermes went with him. Moses eventually returned and played the role of a general leading an army. He did not win the war, but his forces were strong enough for him to negotiate some form of truce.

The scene Ben was shown of Moses leading many thousands of people out of Egypt appeared to represent the Exodus. One problem noted by Ben is that the people Moses was leading to the Promised Land were Egyptians and not Jews. It just didn't make sense. At this time Hermes seemed to disappear and Moses was on his own. The time travelers did say that Moses was "divinely inspired," but would not explain further.

I could not ascertain from his regressions whether the time travelers ever explained this contradiction. This scenario certainly went against anything I ever read about Moses or the Exodus. The fact remained that Moses was a loyal Egyptian attempting to establish his king's theology of a belief in one god, a belief that initiated some sort of civil war in Egypt.

In addition to playing the role of a divinely inspired prophet (with a little help from Hermes), Moses came across as an Egyptian priest who was absolutely loyal to his pharaoh and a politician seeking to rule Egypt following the king's death. His people were Egyptians not Jews. Moses' karmic purpose seemed to revolve around establishing monotheism in Egypt.

Ben did not displace his anger toward me concerning the data he related, he was simply annoyed by the fact that he could not possibly reconcile this material with his religious training. We must understand that Ben was not a Jewish scholar, merely a devoutly practicing Jew who attended services regularly and read the Torah. Neither he nor I had read Josephus' Osarseph story (we will discuss this shortly), nor any other theory expressing this scenario.

I quickly deduced that he had no background in Egyptology, and even less interest. Most people I know are very interested in Egyptian history. They may not know much about it, but most definitely are at least curious. Ben's lack of interest was due to theological reasons. As a Jew I suspected he felt ancient Egypt was the enemy. At least that is how the *Old Testament* portrayed Egypt in relationship to the ancient Hebrews.

What do we make of this? I began doing some research following the completion of Ben's case and uncovered some startling data which supports what the time travelers told Ben, and literally rewrites Jewish history!

Please bear in mind as I relate this supporting data that my agenda is strictly scientific. I have no ax to grind. There is no self interest or prejudicial theme to this reporting. My references come from the theological and historical literature with minimal interpretation on my part.

If you have ever wondered about the inconsistencies in the Bible and the true story of Moses and Exodus, then read on. The story may be controversial, but I absolutely believe it to be factual.

First, let us review what the *Old Testament* tells us about the Jewish people and the Exodus. Abraham of Ur of the Chaldees in Mesopotamia began the Hebrew nation. His family migrated to Canaan, where he was promised that land by God himself. This covenant later passed to Abraham's sons Isaac and the latter's son Jacob. Jacob fathered twelve sons (each son creating one of the Twelve Tribes of the Hebrews)and his progeny, Joseph, became an Egyptian official.

Joseph took his family to Egypt, but later his people were enslaved. One of the Jews, Moses, confronted the pharaoh and successfully freed the Jews from Egypt and led them to the promised land of Canaan forty years later. With the single exception of the Bible, there is no archaeological or historical evidence to support this story.

Scholars suggest that a confederation of Semitic tribes existed before the Hebrew monarchy of David, Solomon and others. A gradual evolution supposedly took place with these nomads and, following the Exodus, a Jewish empire was formed. It is true that hundreds of new settlements were founded in central Canaan during the twelfth and eleventh century B.C. What is missing is any evidence of these Twelve Tribes prior to the thirteenth century B.C.

There is no linkage of any specific Semitic tribe to the ancient Jews. We have no evidence that they lived in Palestine, or any place else other than Egypt, outside of the Bible. I previously discussed the fact that the Bible was organized at least eight hundred years after it was written. The events depicted in these holy scriptures were edited and embellished nearly one thousand years after the events relating to Moses and the Exodus actually took place.

A summary of what really happened is that the Jews living in Egypt were native Egyptians who were devoted followers of pharaoh Akhenaten. Within twenty years following this king's death, Horemheb executed a massive campaign aimed at eliminating all references to Akhenaten and persecuting his followers (the Jews). My use of the term Jews is inaccurate, since these people were Egyptian. I apply this convention to reduce confusion. Moses led these Egyptians out of Egypt and they comprised the House of Israel (Jacob later changed his name to Israel) that settled in Canaan.

We know from Egyptian records that pharaoh Akhenaten was the ninth king of the Eighteenth Dynasty. He ruled as king for eighteen years during the middle of the fourteenth century B.C. Some scholars use the date of 1374-73 as the beginning of his reign.[86]

Akhenaten worshipped only the sun god Re-Herakhty, manifested in the form of Aten, the solar disc. He changed his name from Amenhotep IV to Akhenaten to reflect this belief.

This king was the first Egyptian monarch to preach monotheism. He particularly disdained the worship of Amen, the Thebian chief god. Akhenaten sent agents throughout Egypt to close all of these other god's temples and delete their names wherever they appeared. He was the first Egyptian king to initiate such action.

Osirian funerary practices were also forbidden. This was central to the Egyptian way of life. Despite his attempt to remove polytheism from Egypt, a succeeding pharaoh Horemheb ordered all references that Akhenaten ever existed removed from Egyptian records, and destroyed the capital city built by Akhenaten. The latter's name was omitted from the list of Kings.

Egyptologists did not become aware of Akhenaten or his wife Nefertiti until the late nineteenth century, when ruins in a region called Amarna were examined. Certain Amarna letters gave detailed accounts of the events transpired during the reign of Amenhotep III, his son and the turbulent sate of Egypt at that time.[87]

My thesis is simply that the people who later became the Jews were native Egyptians (and that includes Moses) that were forced out of Egypt. They were all loyal followers of Akhenaten and his sun god.

Horemheb was a strong king who assumed the throne about fourteen years

[86] Donald B. Redford, *Akhenaten: The Heretic King*. (Princeton: Princeton University Press, 1984).
[87] William F. Albright, "The Amarna Letters From Palestine." In *Cambridge Ancient History*. (Cambridge, England: Cambridge University Press, 1971).

following the death of Akhenaten. This subsequent pharaoh destroyed Akhenten's capital city, removed his names from Egyptian records, persecuted all of his followers and eventually either killed or banished them from Egypt. As Horemheb had no royal blood and left no heirs, Ramesses I, another soldier, succeeded him as king.

## WHEN DID THE EXODUS OCCUR?

The *Old Testament* is the only evidence of an Exodus. Scholars like to date the Exodus during the reign of Ramesses II because it removes any link between Moses and Akhenaten. Such an association is offensive to any Jew. After all, their prophet and liberator Moses must not be associated with an Egyptian pharaoh, the arch enemy, according to the Bible.

An archaeological discovery known as the Merneptah victory stele makes this Exodus impossible unless it took place prior to the reign of Ramesses II. Scholars point to the Bible's reference to the enslaved Hebrews building the city of Rameses. This city is equated with the city of Pi-Ramesse, which was the royal home of Ramesses II.[88]

Prior to Ramesses' II reign, this city was called Avaris. The pharaoh who ordered the enslaved Jews to construct the city of Raamses could not have been the same pharaoh at the time of the Exodus. These events transpired prior to the birth of Moses, and Moses was eighty at the time of the Exodus, according to the Bible. Since Ramesses' II reign lasted for only sixty-seven years, he could not have been the pharaoh at the time of Moses' birth and the Exodus.

The Bible clearly states that the pharaoh died when Moses was in exile from Egypt and the succeeding king was in power at the time of the Exodus. We can't have Rameses' II successor on the throne during the Exodus due to the Merneptah victory stele inscriptions. Here is a sample of what this stele contains:

*The princes are prostrate, saying: "Mercy!"*
*Not one raises his head among the Nine Bows.*
*Desolation is for Tehenu; Hatti is pacified;*
*Plundered is the Canaan with every evil;*
*Carried off is Ashkelon; seized upon is Gezer;*
*Yanoam is made as that which does not exist;*
*Israel is laid waste, his seed is not;*
*Hurru is become a widow for Egypt!*
*All lands together, they are pacified;*

---

[88] Exodus 3:23.

*Everyone who was restless, he has been bound.*[89]

This poem describes Merneptaha's victory over a combined force of Libya and the Sea Peoples. We will discuss these Sea Peoples later in this chapter. In his stele we find Israel as the sole name with a grammatical determinative, indicating people and not a land. This suggests a post-Exodus Israel long before it became a significant power.

Egyptian historians accurately place the people who participated in the Exodus in the city of Avaris, not Pi-Ramesse. Since the *Old Testament* was organized over 800 years later, the author simply substituted the name he was most familiar with (Pi-Ramesse) for Avaris.

Another factor that nullifies the Exodus in the Ramesses II era is that this pharaoh was a strong military leader. There is no way the Jews could have stood up to him and leave absolutely no record of this confrontation. Only a much weaker king, such as Horemheb, would have allowed this to occur. There were but fifteen years between Horemheb's death and Ramesses II ascending to the throne.

No official Egyptian records exist of the Exodus because Akhenaten was a pharaoh. Horemheb ordered all references to Akhenaten's very existence removed upon Horemheb's ascension to the throne. This most definitely would have included any confrontation with the Israelites. Even claiming victory over such a heretic as Akhenaten would simply perpetuate his memory. This is the last thing that Horemheb wanted.

The Merneptah victory stele and other evidence I have so far presented strongly suggests that the Exodus took place during the reign of Akhenaten. This would imply that Moses and Akhenaten were childhood and adolescent comrades, both being raised in the pharaoh's house. They would have received the same religious training in the Egyptian temple of Annu, also known as On in the Bible and Heliopolis in Greek.

This stele is evidence that Israel emerged suddenly in the fourteenth century B.C., and not by a gradual evolution over several centuries by nomadic tribes of Semite-speaking peoples. We have absolutely no archaeological records of Israel, or any of their Twelve Tribes, prior to the Merneptah stele.

According to the Merneptah inscription, Israel was a powerful military force. It simply wouldn't have been listed with the Hatti (Hittites), Hurru (Hurrian kingdom) or the powerful Canaan city-states of Ashkelon and Gezer if it wasn't. The fact that it was mentioned without a specific territory suggests that Israel originated from another location.

---

[89] James P. Pritchard, ed., *The Ancient Near East: An Anthology of Texts and Pictures*, 2 vols. (Princeton: Princeton University Press, 1958), 1:231.

If Israel arrived there much earlier than the middle of the reign of Ramesses II, then it most surely would have been identified with the territory in which it was found. By arriving within forty years of the death of Horemheb, this scenario is compatible with my implication that the Exodus occurred shortly after the death of Horemheb and the Bible's portrayal that Israel entered Canaan forty years following the Exodus.

Another Biblical problem that confounds historians is that there is no evidence, outside of the *Old Testament*, that David, Solomon or their empire ever existed. We know a Hebrew nation existed, but if it was such an extensive kingdom we should find references to it among the records of the Phoenicians, Egyptians, Assyrians, Babylonians, Amorites, Canaanites, Edomites and Morabites. All of these were Israel's neighbors. No such records exist. It is not uncommon for history to contain accounts of large kingdoms that never existed (some would apply this to Atlantis and Mu – I do not), but I have never heard of absolutely no records from contemporaries of a mighty kingdom that *did* exist!

There are other structural problems with the Bible. We find *Genesis* ending with Joseph's death and continuing in *Exodus* with the birth of Moses. Several hundred years elapsed, and Israel evolved form a few people to over 600,000 men and their families. Yet nothing else is depicted during this gap, except the pharaoh placing them in bondage because he feared their numbers.

The Bible presents details on the creation through the death of Joseph and from Moses' birth on. Did nothing take place during these gap years worthy of noting from this small number of people to a mighty kingdom and finally to its enslavement? Nothing was recorded because there was no prehistory of the Jews. They were native Egyptians living in Egypt.

## WHO WROTE THE BIBLE?

It has been accepted that Moses was the divinely inspired prophet who authored the first five books of the Bible. These are known as *Genesis, Exodus, Leviticus, Numbers* and *Deuteronomy*, called the *Five Books of Moses*, the *Torah* in Hebrew and the *Pentateuch* in Greek.

In certain parts of the Bible the term "unto this day" appears, clearly proving that these passages were written well beyond Moses' death. For example, in *Deuteronomy* 3:14 we are told that Jair, a son of Manasseh, captured the territory of Argob and called it Bashanhavothiair. The details depict the story of Israel's wanderings in the wilderness. But after stating that Jair renamed the territory, the author adds that the city is still called by the new name "unto this day."

There were two stories of Creation, two stories of the covenant between God and Abraham, two stories in which Abraham told a foreign king that his wife was his sister, two stories of Abraham naming Isaac, and two stories about how many animals were taken aboard Noah's ark. This retelling of the same story with somewhat different details reinforces the hypothesis that there were several authors to the Bible.

Richard Elliot Friedman is a biblical scholar who has devoted many years to determining the authorship of the Bible. He points out that nowhere in the *Five Books of Moses* does Moses state he is the author. The *Pentateuch* includes items Moses could not possibly have known, such as a list of Edomite kings (Genesis 36) who lived long after Moses was dead.

Since different names were used to refer to God (Jaweh and Elohim), Friedman divides the authors using Jaweh as the "J" source and the "E" source for those manuscripts using Elohim. The "E" documents were derived form a third source concerned mostly with matters relating to the priesthood and the laws. This third source was called "P." The fourth source, known as "D," is confined to the Book of Deuteronomy. Friedman also suggests a fifth source he calls the *Book of Generations* that refers to the Genesis chronology located mostly in chapters 5 and 11.

As far as the dates when these components were written, Friedman states that the J author wrote between 922 and 722 B.C., before the Assyrian destruction of the northern kingdom of Israel; E was written between 848 and 722 B.C., also before the Assyrian conquest; D was authored during the reign of Josiah, king of Judah about 622 B.C., and P appeared between 722 and 609 B.C.[90]

The Torah was edited and completed no earlier than the sixth century B.C., and very probably in the fifth century B.C., though not without a *significant* amount of editing and embellishing.

It involved a major effort of attempting to resolve the various conflicts presented from the four or five authors, in addition to Moses himself.

We find references in the Bible to earlier works called the *Book of Jasher* and the *Second Book of Kings* in Joshua 10:14. No such books have been discovered, but we know that earlier sources did exist.

## THE PHARAOH CHRONOLOGY

We can be fairly certain about the dates of the pharaohs within a few years from the three main sources. These are Josephus, the Jewish historian of the first century A.D. for Manetho, and two chronological summaries by the Christian

---

[90] Richard Elliot Friedman's, *Who Wrote the Bible*. (New York: Summit Books, 1987).

historians Africanus (in the third century A.D.) and Eusebius (in the fourth century A.D.). From various archaeological finds, particularly other ancient king lists and monumental inscriptions, indicate that Manetho must have worked from genuine sources. The *Turin Papyrus*, written during the reign of Ramesses II, is the most valuable of the king lists.

The Exodus can be dated at 1315 B.C., as indicated in *Genesis*. While *Exodus* suggests the date of 1310 B.C., scholars now favor the Genesis date from other clues mentioned in the Bible.[91] Exodus states that Moses fled Egypt following his killing an Egyptian soldier. The sitting pharaoh died and Moses returns to Egypt to liberate his people. The new pharaoh probably died as a result of the Red Sea parting and closing again.

Considering the Exodus dates of 1315 B.C. and 1310 B.C., we must consider the pharaoh sequence which is: Horemheb, Ramesses I, and Sethos I. Horemheb's reign ended at about 1315 B.C. and Sethos I's began at about 1314; Ramesses I overlapped the two. This coincides with the Genesis dating of the Exodus in 1315. The first pharaoh to die would have been Horemheb. This would leave Ramesses I as the monarch whom Moses confronted. He would also be the briefly ruling king who died during the Exodus.

Since we know Moses was eighty during the Exodus, he had to have been born in 1395 B.C. Akhenaten became king between 1375 and 1372 B.C., sometime between his late teens and early twenties. This would place Akhenaten with Moses being raised in the pharaoh's house, since Moses was about the same age as Akhenaten.

Rabbinical tradition states that Moses was forty years old when he fled Egypt. That would date this departure at 1355 B.C., between the reigns of Smenkhkare and Tutankhamen.[92] We know that a revolt against Akhenaten's monotheism began immediately upon Tutankhamen's ascension to the throne by the fact that he changed his name from Tutankha*ten* (the *aten* component refers to the Aten worship by Akhenaten) to Tutankha*men* (this *amen* suffix signified the god Amen – the very Theban deity that Akhenaten attempted to eliminate from Egyptian theology).

The first century Jewish historian Josephus' account of Moses' flight clearly stated that political enemies plotted to assassinate Moses, and this was the reason he left Egypt. This is quite different than the Bible's version alleging Moses' flight due to his killing an Egyptian soldier who was beating a Hebrew slave.[93]

---

[91] J. H. Hertz, ed., *The Pentateuch and Haftorahs, 2nd ed.* (London: Soncino Press, 1976).

[92] Ibid.

[93] Josephus, "Jewish Antiquities." 9 vols. From *Josephus.*, vol. 4. Translated by H. J. Thackeray. (Cambridge, Mass.: Harvard University Press, 1930).

What most likely took place is that a political struggle for the throne occurred following Smenkare's death. Moses was in line to succeed this pharaoh, being Akhenaten's chief priest. Old guard polytheists seized control of Egypt and Moses was forced to flee in order to avoid execution.

## OSARSEPH

Josephus related a story of a man called Osarseph when he translated Manetho's writings. We must recall that neither Manetho nor Josephus knew of Akhenaten, since this pharaoh was not discovered until the end of the nineteenth century. Both historians call him Amenophis. Manetho also places Akhenaten after Ramesses I and before Sethos I. He incorrectly makes Akhenaten the father of Sethos and refers to Sethos as "Sethos also called Ramesses."

We must remember that Moses departed Egypt twice, once after Akhenaten died and once at the beginning of the reign of Sethos and during the Exodus. The Egyptian scribes placed the end of Akhenaten's reign immediately before the start of Sethos's. This resulted in dating Moses' two departures at about the same time allowing for no intervening period. It is no wonder Manetho was confused and fused these two departures into a single event distorting the chronology of these pharaohs.

Josephus assumes Amenophis was a fictitious king, and places the Osarseph story during this monarch's reign. The Jewish historian reasons that Amenophis must be fictitious because "[Manetho] did not venture to define the length of his reign although in the case of the other kings he adds their years precisely." This charge is ridiculous, as Manetho's king list notes three rulers named Amenophis and each has a precisely defined reign.[94]

In the Osarseph story Josephus assumes that the Hyksos and the Hebrews were the same entity so that the expulsion of the Hyksos constituted the Exodus. He also places Amenophis (Akhenaten) just before a king named "Sethos also called Ramesses."

With this in mind here is Josephus' Osarseph Story:

*The first writer upon whom I shall dwell is one whom I used a little earlier as a witness to our antiquity. I refer to Manetho. This writer, who had undertaken to translate the history of Egypt from the sacred books, began by stating that our ancestors came against Egypt with many tens of thousands and gained the mastery over the inhabitants; and then he himself admitted that at a later date again they were driven out of the country, occupied what is now Judaea, founded Jerusalem,*

---

[94] W. G. Waddell, ed., *Manetho.* (London: Loeb Classical Library, 1940) p. 121.

*and built the temple. [Here Josephus equates the Hyksos with the Israelites and their expulsion with the Exodus.]*

*Up to this point he followed the chronicles: thereafter, by offering to record the legends and current talk about the Jews, he took the liberty of interpolating improbable tales in his desire to confuse us with a crowd of Egyptians, who for leprosy and other maladies had been condemned, he says, to banishment from Egypt. After citing a king Amenophis, a fictitious person—for which reason he did not venture to define the length of his reign, although in the case of the other kings he adds their years precisely—Manetho attaches to him certain legends, having doubtless forgotten that according to his own chronicle the exodus of the Shepherds [i.e., Hyksos] to Jerusalem took place 518 years earlier. For Tethmosis was king when they set out; and, according to Manetho, the intervening reigns thereafter occupied 393 years down to the two brothers Sethos and Hermaeus [later in the text the spelling changes from Hermaeus to Harmais], the former of whom, he says, took the new name Aegyptus, the latter that of Danaus. Sethos drove out Hermaeus and reigned for fifty-nine years; then Rampses [Ramesses II], the elder of his sons, for sixty-six years. Thus, after admitting that so many years had elapsed since our forefathers left Egypt, Manetho now interpolates this intruding Amenophis. This king, he states, conceived a desire to behold the gods, as Or, one of his predecessors on the throne, had done; and he communicated this desire to his namesake Amenophis, Paapis's son, who, in virtue of his wisdom and knowledge of the future, was reputed to be a partaker in the divine nature. This namesake, then, replied that he would be able to see the gods if he cleansed the whole land of lepers and other polluted persons. The king was delighted and assembled all those in Egypt whose bodies were wasted by disease: they numbered 80,000 persons. These he cast into the stone-quarries to the east of the Nile, there to work segregated from the rest of the Egyptians. Among them, Manetho adds, there were some of the learned priests, who had been attacked by leprosy. Then this wise seer Amenophis was filled with dread of divine wrath against himself and the king if the outrage done to these persons should be discovered; and he added a prediction that certain allies would join the polluted people and would take possession of Egypt for thirteen years [Akhenaten's reign in his new capital was 13 years]. Not venturing to make this prophecy himself to the king, he left a full account of it in writing, and then took his own life. The king was filled with despondency.* Then Manetho continues as follows (I quote his account verbatim):

*When the men in the stone-quarries had suffered hardships for a considerable time, they begged the king to assign to them as a dwelling-place and a refuge the deserted city of the Shepherds, Auaris [Avaris], and he consented. According to religious tradition this city was from earliest times dedicated to*

*Typhon [Seth]. Occupying this city and using the region as a base for revolt, they appointed as their leader one of the priests of Heliopolis called* **Osarseph,** *and took an oath of obedience to him in everything. First of all,* **he made it a law that they should neither worship the gods nor refrain from any of the animals prescribed as especially sacred in Egypt,** *but should sacrifice and consume all alike, and that they should have intercourse with none save those of their own confederacy. After framing a great number of laws like these, completely opposed to Egyptian custom, he ordered them with their multitude of hands, to repair the walls of the city and make ready for war against King Amenophis. Then, acting in concert with certain other priests and polluted persons like himself, he sent an embassy to the Shepherds who had been expelled by Tethmosis, in the city called Jerusalem; and, setting forth the circumstances of himself and his companions in distress, he begged them to unite wholeheartedly in an attack upon Egypt. He offered to conduct them first to their ancestral home at Auaris [Avaris], to provide their hosts with lavish supplies, to fight on their behalf whenever need arose, and to bring Egypt without difficulty under their sway. Overjoyed at the proposal, all the Shepherds, to the number of 200,000, eagerly set out, and before long arrived at Auaris. When Amenophis, king of Egypt, learned of their invasion, he was sorely troubled, for he recalled the prediction of Amenophis, son of Paapis. First, he gathered a multitude of Egyptians; and having taken counsel with the leading men among them, he summoned to his presence the sacred animals which were held in greatest reverence in the temples, and gave instructions to each group of priests to conceal the images of the gods as securely as possible. As for his five-year old son Sethos, also called Ramesses, after his grandfather Rapses, he sent him safely away to his friend. He then crossed the Nile with as many as 300,000 of the bravest warriors of Egypt, and met the enemy. But, instead of joining the battle, he decided that he must not fight against the gods, and made a hasty retreat to Memphis. There he took into his charge Apis and the other sacred animals which he had summoned to that place; and forthwith he set off for Ethiopia with his whole army and the host of Egyptians. The Ethiopian king, who, in gratitude for a service, had become his subject, welcomed him, maintained the whole multitude with such products of the country as were fit for human consumption, assigned to them cities and villages sufficient for the destined period of thirteen years' banishment from his realm, and especially stationed an Ethiopian army on the frontiers of Egypt to guard King Amenophis and his followers. Such was the situation in Ethiopia. Meanwhile, the Solymites [people of Jerusalem] made a descent along with the polluted Egyptians, and treated the people so impiously and savagely that the domination of the Shepherds seemed like a golden age to those who witnessed the present enormities. For not only did they set towns and villages* *on fire, pillaging the temples and mutilating images of the gods without restraint, but they also made a **practice of using the sanctuaries as kitchens to roast the sacred animals which the people worshipped: and they would compel the priests and prophets to sacrifice and butcher the beasts, afterwards casting the men forth naked. It is said that the priest who framed their constitution and their laws was a native of Heliopolis, named Osarseph after the god Osiris, worshipped at Heliopolis; but when he joined_this people, he changed his name and was called Moses.***

*Such, then, are the Egyptian stories about the Jews, together with many other tales which I pass by for brevity's sake. Manetho adds, however, that, at a later date, Amenophis advanced from Ethiopia with a large army, his son Rampses—[referred to earlier as "Sethos Also Called Ramesses, after his grandfather, Rapses"]—also leading a force, and that the two together joined battle with the Shepherds and their polluted allies, and defeated them, killing many and pursuing the others to the frontiers of Syria. This then, with other tales of a like nature, is Manetho's account.[95]*

We can see from this story that Osarseph banned the worship of Egyptian gods and destroyed the images of the gods, one of the most important goals of Akhenaten's reforms. We also note the period of exile lasted thirteen years, the number of years Akhenaten ruled in his newly built capital city completed in the fifth year of his reign. Manetho describes the child "Sethos also called Ramesses" as five years old, which corresponds to the fifth year of Akhenaten's reign.

"The thirteen years of woe wrought by lepers and shepherds" (Hyksos) must refer to Akhenaten's duration in his newly built capital city. Manetho clearly places the responsibility of administering the heretic monotheistic religion on Osarseph (Moses). Another piece of evidence that Akhenaten was Amenophis comes from the claim that he wanted an audience with God, as did his predecessor Or. Orus in the Josephus king list is equated with Amenhotep III. Since the only king Amenophis (Amenhotep) to rule after Orus (Amenhotep III) was Amenhotep IV, Amenophis had to be Akhenaten. The Egyptian god Heru in Greek translates as Or, Orus and Horus.

## THE NEGATIVE CONFESSIONS

To show the origin of the Ten Commandments we can point to the ethical doctrine of the Eighteenth Dynasty known as the *Negative Confessions*. This series of forty-two principles (remember Egypt had forty-two nomes) defined the

---

[95] Josephus, op. cit.

proper moral conduct that would assure ascension and joining Osiris in Paradise.

At this time let me point out that Akhenaten worshipped Aten (the solar disc) only as a representation of the true Creator Re-Herakhte, the invisible source of the sun's creative power. Although this may appear as a dual god belief, Re-Herakhte was self-created, brought no other gods into existence and used Aten merely as a supernatural force in dealing with humankind.[96]

Osiris and forty-two Assessor Judges (one for each confession) weighed the heart of the deceased against the feather of Maat as we have discussed to determine the afterlife fate of the voyaging soul. Akhenaten eliminated Osiris from this paradigm, but most certainly would have kept these confessions. Moses, as Akhenaten's chief priest, would also follow these principles. Note how these confessions form the basis of the Ten Commandments:

1.      I have not done iniquity.
2.      I have not robbed with violence.
3.      I have not done violence to any man.
4.      I have not committed theft.
5.      I have slain neither man nor woman.
6.      I have not made light the bushel.
7.      I have not acted deceitfully.
8.      I have not purloined the things which belong to God.
9.      I have not uttered falsehood.
10.     I have not carried off goods by force.
11.     I have not uttered vile words.
12.     I have not carried off food by force.
13.     I have not acted deceitfully.
14.     I have not lost my temper and become angry.
15.     I have invaded no man's land.
16.     I have not slaughtered animals which are the possession of God.
17.     I have not laid waste the lands which have been ploughed.
18.     I have not pried into matters to make mischief.
19.     I have not set my mouth in motion against any man.
20.     I have not given way to wrath without due cause.
21.     I have not committed fornication, and I have not committed sodomy.
22.     I have not polluted myself.
23.     I have not lain with the wife of a man.
24.     I have not made any man to be afraid.
25.     I have not made my speech to burn with anger.

---

[96] Cyril Aldred, *Akhenaten: King of Egypt.* (London: Thames & Hudson, 1988), p. 239.

26.    I have not made myself deaf unto the words of right and truth.

27.    I have not made another person to weep.

28.    I have not uttered blasphemies.

29.    I have not acted with violence.

30.    I have not acted without due consideration.

31.    I have not pierced my skin and I have not taken vengeance on the God.

32.    I have not multiplied my speech beyond what should be said.

33.    I have not committed fraud, and I have not looked upon evil.

34.    I have never uttered curses against the king.

35.    I have not fouled running water.

36.    I have not exalted my speech.

37.    I have not uttered curses against God.

38.    I have not behaved with insolence.

39.    I have not been guilty of favoritism.

40.    I have not increased my wealth except by means of such things as are mine own possessions.

41.    I have not uttered curses against that which belongeth to God and is with me.

42.    I have not thought scorn of the god of the city.[97]

Now compare these to Moses' Ten Commandments:

1.    Thou shalt have no other gods before me.

2.    Thou shalt not make unto thee any graven image, or any likeness of any thing that is in heaven above, or that is in the earth beneath, or that is in the water under the earth: Thou shalt not bow down thyself to them, nor serve them: for I the LORD thy God am a jealous God, visiting the iniquity of the fathers upon the children unto the third and fourth generation of them that hate me; And showing mercy unto thousands of them that love me, and keep my commandments.

3.    Thou shalt not take the name of the LORD thy God in vain; for the LORD will not hold him guiltless that taketh his name in vain.

4.    Remember the sabbath day, to keep it holy. Six days shalt thou labor, and do all they work: But the seventh day is the sabbath of the LORD thy God: in it thou shalt not do any work, thou, nor thy son, nor thy daughter, thy manservant, nor thy maidservant, nor thy cattle, nor thy stranger that is within thy gates: For in six days the LORD made heaven and earth, the sea, and all that in them is, and rested the seventh day: wherefore the LORD blessed the sabbath day, and hallowed it.

5.    Honour thy father and thy mother: that thy days may be long upon the land

---

[97] A. S. Mercantante, *Who's Who in Egyptian Mythology,* s.v. "Negative Confessions," (New York: Potter, 1978).

which the LORD thy God giveth thee.

6.     Thou shall not kill.

7.     Thou shalt not commit adultery.

8.     Thou shalt not steal.

9.     Thou shalt not bear false witness against thy neighbor.

10.    Thou shalt not covet thy neighbor's house, thou shalt not covet thy neighbor's wife, nor his manservant, nor his maidservant, nor his ox, nor his ass, nor anything that is thy neighbor's.[98]

From these principles we can see an interesting correlation. The first two commandments reflect the heart of Akhenaten's monotheistic beliefs. Upon review of the twenty-eighth, thirty-seventh and forty-first Negative Confessions, we find a source for the Third Commandment. Further review of these confessions demonstrates a source for the sixth through tenth commandments. It is only the fourth and fifth commandments that show no origin in the Negative Confessions. We find in both the Negative Confessions and the Sixth through Tenth Commandments the basis of moral principles in most civilizations and cultures.

Further support for this paradigm of Moses as a potential king in line for the Egyptian throne comes from the Bible's references to a close tie between the Hebrews and Shechem following the Exodus. Shechem was a powerful Canaante tribe at that time. King Labaya of Shechem rebelled against Egypt and established a small kingdom in central Palestine during Akhenaten's tenure. Horemheb failed to reestablish control over this religion, as evidenced by Sethos' I trouble in recapturing southern Palestine. Shechem remained very anti-Egypt.

We find in Exodus, And it came to pass in process of time, that the king of Egypt died; and the children of Israel sighed by reason of the bondage, and they cried, and their cry came up unto God by reason of the bondage.[99] The king who died as Horemheb, who was very much persecuting the followers of Akhenaten. Whereas the Bible refers to these people as the children of Israel, Egyptian scribes described them as the victims of the followers of Aten.

What we have following Horemheb's death is a group of persecuted monotheistic Egyptians, a demolished capital city that was its religious center, a dispensed population of heretics, many Egyptian soldiers banished to the Sinai desert and powerful nations like Shechem openly hostile to Egypt's authority. Could not this combination of Shechem rebels and Aten followers rise up under the only Aten religious/political leader, namely Moses, and attempt a coup?

Manetho's reference to Osarseph (Moses) entering into an alliance with the

---

[98] Harper's Bible Dictionary, s.v. *Ten Commandments*. (New York: Harper & Row, 1975).

[99] Exodus 2:23

Hyksos can be any group of Syrian or Canaanite chieftains. Jerusalem is the source of these allies, according to Josephus. Shechem's kingdom extended to the borders of Jerusalem, so much so that Josephus reported that the rulers of Jerusalem were very much concerned about this presence. We also know that Shechem maintained close ally relationship with the Hebrews during the latter's conquest of Canaan.

Another interesting parallel exists between the Egyptian and biblical accounts of the Exodus. In the Egyptian version, the Egyptian throne is stolen from the rightful ruler and the evil king persecutes the Egyptians. The pharaoh (rightful ruler) is forced to flee Egypt, has a son, Ramesses ("Rameses also called Sethos") born in secrecy and is hidden by his mother. As an adult this now grown child defeats the evil king and liberates his people.

The biblical account states that Moses was hidden shortly after his birth and later raised as the adopted son of the pharaoh, and a possible heir to the throne. After killing an Egyptian soldier he is forced to flee, but returns to confront an evil pharaoh and lead his people out of Egypt to freedom.

We can see an obvious common theme in these two stories. The fact the identities of the hero and villain have been reversed, with the other factors nearly identical, reflects upon a common source.

We can look to the Seth murdering Osiris and Horus avenging his father's death theme of the Osirian cult as this antecedent. This story originated on Mu, as we have discussed in chapter 2, with Hermes keeping it alive in Atlantis and ancient Egypt. The displaced king in the Egyptian version is Osiris, whereas Seth is the usurping king and Horus the hero who defeats the usurping king.

## WAS MOSES HERMES?

I have already stated that Hermes was not Moses. Ben's case establishes that conclusion, but so does several other time traveler revelations from different patients.

What the biblical scholars have to say on this topic is most enlightening. We can trace the origin of the name Moses to the Egyptian word *ms*, which means "is born." The anglicized version of the Hellenistic translation of *mosis* gives us Moses.

My point here is that, contrary to the Bible, Moses is not a Hebrew name. Why would an Egyptian princess give an infant a Hebrew name when an order was issued by the pharaoh to kill all first born Hebrew male children at birth?

The Egyptian custom was to precede the name of a member of royalty with that of a god. Osarseph (Moses) in Josephus' account of Manetho's records shows that Osarseph (named after the god Osiris) changed his name to ms (Moses) to follow suit with Akhenaten's monotheism.

We know that Akhenaten worshipped the god Re-Herakhte. There was an important official in Akhenaten's court named Ramose. Moses may have been Ramose, but he could have been Hormose or Harmose. These names would appear in Egyptian as Rms or Hrms. There are no vowels in the Egyptian language.[100]

The problem some scholars have with the Moses/Hermes question relates to the writings of the second century B.C. historian Artapanus. This historian stated that Moses was honored for his skills in hieroglyphics when he was in the Egyptian court by being given the name Hermes.

The problem with this story is that the Egyptian priests in Moses' time would never have called him Hermes, but Thoth. Furthermore, any such name of another god would be blasphemy to Akhenaten. Artapanus probably saw the name *Hrms* and added the two e's to obtain Hermes (it should have been Hermose). This no doubt excited him and led to his erroneous conclusion. I can just imagine his exuberance over uncovering the one and only Hermes in a pharaoh's court and having him be an equally famous Hebrew prophet Moses.

## THE TEN PLAGUES

An archaeological find known as the Ipuwer Papyrus, or "Admonitions of an Egyptian Sage," dates from the Nineteenth Dynasty, but its writing embraces earlier styles indicating that it was copied from previous works. This document describes a period of anarchy that many scholars refer to as the First Intermediate Period.[101]

Compare sections of this papyrus to those of Exodus:[102]

**Papyrus:** *Indeed the river is blood, yet the men drink of it. Men [shrink] from human beings and thirst after water.*

**Exodus:** *And all the waters that were in the river were turned into blood. . . . The Egyptians could not drink of the water of the river; and there was blood throughout all the land of Egypt.*[103]

**Papyrus:** *Indeed, gates, columns, and [walls] are burnt up. . . . Behold, the fire has gone up on high, and its burning goes forth against the enemies of the land.*

**Exodus:** *[A]nd the fire ran along upon the ground.*[104]

---

[100] Cyril Aldred, op. cit.

[101] R. O. Faulkner, trans. "Admonitions of an Egyptian Sage" in *The Literature of Ancient Egypt*, ed. William Kelly Simpson (New Haven and London: Yale University Press, 1972), 210.

[102] All Papyrus quotes are from Faulkner, *The Literature of Ancient Egypt.*

[103] Exod. 7:20-21.

[104] Exod. 9:23.

**Papyrus:** *Indeed, trees are felled and branches are stripped off.*

**Exodus:** *And the hail smote every herb of the field and brake every tree of the field.*[105]

**Papyrus:** *Neither fruit nor herbage can be found . . . everywhere barley has perished.*

**Exodus:** *And there remained not any green thing in the trees, or in the herbs of the fields, through all the land of Egypt.*[106]

**Papyrus:** *[The land] is not bright because of it.*

**Exodus:** *And there was a thick darkness in all the land of Egypt.*[107]

**Papyrus:** *Indeed, all animals, their hearts weep; cattle moan because of the state of the land.*

**Exodus:** *And all the cattle of Egypt died.*[108]

**Papyrus:** *Indeed men are few, and he who places his brother in the ground is everywhere. . . . Indeed [hearts] are violent, pestilence is throughout the land, blood is everywhere, death is not lacking, and the mummy-cloth speaks even before one comes near it.*

**Exodus:** *And all the firstborn in the land of Egypt shall die. . . .*[109]

I must point out that most scholars don't agree that the Exodus rendition of the Ten Plagues originated from the Ipuwer Papyrus. You can decide for yourself whether you agree with the scientific establishment.

## ATLANTEAN SEA PEOPLES RECORDED IN ANCIENT EGYPT

Archeologists have discovered ancient Egyptian inscriptions describing a powerful force of Greek warriors and other aggressive invaders attempting to establish themselves in several city-states along the Canaanite coast. These Sea Peoples, as they were called, attacked Egypt. The Merneptah stele we discussed earlier describes such a confrontation.

The Philistines were the most powerful and famous of these invaders. The ancient Jews formed a confederation with the other Sea People states and local Canaanites, and out of this confederation came a new nation of Israel. The Dan tribe of Israel may have arisen from the Denyen branch of the Sea Peoples. Samson was the most famous Danite in Hebrew history.[110]

The Hebrew tribe of Asher encompassed territory occupied by the southern

---

[105] Exod. 9:25.
[106] Exod. 10:15.
[107] Exod. 10:22.
[108] Exod. 9:6.
[109] Exod. 11:15.
[110] N. K. Sandars, *The Sea Peoples*. (London: Thames and Hudson, 1985).

part of Phoenicia. We have already discussed that the Phoenicians were displaced Atlanteans. It is also known that the Sea Peoples were aggressive and fierce warriors, another Atlantean trait.

In reality these Sea Peoples were all Atlanteans. They were either exiled from other civilizations, or simply exercising their seafaring and militaristic skills at attempting to obtain a piece of Egypt and another homeland. Several patients have described these Sea Peoples as direct Atlantean offshoots.

The Twelve Tribes of Israel never existed. An Egyptian mythology was the source of the *Old Testament*. Moses was a native born Egyptian who served as Pharaoh Akhenaten's chief priest. The first Israelites were persecuted Egyptians and followers of Akhenaten. Lastly, the Exodus took place during the reigns of Ramesses I and Sethos I. These are documented historical facts.

The only people who will resent my data and conclusions have a prejudicial personal or ideological antipathy to a Moses association with Akhenaten and the startling fact that basically all of the Jews we see today can trace their bloodline back to ancient Egypt.

The main reason the Bible is so inaccurate is due to the long period of time that elapsed when it was compiled, along with its tendency to use tradition and myths instead of historical fact as its basis. Local cultural influences and the destruction of the northern kingdom of Israel, coupled with the Babylonian captivity of the Judah kingdom in the south did not help matters.

## WAS MOSES DIVINELY INSPIRED?

My conclusion to Moses' true role may surprise you based on the data I have presented. I do not feel Moses was a mere follower of Akhenaten. Yes, he most definitely supported his pharaoh, but his belief in God was far greater than his relationship with his lifetime friend and king.

Karmically, if Akhenaten was supposed to rid Egypt of its polytheistic beliefs he would have succeeded. Hermes advised Akhenaten as well as Moses. The pharaoh's death set the karmic mechanism in motion for Moses to establish monotheism.

Moses was divinely inspired. He was a talented scribe, brilliant scholar and a moral leader. The universe showed him that Egypt was not the place to be. When he heard the cry of his persecuted people, this prophet waited for a signal from God to lead them to freedom.

When Horemheb died in 1315 B.C., Ramesses I was appointed to the throne. Ramesses was a northerner, not from Thebes, and represented a worshiper of the god Seth. He named his son Sethos I in honor of Seth.

The sign Osarsepth (Moses) was looking for was a Theban priesthood unhappy with the northern, Seth-worshipping pharaoh. Moses formed an alliance with the kingdom of Shechem in the north and Ethiopia in the south. He most likely went to Ethiopia first when he fled Egypt, as we know he had an Ethiopian wife.

A two-front war was launched by Moses. The Shechemites invaded Egypt from the north and Ethiopians assaulted from the south. As Egypt was placed in a stalemate position, a peace was negotiated with Moses allowing him and his people to leave Egypt safely. This departure was the Exodus.

The now divinely inspired, but politically defeated, Moses led his people to the Promised Land, that was never really promised. Later on alliances were formed between the Israelites in central Canaan with the leaders of several northern city-states, some of which were Sea Peoples. The nation of Israel grew out of this alliance and became the foundation for what later would be known as Israel's tribal confederation.

## HERMES AND OTHER MASTERS

Moses wasn't the only Master or sage that Hermes worked with. When Jesus came to Egypt as a youth, Hermes tutored him. He also assisted Jesus up to the end of the latter's life. Hermes worked with Mohammed, Buddha, Krishna and most of the sages we know of.

The question exists how much of the experience of these Masters was due to time traveler communication versus true contact with God? Although it is true that Hermes and other time travelers can communicate with us in our dreams and create any "special effects" they desire (burning bushes, parting of the Red Sea? and so on), these chrononauts most definitely believe in God and attempt to guide us in our spiritual growth.

This is not a "smoke and mirrors" paradigm. My work with time traveler abductees has convinced me there truly is a God, one God. I cannot state just how much of these miracles and revelations are due to divine contact versus time traveler intervention. Most of these reports are probably divinely inspired. All I know is we would be far worse off without the assistance and guidance of these time travelers, especially Hermes.

# CHAPTER 7  HYPNOSIS EXERCISES
## THE HIGHER CHAKRAS LINK

Throughout this book I have promoted the concept of spiritual growth and eventual ascension as the ultimate goal for our sojourn on the physical plane. We owe a great debt to ancient Egypt in establishing many techniques and principles in this regard.

The Hermetic tradition is the foundation for reincarnation and specific beliefs in the afterlife, as far as our written records are concerned. Before I present methods to access the Higher Self and travel back in time and/or leave the physical body, as it is necessary to align the four upper *chakras* (energy centers) of the astral body. I refer to this technique as *higher chakras* link. It functions to maximize and self-hypnosis, meditative, yoga or other alpha approach to spiritual growth.

There are seven major chakras located along the spinal cord of the astral body. A chakra is constantly spinning and functions to recycle the flow of energy to our soul or subconscious. These swirling mini blackholes may be blocked and out of balance. That condition comprises our spiritual growth and may even result in our susceptibility to a psychic attack. A more thorough treatment of this topic is presented in my book *Protected By The Light*.[111]

1.      Sit comfortably or lie down. Breathe deeply and apply protection. Focus your attention on the Third Eye region of your forehead. This is located between your eyes and is the 6th chakra.

2.      Imagine a glowing white light as you inhale being drawn in this Third Eye area and creating a sensation of warmth. Hold this focus for a count of eight. Now exhale and repeat this procedure two more times.

3.      As you inhale again see this glowing white light being drawn up to the crown chakra located at the top of the head. See a rainbow bridge being formed here. Hold this focus on the rainbow bridge for a count of eight at the crown chakra, exhale and repeat this procedure two more times.

4.      Visualize the rainbow bridge moving into the Third Eye chakra and finally into the throat (5th) chakra. As you inhale feel this warm sensation permeating the throat. Hold this focus of the rainbow bridge in the throat chakra for a count of 8, exhale and repeat this procedure two more times.

5.      Imagine this rainbow bridge moving from the throat chakra into the heart (4th) chakra. This is the area in the middle of the chest at the level of the heart.

---

[111] B. Goldberg, *Protected By The Light*, op. cit.

6.    As you inhale feel this warm sensation permeating the heart chakra.  Hold this focus for a count of 8, exhale and repeat this procedure two more times.
7.    Finally, inhale deeply and hold your breath for a count of eight, and as you hold your breath visually link up the rainbow bridges in your heart, throat, Third Eye and crown chakras with a band of glowing white light.  Feel this link as a warm, tingly sensation.  Exhale slowly and repeat this procedure two more times.

    You have activated your higher spiritual centers for receiving communication from your Higher Self and raising the quality of your soul's energy.

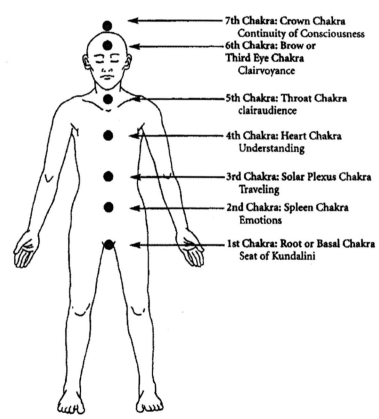

7th Chakra: Crown Chakra
Continuity of Consciousness
6th Chakra: Brow or
Third Eye Chakra
Clairvoyance

5th Chakra: Throat Chakra
clairaudience

4th Chakra: Heart Chakra
Understanding

3rd Chakra: Solar Plexus Chakra
Traveling

2nd Chakra: Spleen Chakra
Emotions

1st Chakra: Root or Basal Chakra
Seat of Kundalini

**Figure 5** The Seven Major Chakras

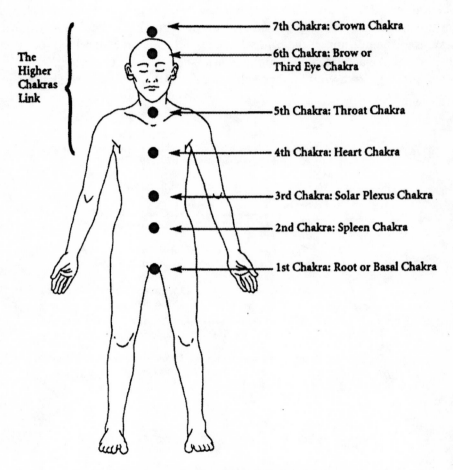

The Higher Chakras Link

7th Chakra: Crown Chakra

6th Chakra: Brow or Third Eye Chakra

5th Chakra: Throat Chakra

4th Chakra: Heart Chakra

3rd Chakra: Solar Plexus Chakra

2nd Chakra: Spleen Chakra

1st Chakra: Root or Basal Chakra

**Figure 6** The Higher Chakras Link

# SUPERCONSCIOUS MIND TAP

The main technique I use in my Los Angeles hypnotherapy practice is something I call the *superconscious mind tap*[112] or *cleansing*. Simply stated, this is a technique designed to train the user to access their Higher Self (superconscious mind) and raise the quality of their soul's energy as a result of exposure to the perfect energy of the Higher Self.

In removing dysfunctional behavior and traits, something I term *self-defeating sequences*,[113] it is not necessary to know or understand the origin of this issue. All that is required is to tap into the divine spark within us known as the Higher Self.

There are many advantages of using this cleansing approach. Some of these are

1.      Receiving spiritual guidance from your Higher Self or Masters and Guides.
2.      Scanning past lives, the future of your current lifetime, and future lifetimes.
3.      Contacting departed loved ones.
4.      Removing attached entities.
5.      Spiritual protection from negative projection techniques.
6.      Contacting the souls of unborn children.
7.      Raising your soul's energy in preparation for ascension.

With this background you are now ready to experience your own Higher Self.

Now listen very carefully. I want you to imagine a bright white light coming down from above and entering the top of your head. Filling your entire body. See it, feel it and it becomes reality. Now imagine an aura of pure white light emanating from your heart region. Again surrounding your entire body. Protecting you. See it, feel it and it becomes reality. Now only your masters and guides and highly evolved loving entities who mean you well will be able to influence you during this or any other hypnotic session. You are totally protected by this aura of pure white light.

In a few moments I am going to count from 1 to 20. As I do so you will feel yourself rising up to the superconscious mind level where you will be able to receive information from your Masters and Guides. You will also be able to overview all of your past, present and future lives. Number 1 rising up. 2, 3, 4 rising higher. 5, 6, 7, letting information flow. 8, 9, 10, you are half way there. 1, 12, 13, feel yourself rising even higher. 14, 15, 16, almost there. 17, 18, 19

---

[112] B. Goldberg, *Soul Healing.* (St. Paul: Llewellyn, 1996).
[113] B. Goldberg, *Past Lives-Future Lives.* (New York: Ballantine, 1988).

number 20 you are there.  Take a moment and orient yourself to the superconscious mind level.

## PLAY NEW AGE MUSIC FOR 1 MINUTE

You may now ask yourself any question about any past, present or future life issue.  Or, you may contact any of your guides or departed loved ones from this level.  You may explore your relationship with any person.  Remember, your superconscious mind level is all knowledgeable and has access to your Akashic Records.

Now slowly and carefully state your desire to information or an experience and let this superconscious mind level work for you.

## PLAY NEW AGE MUSIC FOR 8 MINUTES

You have done very well.  Now I want you to further open up the channels of communication by removing any obstacles and allowing yourself to receive information and experiences that will directly apply to and help better your present lifetime.  Allow yourself to receive more advanced and more specific information from your Higher Self and Masters and Guides to raise your frequency and improve your karmic subcycle.  Do this now.

## PLAY NEW AGE MUSIC FOR 8 MINUTES

Alright now.  Sleep now and rest.  You did very very well.  Listen very carefully.  I'm gong to count forwards now from 1 - 5.  When I reach the count of 5 you will back in the present, you will be able to remember everything you experienced and re-experienced you'll feel very relaxed refreshed, you'll be able to do whatever you have to planned for the rest of the day or evening.  you'll feel very positive about what you've just experienced and very motivated about your confidence and ability to play this tape again to experience the superconscious mind level.  Alright now.  1 very very deep, 2 you're getting a little bit lighter, 3 you're getting much much lighter, 4 very very light, 5 awaken.  Wide awake and refreshed.

If you would like to explore the specific origins of a particular issue, try this modification of the superconscious mind tap.

Now listen very carefully.  I want you to imagine a bright white light coming down from above and entering the top of your head.  Filling your entire body.  See it, feel it and it becomes reality.  Now imagine an aura of pure white light emanating from your heart region.  Again surrounding your entire body. Protecting you.  See it, feel it and it becomes reality.  Now only your Higher Self, Masters and Guides and highly evolved loving entities who mean you well will be able to influence you during this or any other hypnotic session.  You are totally protected by this aura of pure white light.

In a few moments I am going to count from 1 to 20.  As I do so you will feel yourself rising up to the superconscious mind level where you will be able to receive information from your Higher Self and Masters and Guides. You will also be able to overview all of your past, present and future lives. Number 1 rising up. 2, 3, 4 rising higher. 5, 6, 7, letting information flow. 8, 9, 10, you are half way there. 11, 12, 13, feel yourself rising even higher. 14, 15, 16, almost there. 17, 18, 19 number 20 you are there. Take a moment and orient yourself to the superconscious mind level.

## PLAY NEW AGE MUSIC FOR 1 MINUTE

You are now in a deep hypnotic trance and from this superconscious mind level there exists a complete understanding and resolution of the

_____.

You are in complete control and able to access this limitless power of your superconscious mind. I want you to be open and flow with this experience. You are always protected by the white light.

At this time I would like you to ask your Higher Self to explore the origin of

_____.

Trust your Higher Self and your own ability to allow any thoughts, feelings or impressions to come into your subconscious mind concerning this issue. Do this now.

## PLAY NEW AGE MUSIC FOR 3 MINUTES

Now I would like you to let go of this situation, regardless of how simple or complicated it may seem. At this time I want you to visualize yourself in your current life and consciousness free of this issue. Perceive yourself in your daily life now functioning in a happy and empowered manner without any recurrence of this issue. Do this now.

## PLAY NEW AGE MUSIC FOR 4 MINUTES

Alright now. Sleep now and rest. You did very very well. Listen very carefully. I'm going to count forwards now from 1 -5. When I reach the count of 5 you will be back I the present, you will be able to remember everything you experienced and re-experienced you'll feel very relaxed refreshed, you'll be able to do whatever you have to planned for the rest of the day or evening. You'll feel very positive about what you've just experienced and very motivated about your confidence and ability to play this tape again to experience the superconscious mind level. Alright now. 1 very very deep, 2 you're getting a little bit lighter, 3 you're getting much much lighter, 4 very very light, 5 awaken. Wide awake and refreshed.

## PAST LIFE IN EGYPT EXPLORATION

I am not a psychic past life reader.  My approach to eliciting previous incarnations from my patients is to use hypnosis to train them to travel back in time to one of their previous lifetimes.

People often ask me if they lived in a certain country or period of history.  The short answer to that query is that we have all lived in ancient Egypt, Mu and Atlantis.  Out of the 35,000 past life regressions I have conducted on more than 12,000 patients, an Egyptian experience will always be depicted if I do enough of them.

Try this simple self-hypnosis exercise to review one or more of your Egyptian past lives.  I have included instructions to help you relive abductions, just in case the ETs or time travelers paid you a visit.

Now listen very carefully.  I want you to imagine a bright white light coming down from above and entering the top of your head.  Filling your entire body.  See it, feel it and it becomes reality.  Now imagine an aura of pure white light emanating from your heart region.  Again surrounding your entire body.  Protecting you.  See it, feel it and it becomes reality.  Now only your maters and guides and highly evolved loving entities who mean you well will be able to influence you during this or any other hypnotic session.  You are totally protected by this aura of pure white light.  Now listen very carefully in a few minutes I'm going to be counting backwards from 20 - 1.  As I count backwards from 20 - 1 you are going to perceive yourself moving through a very deep and dark tunnel.  The tunnel will get lighter and lighter and at the very end of this tunnel there will be a door with a bright white light above it.  When you walk through this door you will be in a past life scene.  You're going to re-experience one of your past lives in Ancient Egypt.  You'll be moving to an event that will be significant in explaining who you are, where you are and why you are there.  I want you to realize that if you feel uncomfortable either physically, mentally or emotionally at any time you can awaken yourself from this hypnotic trance by simply counting forward  from 1 - 5.  You will always associate my voice as a friendly voice in trance.  You will be able to let your mind review back into its memory banks and follow the instructions of perceiving the scenes of your own Egyptian past lives and following along as I instruct.  You'll find yourself being able to get deeper and quicker in hypnotic trances each time a you practice with this tape or other methods of self-hypnosis.  When you hear me say the words "sleep now and rest" I want you to immediately detach yourself form any scene you are experiencing.  You will be able to wait for further instructions.

You absolutely have the power and ability to go back into a past life as your subconscious minds memory banks remembers everything you've ever experienced in all your past lives as well as your present life.  I want you to relive these

144

Egyptian past life events only as a neutral observer without feeling or emotion just as if you were watching a television show. I want you to choose a past life now in each you've lived to at least the age of thirty.

I'm going to count backwards now from 20 - 1. As I do so I want you to feel yourself moving into the past. You'll find yourself moving through a pitch black tunnel which will get lighter and lighter as I count backwards. When I reach the count of one you will have opened up a door with a bright white light above it and walked into a past life scene. You will once again become yourself at about the age of 15 in a previous lifetime in ancient Egypt. Now listen carefully - - - Number 20 you're moving into a very deep dark tunnel surrounded by grass and trees and your favorite flowers and very very inviting as you feel very calm and comfortable about moving into the tunnel. 19, 18, you're moving backwards in time back, back, 17, 16, 15, the tunnel is becoming lighter now. You can make out your arms and legs and you realize that you are walking through this tunnel and you're moving backwards in time. 14, 13, 12, moving so far back, back, back, 11, 10, 9, you're now so far back - you're over half way there the tunnel is much lighter. You can see around you and you can now make out the door in front of you with the bright white light above it. 8, 7, 6, standing in front of the door now feeling comfortable and feeling positive and confident about your ability to move into this past life scene. 5, 4, now walk up to the door, put your hand on the doorknob, the bright white light is so bright it's hard to look at. 3, open the door 2, step through the door 1, move into the past life scene. Focus carefully on what you perceive before you. Take a few minutes now and I want you to let everything become crystal clear. The information flowing into your awareness the scene becoming visual and visible. Just let yourself orient yourself to your new environment. Focus on it. Take a few moments and listen to my instructions. Let the impression form. First what do you see and what are you doing? Are you male or female? Look at your feet first - what type of footwear or shoes are you wearing? Now move up the body and see exactly how you are clothed. How are you dressed? How old are you? What are you doing right now? What is happening around you? Be able to describe the situation you find yourself in. Are you outdoors or indoors? Is it day or night? Is it hot or cold? What country or land do you live in or are you from? Focus on one of your Egyptian lives at this time. Now focus on this one carefully - what do people call you? What is the year? Take a few moments number may appear right in front of your awareness. You will be informed of exactly what year this is. Take a few more moments and let any additional information crystalize and become clear into your awareness about the events that you find yourself in as well as yourself. Take a few moments. Let any additional information be made clear to you.

**PLAY NEW AGE MUSIC FOR 3 MINUTES**

Very good now. Listen very carefully to my voice now. Sleep now and rest. Detach yourself from this scene just for a moment. I'm going to be counting forward from 1 - 5. When I reach the count of five you're going to be moving forward now to a significant event that's going to occur in this lifetime which will affect you personally. It will also most probably affect those close to you - it may involve your parents, friends, people who are close to you in this lifetime. If you have ever been abducted in this past life, move to this incident now. Focus carefully now. Sleep now and rest and listen now as I count forward from 1 - 5. On the count of five you will be moving forward in time to a significant event that is going to occur to you. 1 moving forward, slowing, carefully, comfortably, 2 feeling good as you move forward in time, 3 half way there, 4 almost there, 5. Now again focus on yourself and the environment you find yourself in. What are you doing now and why are you in this environment? Has anything changed since I last spoke with you? What is happening around you? Are there any other people around you who are important to you? If there are, are they male or female? Are they friends or relatives? How do they relate to you? Why are they important to you? Focus on your clothes now starting with your feet first. How are you dressed? Are you dressed any differently then when I last spoke with you? Move all the way up your body and perceive how you are dressed. Then look at the people next to you - are they dressed any differently? About how old are you now? Focus on that for a moment - a number will appear to you - about how old are you right now? Where exactly are you? Are you outdoors or indoors? Is it day or night? What season is this? What kind of occupation do you have? What do you do to pass the time? What do you do with your day? Focus on how you spend your time in this Egyptian life. Now I want you to focus on an event that's going to be happening right now that you find yourself right in the middle of. I want you to take this event right through to completion. I want you to spend a few moments and whatever this event is I want you to carry it through to completion. If this is an abduction let all of the details unfold safely and comfortably. Take a few moments and carry this event through to completion.

**PLAY NEW AGE MUSIC FOR 3 MINUTES**

All right now. Sleep now and rest. Detach yourself form this scene that you are experiencing and listen to my voice again. You're going to be moving forward now by a period of a minimum of 3 years. It can be as long as necessary but a minimum of three years. You will not have died. It will be at least 3 years further in time. Now I want you to move forward to a significant event which is going to affect not only the kind of work that you do but also yourself personally. It may even be another abduction. I want you to move forward to this very significant time which is going to be at least three years from now. On the count of five move forward very carefully and comfortably. 1 moving forward, 2 moving further forward, 3 half way there, 4 almost there 5. Now perceive what you perceive around you. What has transpired last since I saw you? Focus on yourself first. Perceive where you are, how you are dressed, what environment and who are you with. Take a few moments and let this information crystalize and become clear into your awareness.

## PLAY NEW AGE MUSIC FOR 3 MINUTES

Alright now. Sleep now and rest. Detach yourself form this scene. We're going to be moving forward again on the count of five. This time you're going to be moving forward to a scene which is going to signify or illustrate the maximum achievements that you accomplished in this lifetime. This scene will illustrate the maximum accomplishments personally or professionally. You'll be surrounded by the people that affect you most in this lifetime. You will be achieving the maximum amount of success or goals or whatever else you wanted to accomplish in this lifetime. You will remember any communication from any strange or more advanced beings. Move forward to this maximum accomplishment in this lifetime, on the count of five. 1 moving forward slowly, carefully, comfortably, 2 moving further forward, 3 halfway there, 4 almost there 5. Now take a few moments and see where you find yourself. What is your environment? What has happened and why this time of your life is so important to you? Focus on it and see what you've accomplished and let all the information be made clear to you.

## PLAY NEW AGE MUSIC FOR 3 MINUTES

Now that you've been able to perceive this particular period of your life I want you to be able to evaluate your life. I want you to find out what goals you were suppose to accomplish and what you actually did accomplish. What do you feel that you learned from this lifetime? What do you feel that you have gained from this lifetime - in your own personal goals, family life, relationships. Let the information flow - what did you gain? Now let's focus on what you weren't able to achieve. Focus on what you felt you would have liked more time for. What do you feel that you just weren't able to accomplish and why? Focus on that. Let the information flow. Now remember in this particular lifetime you are still alive now. I want you now to focus upon your activities whatever you're involved in this particular scene to evaluate why this lifetime was important to you. What necessary or needed experience did you gain from this lifetime? Focus on this now. Let the information flow into your awareness.

## PLAY NEW AGE MUSIC FOR 3 MINUTES

Alright now. Sleep now and rest. You did very very well. Listen very carefully. I'm going to count forwards now from 1 -5, one more time. This time when I reach 5 you will be back in the present, you will be able to remember everything you experienced and re-experienced you'll feel very relaxed refreshed, you'll be able to do whatever you have to planned for the rest of the day or evening. You'll feel very positive about what you've just experienced and very motivated about your confidence and ability to play this time again to experience additional lifetimes. Alright now. 1 very very deep, 2 you're getting a little bit lighter, 3 you're getting much much lighter, 4 very very light, 5 awaken. Wide awake and refreshed.

This script may be modified to eliminate the references to ancient Egypt and used to explore any of your past lives. Try this method to explore your earlier incarnation in Mu and Atlantis. The best way to use these self-hypnosis exercises is to make tapes from the scripts I present.

## ASTRAL PROJECTION

The ancient Egyptians were very much involved with out-of-body techniques. Their term *ba* was used to express the concept we refer to as the soul. A human-headed bird was portrayed as this component of our consciousness.

Here is a simple technique that will train you to safely leave and return to your physical body. While out-of-the body you may venture to the Upper Astral plane and sample what it will be like when you eventually cross into spirit from this life following clinical death. One advantage to this approach is that it is evidence of life after death.

For the best results I recommend practicing this self-hypnosis technique in a quiet, darkened and comfortable room.

Let yourself relax completely . . . and breathe quickly . . . in . . . and out.

And as you do so . . . you will gradually sink into a deeper, deeper sleep.

And as you sink into this deeper, deeper sleep . . . I want you to concentrate on the sensations you can feel in your left hand and arm.

You will feel that your left hand is gradually becoming lighter and lighter.

It feels just as though your wrists were tied to a balloon . . . as if it were gradually pulled up . . . higher and higher . . . away from the chair.

It wants to rise up . . . into the air . . . towards the ceiling.

Let it rise . . . higher and higher.

Just like a cork . . . floating on water.

And, as it floats up . . . into the air . . . your whole body feels more and more relaxed . . . heavier and heavier . . . and you are slowing sinking into a deeper, deeper sleep.

Your left hand feels even lighter and lighter.

Rising up into the air . . . as if it were being pulled towards the ceiling.

Lighter and lighter . . . light as a feather.

Breathe deeply . . . and let yourself relax completely.

And as your hand gets lighter and lighter . . . and rises higher and higher into the air . . . your body is feeling heavier and heavier . . . and you are falling into a deep, deep sleep.

Now your whole arm, from the shoulder to the wrist, is becoming lighter and lighter.

It is leaving the chair . . . and floating upwards . . . into the air.

Up it comes . . . into the air, . . . higher and higher.

let it rise . . . higher and higher, . . . higher and higher.

It is slowly floating up . . . into the air . . . and as it does so . . . you are falling into a deeper, deeper trance.

Visualize a floating sensation spreading throughout your entire body. Continue breathing deeply and feel your soul leaving your body through the top of your head, as it rises up beyond the earth plane to the astral plane.

Note the warm feeling now spreading and permeating throughout your entire body. Allow yourself to receive the guidance and love from your Higher Self and spirit guides.

## PLAY NEW AGE MUSIC FOR 2 MINUTES

Experience a feeling of total love and peace. Let yourself immerse your complete awareness in a sense of balance and centering of your soul's energy. Now we're going to send your astral body to the upper astral plane or beyond. If you would like to explore the causal, mental, etheric or even the soul plane, just concentrate on the name of this dimension.

As I count forward from 1 to 10 on the count of 10 you will arrive at your destination. 1, 2, 3 moving toward this plane. 4, 5, half way there. 6, 7, 8, almost there. 9, 10, you are there.

Now begin exploring this dimension at your leisure. Record everything you see, hear, touch, taste and feel in your subconscious, to be remembered later. Do this now.

## PLAY NEW AGE MUSIC FOR 3 MINUTES

Now begin your trip back to Earth by first entering a brilliant white light you now see before you.

Descend back to your room and merge with your physical body.

Note the warm feeling now spreading and permeating throughout your entire body. Stay with this feeling for a few moments.

Alright now. Sleep now and rest. You did very well. Listen very carefully. I'm going to count forwards now from 1 - 5. When I reach the count of 5 you will be back in the body you will be able to remember everything you experienced and re-experienced you'll feel very relaxed refreshed, you'll be able to do whatever you have to planned for the rest of the day or evening. You'll feel very positive about what you've just experienced and very motivated about your confidence and ability to play this tape again to experience leaving your physical body safely. Alright now. 1 very very deep, 2 you're getting a little bit lighter, 3 you're getting much much lighter, 4 very very light, 5 awaken. Wide awake and refreshed.

When you use this technique there are some considerations you need to be aware of:

- Don't become frustrated if you experience your mind wandering during this contemplation.
- Remove any expectation of actually feeling your two bodies separating. What is more likely to occur is a shift in your awareness during the early stages of your first sleep cycle of being out-of-the body.
- Eliminate the tendency to expect a full OBE with this approach. Just relax and enjoy this experience.

## AN EXERCISE TO ACCESS THE AKASHIC RECORDS

All of the records of both our individual past, parallel and future lives, as well as that of the universe, are stored in something known as the *Akashic Records*. The specific location of these memories is on the causal plane[114], but we may access them on any dimension.

When you receive data from the Akashic Records, it may be perceived by you audibly through sounds, visually by way of colors or impressions, or simply as thoughts. Here is an exercise to tap into your Akashic Records to allow you to explore the true karmic purpose you have set for yourself.

1.      Use any of the previous self-hypnosis or other exercises to relax and apply white light protection. Lie down or sit in an easy chair and when you are relaxed turn your attention inward and center it on the area of the third eye. See it glow with a golden white radiance and feel it pulsate with energy. As you do this, your realization of the sounds, colors and temperature in the room around you should gradually fade and as they do so the subtle psychic stirrings will become more noticeable.

2.      At first, this may be only an impression of inner light or of brilliantly illuminated geometrical figures, or of stars shooting by in ordered procession, or

---

[114] In my book, Past Lives——Future Lives, I present a paradigm showing the five lower planes. They are in order from the lowest to the highest the physical, astral, causal, mental and etheric planes.

some other visual appearance which will probably be meaningless. Or your first impression may be of sound, as I have previously described.

3.      Focus your mind, not on the Akashic Records themselves, but on a specific historical event for your initial trials. For example, I suggest you read up on the discovery of radium by Madame Curie or the signing of the Declaration of Independence in 1776 first.

4.      Your next step is to go to that historical event and ask yourself, "what happened that afternoon?" If you have properly prepared yourself, you will find yourself drifting into a scenario-like dream.

In the earlier stages of your development you will not get clearly defined contacts that you can recognize as such, so don't expect them. Accept the dream-like sequence which passes before your consciousness as you sit in reverie. Remember what you observe and write it down as soon as possible thereafter.

5.      During these practice sessions you should "feel" this connection between your waking consciousness and the Akasha. When this has been accomplished and you can recall an incident from the past as simply as you can look up an account in the encyclopedia, you are then ready to move on to the next step.

6.      The next step is to repeat the previous steps, omitting the preparation phase consisting of reading about the historical event beforehand.

7.      Next, check your data with specialty books written about that event in detail, not merely an Encyclopedia summary.

8.      After successful completion of this step, move on to your own future. Begin with a short range, say one week to a month. Log all of your observations into a journal and occasionally verify the accuracy of your prophecies.

9.      With a proven track record you are now ready to venture much further ahead in time in your current life. Try five years, ten years, fifty years and so on.

10.     You may move several hundred years into the future and explore future lives. My books *Past Lives—Future Lives* and *Soul Healing* describe nearly twenty such cases as far forward as the 38th century!

11.     Lastly, tap into the general Akasha and allow your consciousness to tune into future world events, inventions, lifestyle changes and so on.

Again, even of these scripts work best with the use of self-hypnosis tapes. My book *New Age Hypnosis*[115] instructs you step-by-step in this simple art. You do not need to be initiated into the Lesser and the Greater Mysteries to accomplish this. Professionally recorded tapes with my voice and specially designed music are available from my office.

---

[115] B. Goldberg, *New Age Hypnosis*. (St. Paul: Llewellyn, 1998).

# CONCLUSION

Esoteric belief is that our species *Homo sapiens sapiens* has existed on the earth for many millions of years. Mainstream science does not accept that premise and states that our ancestors date back four million years or so. We can refer to "James Law" named after the philosopher and father of American psychology William James who stated that there always seems to be just enough evidence to convince the believers, and never enough to convince the skeptics.

Conventional historians assume that civilization began in Sumeria, some say Egypt. The dates for these cultures go back no further than 5000 B.C. Prior to that date man was merely an ignorant cave man devoid of culture, science or a higher philosophy to guide them.

Recent archaeological findings, to say nothing of the forbidden archaeology examples I presented in chapter 1, have poked more holes in this paradigm then a Swiss cheese factory. We have legends and holy scriptures from nearly every religion in the world that depict earlier advanced civilizations that met their end as a result of cataclysms. This can be found in Chinese mythology, the *Ramayana* of India, Mayan codices, Greek writings, Scandinavian and Welch lore, Tibetan scriptures, Hopi Indian and African tribal legends, the Bible and Egyptian hieroglyphics.

These sources give us evidence of Mu, Atlantis, the ancient Rama Empire of India and other antediluvian advanced civilizations. Before blindly dismissing such reports consider the fact that *all* legends have some basis in reality. I do not doubt they are embellished and used to control the masses, but isn't it interesting how they all seem to refer to the Flood and highly advanced people (gods and goddesses)?

The late Cornell University Carl Sagan believed that a book once existed titled *The True History of Mankind Over the Last 100,000 Years*. It was reportedly kept in Alexandria, Egypt, but was destroyed along with 700,000 other works, as a result of Julius Caesar's and Islamic wanton acts of repression, as I have discussed.

Let us not forget the Roman's senseless destruction of the Library of Carthage (an Atlantean colony) in 146 B.C. with its 500,000 volumes. Fanatical Christians burned another 200,000 books at Pergamus in Asia Minor that contained occult knowledge and pre-Flood history so sought after today. We must not forget the original 42 books written by Hermes, including the *Book of Thoth*. Some say he wrote over 35,000 books!

The few records that escaped this wanton destruction had the misfortune of being guarded by secret societies that perished as each society faded into history – or did some survive? The Moslems did their share of book burning a few hundred years following the Christian affair. After all, the powers that be in their infinite wisdom decided that any knowledge not contained in the Bible or Koran couldn't possibly be anything but evil or of no use.

We should ask ourselves why civilization began in the form of agriculture and the grouping together of our species about 16,000 years ago. Since our species has been around for at least 117,000 years (my thesis is that we have been around for at least 200,000 years), why did it take so long to develop this beginning of civilization? Why not 50,000 or 100,000 years ago?

Many conventional scientists consider Cro-Magnon man our predecessor. Recent DNA studies have eliminated Neanderthal man from this category. We find the remains of Cro-Magnon man in elevated and mountainous regions, showing that their existence in Europe commenced *after* the mountains were raised. Yet remains of our species have been found in gravel beds formed by waters of the last cataclysm (11,000 B.C.) that took place *before* the mountains had gone up. We also have specific bones of our ancestors dating back 113,000 years, long before Cro-Magnon Man spread through Europe about 40,000 B.C. This virtually eliminates Cro-Magnon man as our ancestor. Where did we come from?

Race after race of man have been found only after archeologists uncovered their remains. Churchward supposedly found writings in Tibetan monasteries dating back some 70,000 years describing men from 200,000 B.C. in Mu.

Let us consider some of the traces of our species that date back long before our scientists' "expert" opinion. When palentologists discover fossil human footprints dating back millions of year they explain them away by adopting one of two hypotheses. Either they: (1) declare them to be the distorted tracks of animals; or (2) claim that the tracks were engraved by Indians of yore. Although primitive cultures did carve many footprints in rock, the discovery of footprints in deep underlying rock strata eliminates anything but a human foot made that impression.

In the Paluxy River near Glen Rose, Texas footprints of a modern human were found alongside dinosaur prints in Cretaceous Rock. This dates man back 144 million years! Dr. Clifford L. Burdick, an Arizona geologist, measured these footprints. His data showed they were fifteen inches in length. This man had to have lived at the exact same time as the dinosaurs.

We can add to this list artifacts that appear to defy historical logic. In this category I would include abandoned cities in South and Central America, and the unidentified ruins under both the Atlantic and Pacific Oceans that are made of stones so huge and heavy, that moving them into place would seem to be beyond the abilities of primitive people. We can't even duplicate the construction of the Great Pyramid with modern equipment!

Scientists tell us that we have had the use of fire for 750,000 years. They also state that some measure of organized culture existed between 75,000 and 100,000 years ago. This allows ample opportunity for advanced civilizations such as Mu and Atlantis to develop, decay and disappear as a result of cataclysms.

The legends of the Flood has kept alive the memory of a catastrophe occurring 13,000 yeas ago that destroyed the cultural center and many of the most civilized points of the world. Survivors of that cataclysm carried on some form of their civilization in ancient Egypt. The instinctive memory of the lost world and the golden age of mankind is one of the deepest and most general racial memories.

The prophets who were forewarned about these cataclysms took care to preserve them, although distorted by priests and others in the form of Mystery Schools. We are all in this New Age feeling this ancient knowledge beginning to rise to the surface within us and seeking to find a vehicle through which that memory can be activated. That is why I included the script to my superconscious mind tap and other spiritual growth techniques in this book.

As the memory is activated in each of you, it will not necessarily take form of information. Instead, it will simply take the form of your spiritual and inner wisdom. The ancients all had an inner wisdom and an inner spirituality that was never discussed or argued about. Those beliefs all are the same idea on the most basic level. Those basic beliefs are the belief in a higher power, love and respect for each other and love and respect for the Earth. That is the very basic foundation of spirituality. That was the spirituality of the ancients, and that is the spirituality that is awakening within you. I refer to this concept as psychic empowerment.

The most recent cataclysm of 11,000 B.C. was referred to as *Götterdämmeriung*, or "twilight of the gods" by Teutonic legend. *Genesis* describes the story of the Deluge that annihilated an entire civilization by means of the most destructive flood the world has ever experienced. This civilization flourished during what has been termed the antediluvian era—the period between the earliest recorded Biblical history and the worldwide catastrophe.

*Genesis* describes these antediluvian people as highly knowledgeable, being the first to develop agriculture, animal husbandry, construction, architecture, political organization, metalworking, the abstract arts, mathematics, chronology and astronomy. There were only ten generations of antediluvians, and most of the foundations of civilization were developed by the sixth generation!

Another criticism the scientific establishment has concerning the *Old Testament* relates to the excessive age of the patriarchs depicted. Methuselah lived to be 969 and others far exceeded those of modern civilization. Perhaps this just reflected the long life span of those Muvian and Atlantean citizens that possessed knowledge we are only beginning to comprehend. In my book *Long Younger, Live*

*Longer*, I discuss and present recommendations how we can extend our life to 120 to 140 quality years![116]

Let us compare the antediluvian patriarchs in the *Old Testament* to Egyptian gods:

| BIBLICAL PATRIARCHS | EGYPTIAN GODS |
| --- | --- |
| Adam | Ptah |
| Seth | Ra |
| Enos | Su |
| Cainan | Seb |
| Mahalaleel | Osirus |
| Jared | Seth |
| Enoch | Horus |
| Methuselah | Thoth |
| Lamech | Maat |
| Noah | Horus |

Herodotus visited Egypt at about 350 B.C. and was informed by temple priests that Egypt had been "ruled by pharaohs for 14,340 years." This dates back to 11,700 B.C., which is very close to my date of 11,000 B.C. for the submerging of Mu and Atlantis for the *third* (that magic number again) and final time.

The thirteenth day of the month thout in ancient Egypt was a day in which no work was to be done. The citizens weren't even permitted to eat. Some feel that this was in respect to Mu's submerging on a Friday the thirteenth.[117]

The letter "M" was pronounced "m-a" in ancient Egypt and meant "earth-home" or "country-place." We see the term "Ma" denoting "earth" in ancient Indian Naga-Maya dialects. There were Maya populations in India and Mexico. The "Maya" were Muvian explorers, although some considered it referred to a priestly caste.

An interesting "m-a" root is seen in the words "magnet," "magic," "mahatma" (or "master"), and "man." It could also be present in the *tri*littoral root "mar'," which in ancient times became incorporated into words signifying the sea. Words derived from this root include the Latin "mare" and our "marine" and "maritime." The Egyptian goddess *Mat* (Hermes' wife) means "truth" or "justice." All this suggests a common origin, Mu.

One sadistic custom Egypt never adopted was that of animal and human sacrifice. Sacrifice, both of animals and humans (young maidens were especially

---

[116] B. Goldberg, *Live Younger, Live Longer: Add 25 to 50 quality years to your life, naturally.* (St. Paul: Llewellyn, 1997).

[117] I. Velikovsky, *Worlds in Collision*. (Garden City, N.Y., Doubleday & Co., 1950) p.65.

frequent victims in many cultures) was common among the ancients. In most cases such rites included the use of fire. In Mexico, especially among the Aztecs, human sacrifice was closely connected with the sun. This was a result of Mu's demise by fire. The ancient Mexicans considered the heart the symbol of life, and regarded it as an especially valuable offering.

Aztec priests, when offering a human sacrifice, would begin by cutting the victim's chest open and then extract the still-pulsating heart and hold it up to the sun. According to Cortes, at the time he conquered Mexico, Aztec priests were sacrificing 50,000 human victims a year! It is a testimony to the Egyptian experiment that they didn't degenerate to the level of these ancients, as did the Druids and others.

Today we are practicing sciences that have been developed within the past 500 years. We are probably just retracing the steps of the Muvians over 100,000 years ago. The scientific establishment has exhibited ego, jealousy, a repressive nature, a domineering and selfish attitude craving for prominence and desiring fame, regardless of whether or not it is deserved.

The purpose of the Muvian civilization, and the time travelers who guided and created them, was to assist our species to ascend and end the karmic cycle. These were originally loving, knowledgeable, kind and sympathetic human beings dedicated to helping others journeying along the same path. Unfortunately, the ETs stepped in and made a mess of the human race. Karmically, we asked for this situation.

The founding fathers of the United States included many Masons as well as several Rosicrucians. The history of both of these groups can be traced back to the ancient Mystery Schools of Egypt; the same Mystery Schools that had taught Moses! We can further trace the Mystery Schools back to Atlantis and finally to Mu.

We must consider the Great Pyramid along with the origin of Egyptian Masonry. Conventional scientists simply cannot explain lifting and placing forty-ton blocks side by side, with enough precision to last anywhere from 4,500 to 12,500 years. How do we explain cores of granite drilled without high-speed rotary machines, or the hollowing of thin-necked alabaster vases? What was used in certain rock-temples, walls faultlessly carved with glyphs, where no natural light, direct or reflected, can possibly reach the chamber, and yet not a trace of carbon has been found on walls or ceiling?

Egyptian Masonry was passed on to the Greeks by such people as Thales, Pythagoras and Plato. Its second path was through Egyptian Gnosticism and heretical Christianity; a third through the Tarot whose cards, just as surely as the Emerald Tablet of Hermes, are said to portray the structure of the sacred science of the Egyptians. The Knights Templar of Europe borrowed these masonic principles as a result of the Crusades. They used this science to build cathedrals and used symbols, such as colored glass, which become known as the reds and blues of Chartres.

We can learn from Egyptian temple inscriptions that our own body is a microcosm of the universe. The temple is merely a projection of Heaven upon Earth. The true living temple of Egyptian Wisdom is *Man*, who embodies the cosmic principles and functions, the *Neters*. And temples are "houses" in which the symbols of these *Neters* can be seen in order to teach man to recognize within himself the elements of the great world whose image and epitome he is.

The whole of Egypt is the "Temple," and its entire history the history of man, of the living symbol of all cosmic functions. The crowns and the sceptres of the King represent the powers acquired through the development of consciousness by which he becomes the King of Nature and of all inferior creatures.

To reach our spiritual, potential the ancient Egyptians used their Temple to teach *three* stages of growth. The first stage is to experience life by observation. A progressive initiation into the *causal laws* represent the second and third stages. We see another example of the number three.

The second stage more specifically involved lessons portrayed by the temple religious and funeral rites in the form of hieroglyphics. Symbolism was always a component to this Mystery School approach. Supreme questions posed to the various deities comprised the third stage.

To truly understand the causal laws, the initiate needs to use a simplicity of heart and mind (the factor opposed to the complexity of modern thought). A spirit of synthesis, as opposed to our analytical mentality, is also required. The ancient Egyptian wisdom left its testimony in the language of architecture, sculpture, and hieroglyph.

An interesting, yet unexplainable pattern occurred less than 16,000 years ago. The Russian botanist Nikolai Ivanovitch collected over 50,000 wild plants from around the world and traced their origin to eight mountainous regions. Agricultural cultures date from this period and the mountainous regions suggest the humans here survived a great flood.

These sites included Lake Titicaca in South America and the highlands of Thailand. Prior to the crust displacement, Crete, Sumeria, India, China and Egypt were tropical. Now they became temperate and civilization flourished in each place.[118]

In reference to ETs in Egypt, we can observe a link between UFO events and

---

[118] Rand Flem-Ath and Rose Flem-Ath, *When the Sky Fell*. (Canada: Studdart, 1995).

occult phenomena. For example, abductees commonly report levitation, psychic control, healing, and out-of-body experiences: things quite familiar to those who know the occult literature. The various offshoots of the Hermetic Order of the Golden Dawn have inspired not only the witchcraft revival, but also the current generation of metaphysical writers and many of today's scientific parapsychologists. These scientists will deny such affiliations to prevent professional censure.

The basis of almost all esoteric teachings is that ordinary reality is an illusion, called *maya* by the East Indians. Modern quantum physics has confirmed this hypothesis. One supplement to this paradigm by esoteric schools is that an adept can consciously manipulate reality by understanding its causal laws (higher nature).

Unfortunately, these groups say that the actual techniques for manipulation have to be kept secret and constitute the core of the "occult tradition." The weakness of the esoteric philosophy lies in the fact that it will not submit its tenets to critical inquiry. It will only "reveal" them to selected initiates. This reflects the Mystery School mentality that has contributed to the failure of the ET-influenced Egyptian experiment. Not even the time travelers could save it.

Today and throughout history scientists have distorted, ignored and destroyed the very facts they should have investigated to protect their turfs. A complete reexamination of the enter UFO problem of millions of unexplained observations by reliable witnesses has led to private research groups known as the Invisible College.

An interesting item appeared in the FBI Bulletin in 1975. Here is a sample of it:

*Way back in the "dark ages" of science, when scientists themselves were suspected of being in league with the Devil, they had to work privately. They often met clandestinely to exchange views and the results of their experiments. For this reason, they called themselves the Invisible College. And it remained invisible until the scientists of that day gained respectability when the Royal Society was chartered by Charles II in the early 1660's.*[119]

The ETs were involved with the earliest development of Egypt and the antediluvian civilizations of Mu and Atlantis. The fact that Egypt and or current civilization were the result or *gradual* development from primitive beginnings—can now seriously be challenged. Biblical history, archaeology, geology, paleontology, and ordinary level-headed thinking most definitely point us in a completely different direction. Our early ancestors created a society that surpassed

---

[119] "The UFO Mystery", *FBI Bulletin*, February, 1975.

ours in all aspects of development.

The world has undergone a number of important transitions, with still more to come. Between 1950 and 220 B.C. marked a period of transition for almost every civilization of the Old and New worlds. During this time, Egypt's first kingdom slipped into deterioration; Sumeria and India were overwhelmed by barbaric invaders; China and the rest of the Far East suffered a disastrous flood; and in the Americas, the primitive cultures were suddenly followed by more advanced ones. In many instances, the societies that collapsed and disappeared had had historical ties of one kind or another with scattered remnants of the lost super-civilization.

Historians can't explain this occurrence. There was no single cause that could account for their sudden decline. The keepers of the knowledge from Mu and Atlantis safeguarded their secrets and fused it with these new colonies. We can see from 250 B.C. to the beginning of the Christian era a technological rekindling in Egypt.

One common factor we must never forget is Taatos and the other time travelers. They, along with the ETs, sporadically came and went. Each time they were around civilization benefitted technologically. The reverse transpired when they left.

The greatest threat to our safety is not atom bombs or terrorism, but neglect of the spiritual forces that make us wish to be right and noble. Let us learn from the ancient Egyptians and both rediscover and reassert in the spiritual values on which life has really rested from its beginning.

My conclusions about current civilization and the true history of Egypt may be summarized as follows:

- Man has been present on this planet for a minimum of 10,000,000 years.
- Mu was the true origin of modern man.
- ETs genetically altered our ancestors to speed up our evolution.
- Time travelers tried to repair the damage created by the ETs, but so far have failed in that regard.
- Mu and Atlantis were technologically superior civilizations, with Mu showing almost ideal spiritual characteristics for the first 50,000 to 75,000 years of its existence.
- The misuse of spiritual powers and materialistic tendencies brought on a karmic necessity of cataclysms to destroy these advanced civilizations.
- Egypt was a colony first of Mu and then of Atlantis combined with Muvians. ETs supervised and interfered with Egypt's development at that time.
- The time travelers, particularly Taatos, did their best to salvage the Egyptian

experiment, but failed.

- The entire history of Egypt and all of civilization is stored in the Akashic Records, or "Book of Life." We each have the ability to read these records. The accuracy with which these records reveal depends on the level of spiritual development of the reader.

Remember the old saying, "He who forgets his past is doomed to repeat it." We must never forget that we have an immortal soul (the Egyptian *ba*) that is created from the substance of the macrocosm/universal mind/God and in the image or pattern of this universal mind. The theology and cosmology of the ancient Egyptians taught us that.

Our soul periodically reincarnates into a physical body, but this is not our true purpose. We are all destined to ascend, but must earn that privilege. Living a self-centered life has distracted us from our greater awareness (Higher Self).

We must rejoin with our Higher Self and take responsibility for our actions and our lives. As long as we use alcohol, drugs, war, and even work, games, and sex to help us forget our lonely, alienated existence that will soon be ended "forever" by death, we will never attain the state of Grace.

When each of us can, at last, remember the oneness with All That Is (God), all that was, and all that ever will be, we will no longer be able to blame others for our own misfortunes. And most importantly, when we have expanded our awareness to the point where we can remember our own past lives, we will know that we alone created our destiny through our own choosing. We will then realize that we alone are responsible for all of our experiences. This spiritual awareness will initiate great steps forward in eliminating all conflict between individual races and nations. I present several ascension techniques in my book *Peaceful Transitions*.[120]

Egypt was a failed experiment because of the lack of true spiritual growth that came from its reign. The Muvians, Atlanteans, ETs and time travelers failed to facilitate our ascension. The evidence is we are still on the Earth plane.

The time travelers are the most important influence on Egypt as well as modern society. In ancient Egypt they spent most of their time correcting the mistakes and manipulation attempts of the ETs, and of our own race. Even when they did have time to assist us, we didn't listen.

A time traveler can enter our consciousness through our thoughts, dreams or appear in physical form. We can't blame them for Egypt's failure. Each of us has free will and the right to choose between good and evil, or whatever is in between.

---

[120] B. Goldberg, *Peaceful Transition: The Art of Conscious Dying and the Liberation of the Soul*. (St. Paul: Llewellyn, 1997).

The same pattern of secrecy, distrust, selfishness, cruelty, power and control dominated ancient Egypt. Slavery, killing pharaohs, inventing the Devil and Hell were just some of the atrocities initiated by the High Priests. Who died and made them God? Even their own theology limited that right to their king.

These ancients ignored the Muvians and their attempt at spirituality. Granted that by about 16,000 B.C. the Muvian who colonized Egypt was quite different than the spiritual adept of 200,000 B.C., but these primitive people still could have listened.

We see a degeneration in technical and artistic skills in pyramid construction and hieroglyphic art respectively following the Pyramid Age. This great skill lasted a mere hundred years out of a possible 2200 years until Alexander the Great conquered them.

Still, we can look at the achievements of a truly great civilization. The Pyramid of Giza is a model for human consciousness resurrection. It is an ascension device for the pharaoh. This great structure bears the mark of the ETs who used their home planet to indicate Osiris' Paradise. There is a sad aspect of this. Perhaps these ETs were just homesick.

Let us not forget Egypt's contribution to alchemy and subsequently modern chemistry. This provided the basis for modern medicine. Just as the ancient Egyptian alchemists believed in a transmutation of matter into gold, we today can undergo a personal transformation by accessing our Higher Self.

The mistake of the Egyptian Mystery Schools was in its secrecy and limited availability. Let us learn from the ancients and open up doorways that are not sealed by dogma or religious authority, so that we may all master a deeper wisdom and ascend from this dimension. Using the techniques I presented in chapter 7 will assist you in tapping into your time energy points.

I propose that we all access our Higher Self and concentrate on the universal number three. Let us together practice the superconscious mind tap and conscious dying techniques. With a little conscientiousness each of us, you, me and Hermes, can drink a glass of herbal Egyptian tea on the soul plane and laugh about the "old days" when we all actually *had* a karmic cycle.

# BIBLIOGRAPHY

Abetti, Giorgio. *The History of Astrology*. New York: Henry Schuman, 1952.

Albright, William F. "The Amarna Letters From Palestine." In *Cambridge Ancient History*. II:2A, 3rd ed. Cambridge, England: Cambridge University Press, 1971.

Alcubierre, M. "The Warp Drive: Hyperfast Travel Within General Relativity." *Classic and Quantum Gravity*. 1994, *11*, 73.

Aldred, Cyril. *Akhenaten: King of Egypt*. London: Thames and Hudson, 1988.

Allegro, J. M. *Mystery of the Dead Sea Scrolls Revealed*. New York: Gramercy Pub. Co., 1981

Anonymous. "The Little Wooden Airplane." Pursuit, 1972, *5*, 88.

Apollodorus. *Apollodorus*, Trans. James George Frazier. London: Loeb Classical Library, 1921.

Ardrey, Robert. *African genesis; a personal investigation into the animal origins and nature of man*. New York: Antheneum, 1961.

Aubet, Maria Eugenia. *The Phoenicians and the West*. Boston: Cambridge University Press, 1993.

Baldwin, John D. *Pre-Historic Nations*. New York: Harper and Brothers, 1869.

Bailey, James. *The God-Kings and the Titans*. London Hodder & Stoughton, 1972.

Baines, John and Malek, Jaromir. *Atlas* of Ancient Egypt. Virginia: Time-Life Books, 1990.

Baring-Gould, S. *Legends of the Patriarchs and Prophets*. New York: Henry Regnery Company, 1872.

Barr, James. *Biblical Chronology: Legend or Science*. London: University of London, 1987.

Bauval, Robert and Gilbert, Adrian. *The Orion Mystery*. London: Wm. Heinemann, 1994.

Bergier, Jacques. *Extraterrestrial Invention: The Evidence*. Chicago: Henry Regnery Company, 1974.

Berlitz, Charles. *The Bermuda Triangle*. Garden City, N.Y.: Doubleday and Company, 1974.

_____. *Mysteries from Forgotten Worlds*. New York: Dell Publishing Co., Inc., 1972.

_____. *Without a Trace*. New York: Ballantine Books, 1985.

Binder, Otto. *Mankind—Colony of the Stars*. New York: Tower Publications, Inc., 1974.

_____. *Unsolved Mysteries of the Past*. New York: Tower Publications, Inc., 1970.

Braidwood, Robert J. *Prehistoric Man*. New York: William Morrow & Co., 1967.

Breasted, James Henry. *Ancient Records of Egypt: Historical Documents from the Earliest Times to the Persian Conquest*. London: Histories and Mysteries of Man Ltd., 1988.

Brown, H. A. *Cataclysms of the Earth*. New York: Twayne, 1967.

Brownlee, W. H. "A Comparison of the Covenanters of the Dead Sea Scrolls with Pre-Christian Jewish Sects." *The Biblical Archeologist*. 1950, *13*, 50-72.

Bryan, P. W. *The Papyrus Ebers*. London: Geoffrey Bles, 1930.

Budge, E.A.W. *Egyptian Magic*. London: Kegan Paul, 1901.

_____. *From Fetish to God in Ancient Egypt*. London: Oxford University Press, 1934.

_____. *Gods of the Egyptians*. London: Methuen & Co., 1904.

_____. *Egyptian Book of the Dead*. London: Longman & Co., 1895.

Burroughs, W.G. "Human-like footprints, 250 million years old." *The Berea Alumnus*. Berea College, Kentucky, November, 1938, 46-47.

Campbell, Joseph. "The Hero with a Thousand Faces" London: Paladin Books, 1988.

Cayce, Edward Evans. *Edgar Cayce on Atlantis*. Virginia Beach: A.R.E. Press, 1968.

Cerve, Wishar. *Lemuria: The Lost Continent of the Pacific*: San Jose, California: AMORC, 1931.

Charroux, Robert. *Forgotten Worlds*. New York: Walker and Company, 1973.

_____. *The Gods Unknown*. New York: Berkeley Publishing, 1974.

_____. *Legacy of the Gods*. New York: Berkeley Publishing, 1974.

_____. *One Hundred Thousand Years of Man's Unknown History*. New York: Berkeley Publishing, 1971.

Chatelain, Maurice. *Our Ancestors Came from Outer Space*. Garden City, New York: Doubleday & Co., 1978.

Churchward, James. *The Lost Continent of Mu*. New York: Ives Washburn, 1931.

_____. *The Children of Mu*. New York: Ives Washburn, 1931.

_____. *The Sacred Symbols of Mu*. New York: Ives Washburn, 1933.

_____. *The Cosmic Forces of Mu*. New York: Ives Washburn, 1934.

_____. *The Second Book of the Cosmic Forces of Mu*. New York: Ives Washburn, 1934.

Cockren, Archibald. *Alchemy Rediscovered and Restored*. Kala, Montana: Life Sciences Pub., 1991.

Cremo, M. A. and Thompson, R. L. *Forbidden Archaeology: The Hidden History of the Human Race*. Los Angeles: Bhaktivedanta Book Pub., Inc., 1993.

Davidovits, Joseph and Morris, Margie. *The Pyramids: An Enigma Solved*. New

York: Dorset Press, 1988.

DeCamp, L. Sprague and Catherine C. *Ancient Ruins and Archaeology*. Garden City, N.Y.: Doubleday and Co., 1962.

de Freycinet, Louis-Claude. *Voyage Autour du Monde plus Atlas Historique*. Paris, 1825.

Diodorus. *Diodorus Siculus* (trans. C.H. Oldfather). London: Loeb Classical Library, 1989.

Donnelly, Ignatius. *Atlantis: The Antediluvian World*. New York: Harper & Brothers, 1882.

_____. *Ragnarok*. Blauvelt, New York: Rudolf Steiner Pub., 1971.

Drake, W. Raymond. *Gods and Spacemen in the Ancient East*. New York: New American Library, Inc., 1973.

_____. *Gods and Spacemen in the Ancient West*. New York: New American Library, Inc., 1974.

Earll, Tony. *Mu Revealed*. New York: Paperback Library, 1970.

Edwards, I.E.S., *The Pyramids of Egypt*. London: Penguin, 1949.

"Electric Battery of 2,000 Years Ago." *Discovery*. March 1939.

Emery, W. B. *Archaic Egypt*. London: Penguin Books, 1987.

Eusebius. *Preparation for the Gospel*. 2 vols. Translated by Edwin Hamilton Gifford. Grand Rapids, Mich.: Baker Book House, 1981.

Faulkner, R. O., trans. "Admonitions of an Egyptian Sage." In *The Literature of Ancient Egypt*. Edited by William Kelly Simpson. New Haven: Yale University Press, 1972.

_____. *The Ancient Egyptian Book of the Dead*. London: British Museum Press, 1969.

_____. *Ancient Egyptian Pyramid Texts*. London: Oxford University Press, 1969.

Fears, J. Rufus. *Atlantis: Fact or Fiction?* Bloomington, Indiana: Indiana Univ. Press, 1978.

Feinberg, Gerald. *T. D. Lee: Selected Papers*. Boston: Birkhauser, 1986.

Filby, Frederick A., *The Flood Reconsidered: A Review of the Evidences of Geology, Archaeology, Ancient Literature and the Bible*. London: Pickering & Inglis, 1970.

Flem-Ath, Rand and Rose. *When the Sky Fell*. Canada: Stoddart, 1995.

Fowden, Garth. *The Egyptian Hermes*. Cambridge, England: Cambridge University Press, 1987.

Friedman, Richard Elliot. *Who Wrote the Bible*. New York: Summit Books, 1987.

Goedicke, Hans. "The End of the Hyksos in Egypt." In *Egyptological Studies in Honor of Richard A. Parker*. Edited by Leonard H. Lesko. Hanover and

London: Brown University Press, 1986.

Goetz, Delia and Morley, S. G. *Popol Vuh: The Sacred Book of the Ancient Quiche Maya*. Norman, Oklahoma: University of Oklahoma Press, 1991.

Goldberg, B. *Soul Healing*. St. Paul: Llewellyn Pub., 1996.

_____. *The Search for Grace: A Documented Case of Murder and Reincarnation*. Sedona, AZ: In Print Pub., 1994.

_____. *Past Lives-Future Lives*. New York: Ballantine Books, 1988.

_____. *Peaceful Transition: The Art of Conscious Dying and the Liberation of the Soul*. St. Paul: Llewellyn Pub., 1997.

_____. *Astral Voyages: Mastering the Art of Interdimensional Travel*. St. Paul: Llewellyn, 1999.

_____. *New Age Hypnosis*. St. Paul: Llewellyn Pub., 1998.

_____. *Protected by the Light: The Complete Book of Psychic Self-Defense*. Tucson, AZ: Hats Off Press, 2000.

_____. *Time Travelers from Our Future: A Fifth Dimension Odyssey*. Woodland Hills, CA: BG, Inc., 2006.

_____. *Custom Design Your Own Destiny. Woodland Hills, CA: BG, Inc. 2007.*

_____. "Quantum Physics and its application to past life regression and future life progression hypnotherapy." *Journal of Regression Therapy*, 1973, 7 (1), 89-93.

Good, Timothy. *Alien Update*. New York: Avon, 1995.

Goodman, Jeffrey. *American Genesis*. New York: Summit, 1981.

Graves, Robert, and Patai, Ralph. *Hebrew Myths: The Book of Genesis*. New York: McGraw-Hill, 1966.

Hall, Richard. *Uninvited Guests: A Documented History of UFO Sightings, Alien Encounters and Coverups*. Santa Fe, New Mexico: Aurora Press, 1988.

Hancock, Graham. *Fingerprints of the Gods*. London: Heinemann, 1995.

_____. *The Sign and the Seal*. London: Mandarin, 1993.

Hapgood, Charles H. *Earth's Shifting Crust: A Key to Some Basic Problems of Earth Science*. New York: Pantheon Books, 1958.

_____. *Maps of the Ancient Sea Kings*. London: Turnstone Books, 1979.

_____. *The Path of the Pole*. New York: Chilton Books, 1970.

*Harper's Bible Dictionary*. New York: Harper & Row, 1975.

Harrison, W. "Atlantis Uncovered-Bimini, Bahamas." *Nature*, 1971, *230*, 287-289.

Hart, George, *Egyptian Myths*. London: British Museum Publications, 1990.

_____. *Pharoahs and Pyramids*. London: Guild Publishing, 1991.

Hawkins, Gerald S. *Beyond Stonehenge*. London: Arrow Books, 1977.

Hayes, William C. *Cambridge Ancient History*. 3rd ed., Cambridge, England:

Cambridge University Press, 1970.

Herm, Gerard, *The Phoenicians*. London: BCA, 1975.

Herodotus, *The History* (trans. David Grene). Chicago: University of Chicago Press, 1987.

Hertz, J. H., ed. *The Pentateuch and Haftorahs*, 2nd ed. London: Soncino Press, 1976.

Heyerdahl, Thor, *The Ra Expeditions*. London: BCA, 1972.

Hodges, Peter and Keable, Julian, *How the Pyramids Were Built*. Shaftsbury, England: Element Books, 1989.

Hutlin, Serge. *Alien Races and Fantastic Civilizations*. New York: Berkeley, 1975.

Josephus: *Against Apion*. 9 vols. From *Josephus*, vol. 1. Translated by H. St. J. Thackeray. Cambridge, Mass: Harvard University Press, 1926.

_____. *Jewish Antiquities*. 9 vols. From *Josephus*, vol. 4. Translated by H. St. J. Thackeray. Cambridge, Mass.: Harvard University Press, 1930.

Kanjilal, Dileep Kumar, *Vimana in Ancient India*. Calcutta: Sanskrit Pustak Bhandar, 1985.

Kirkpatrick, R. "Witchcraft and Lupus Erythematosus." *Journal of the American Medical Association.* May 15, 1981.

Landsburg, Alan and Landsburg, Sally. *In Search of Ancient Mysteries*. New York: Bantam Books, 1974.

Lear, John. Flying Saucers: Government Cover-up. VHS. Lightworks Audio & Video, 1996.

Le Plongeon, August. *Sacred Mysteries Among the Mayas and the Quiches 11,500 Years Ago*. New York: R. Macy, 1886.

Lewin, Roger. *Human Evolution*. Oxford, England: Blackwell Scientific Pub., 1984.

Mackenzie, N. *Dreams and Dreaming*. London: Bloomsbury Books, 1989.

Marshak, Alexander. *The Roots of Civilization: the cognitive beginnings of man's first art, symbol and notation*. Mount Kisco, New York: Moyer Bell, 1991.

Maziere, Francis. *Mysteries of Easter Island*. New York: Tower Publications, Inc. 1965.

Mercantante, A. S. *Who's Who in Egyptian Mythology*. New York: Potter, 1978.

Mertz, Henriette. *Gods from the Far East*. Ballantine Books, 1972.

Michanowsky, George. *The Once and Future Star*. New York: Hawthorn Books, 1977.

Michell, John. *The New View Over Atlantis*. San Francisco: Harper & Row, 1993.

Miller, Hugh. *The Testimony of the Rocks*. New York: John B. Alden, 1892.

Morentz, Siegfried. (trans. Ann E. Keep). *Egyptian Religion*. Ithaca: Cornell Paperbacks, 1992.

Morris, M. S. and Thorne, K. s. "Wormholes in Spacetime and Their Use for Interstellar Travel: A Tool for Teaching General Relativity." *American Journal of Physics*, 1988, *56*, 411.

Morris, M. S., Thorne, K. S. and Yortsever, U. "Wormholes, Time Machines, and the Weak Energy Condition." *Physical Review Letters*, 1988, *61(13),* 1446-1449.

Neil, W. *Harper's Bible Commentary*. New York: Harper and Row, 1975.

*New Energy News*. February, 1997, *4(10),* 12.

Newton, Robert. *The Crime of Claudius Ptolemy*. Baltimore: Johns Hopkins University Press, 1977.

Nunn, J. F. *Ancient Egyptian Medicine*. Norman, Oklahoma: University of Oklahoma Press, 1996.

Patten, Donald W., The Biblical Flood and the Ice Epoch: A Study in Scientific History. Seattle: Pacific Meridian Publishing Co., 1966.

Petrie, W. N. Flinders. *The Pyramids and Temples of Gizeh*. London: History and Mysteries of Man Ltd., 1990.

Pike, A. Morals and Dogma of the Ancient and Accepted Scottish

Rite of Freemasonry. Charleston, South Carolina: A.M. 5632, 1950.

Plato, *Timaeus and Critias*. London: Penguin Classics, 1977.

Pritchard, James P. *The Ancient Near East: An Anthology of Texts and Pictures, 2 vols.* Princeton, New Jersey: Princeton University Press, 1958.

Ptolemy. *Geographia* (trans. Edward L. Stevenson). London: Constable, 1991.

Puthoff, H. "SETI, the velocity-of-light limitation and the Alcubierre Warp Drive: An Integrating Overview." *Physics Essays*, 1996, *9 (1)*.

Rau, Jack, *The Codex as a book form: three Maya Codices*. New York: Pre-Columbian Press, 1976.

Redford, Donald B. *Akhenaten: The Heretic King*. Princeton: Princeton University press, 1984.

_____. *Pharaonic King Lists, Annals, and Day Books*. Mississauga: Benben publications, 1986.

Rehwinkel, Alfred M. *The Flood*. St. Louis: Concordia Publishing House, 1951.

Riem, Johannes. *Die Sinflut in Sage und Wissenschaft*. Hamburg: Agentur des Rauhen Hauses, 1925.

Rothovius, Andrew. "The Mysterious Cement Cylinders of New Caledonia." *INFO Journal*, 1967, *1*, 15-16.

Roy, P. *Mahabharata*. Calcutta: Bharata Press, 1978.

Sandars, N. K. *the Sea Peoples*. London: Thames and Hudson, 1985.

Sanderson, Ivan. *Uninvited Visitors: A Biologist Looks at UFOs*. New York: Cowles Educational Corp., 1967.

Savill, Shelia. *Pears Encyclopedia of Myths and Legends: Oceania, Australia and the Americas*. London: Pelham Books, 1978.

Scanlin, Harold. *The Dead Sea Scrolls & Modern Translations of the Old Testament*. Wheaton, Illinois: Tyndale, 1993.

Schueler, G. and Schueler, B. *Egyptian Magick: Enter the Body of Light and Travel the Magickal Universe*. St. Paul: Llewellyn, 1989.

Schwaller de Lubicz, R. A., *Sacred Science: The King of Pharaonic Theocracy*. Rochester, Vermont: Inner Traditions International, 1988.

Seike, S. *Principles of Ultrarelativity*. Tokyo: G Research Laboratories, 1982.

Sellers, Jane B., *The Death of Gods in Ancient Egypt*. London: Penguin Books, 1992.

Seton-Watson, M. V., *Egyptian Legends and Stories*. London: Rubicon Press, 1990.

Singer, J. D. "The Origins of Lemuria." *Pursuit*, Fall, 1982, p. 124.

Smith, W. Stevenson. "The Old Kingdom in Egypt and the Beginning of the First Intermediate Period." In *Cambridge Ancient History*. 3rd ed., 1:2A. Cambridge: Cambridge University Press, 1971.

Smyth, Piazzi, *The Great Pyramid: Its Secrets and Mysteries Revealed*. New York: Bell Publishing Co., 1990.

Sparks, H.F.D., ed. *Apocryphal Old Testament*. Oxford: Clarendon Press, 1989.

Spencer, A. J. *Death in Ancient Egypt*. Harmondsworth, England: Penguin Books, 1988.

Stemman, Roy. *Atlantis and the Lost Lands*. London: Aldus Books, 1976.

Straus, W. L., Jr. and Cave, A.J.A. "Pathology and the Posture of the Neanderthal Man." *Quarterly Review of Biology*, 1957, <u>32</u>, 348-63.

Temple, Robert K. G., *The Sirius Mystery*. Rochester, Vermont: Destiny Books, 1987.

"The UFO Mystery." FBI Bulletin, February, 1975.

Thompson, J. Eric, *Maya Hieroglyphic Writing*. Washington, D.C.: Carnegie Institution, 1950.

Thorne, K. S. Black Holes and Time Warps: Einstein's Outrageous Legacy. New York: W. W. Norton & Co., 1994.

Tompkins, Peter, *Secrets of the Great Pyramid*. New York: Harper & Row, 1978.

Trismegistus, Hermes. *Corpus Hermeticum*. Trans. A. J. Festugiere and A. D. Nock. Paris: Societe Edition Les Pelles Lettres, 1945-1954.

Turbott, I. G. "The Footprints of Tarawa." *Journal of the Polynesian Society*, 1949, *58 (4)*.

Valee, Jacques. *The Invisible College: What a Group of Scientists Has Discovered About UFO Influences on the Human Race*. New York: Dutton, 1975.

Valmiki. *Ramayana: the concise Ramayana of Valmiki*, trans. by Swami Venkatesananda. Albany: State University of New York Press, 1988.

Vankin, Jonathan and Whalen, John. *60 Greatest Conspiracies of All Time*. New York: Citadel press, 1995.

Velikovsky, I. *World in Collision*. Garden City, New York: Doubleday & Co., 1950.

Waddell, W. G., ed. *Manetho*. London: Loeb Classical Library, 1940.

Waddell, L. A. *Lhasa and its mysteries with a record of the Expedition of 1903-1904*. London; Methuen, 1929.

Waters, Frank. *The Book of the Hopi*. London: Penguin Books, 1977.

Wente, E.F., trans. "The Contendings of Horus and Set." In *The Literature of Ancient Egypt*. Edited by William Kelly Simpson. New Haven: Yale University Press, 1972.

West, John. *Serpent in the Sky*. New York: Harper & Row, 1979.

Wilson, Colin. *Atlantis and the Lost Lands*. London: Aldous Books, 1976.

Wise, M. O., Abegg, M. and Cook, E. *The Dead Sea Scrolls: A New Translation*. San Francisco: Harper San Francisco, 1996.

Wolfe, F. A. *Parallel Universes*. New York: Simon and Schuster, 1988.

Yurco, Frank J. "3,200-Year-Old Picture of Israel Found in Egypt." *Biblical Archaeological Review*, September/October, 1999.

Printed in the United States
148929LV00002B/36/A